DIXIE DEAN

*The life story
of a goal scoring legend*

Nick Walsh

READERS UNION
Group of Book Clubs
Newton Abbot 1978

Publisher's note:

Nick Walsh
Shortly before publication of this book, the author, Nick
Walsh, died suddenly at his home in Liverpool. The
publishers wish to express their sympathy to his family. His
untimely death has meant that the publishers have been
unable to credit all the photographs used, but most of them
were supplied by the *Liverpool Echo* and *Liverpool Daily Post*,
and our thanks are due to them. Thanks also to Mr Bryan
Horsnell, for loaning the cap incorporated in the jacket
design.

First published by Macdonald and Jane's Limited

This edition was produced in 1978 for sale to its members
only by the proprietors, Readers Union Limited,
PO Box 6, Newton Abbot, Devon, TQ12 2DW.
Full details of membership will gladly be sent on request

Reproduced and printed in Great Britain
by A. Wheaton & Co Ltd Exeter
for Readers Union

1 Before the Kick-off

Then strip lads and to it though sharp be the weather
And if by mischance you should happen to fall
There are worse things in life than a tumble on heather
And life is itself but a game of football

Sir Walter Scott

IN THESE DAYS of the philosophy which encourages the desire for the 'instant' in everything, from coffee to culture, it is to some extent satisfying to know that sport at least retains some measure of immunity from such uncivilising influences. Of course, there are those followers of cricket, appreciating the more profound aspects of the game, who complain that the trend has already invaded their sport, producing condensed versions of the play via the increasing attraction of one-day fixtures. Depending on your point of view, you may be thankful that soccer matches have not yet been reduced to half-hour periods, with 15 minutes play in each direction and modified rules to produce more goals in the shorter time. Perhaps a goal scored from a distance of 30 yards or more would count as three! Thank goodness that 'instant' soccer is not yet with us.

The media, particularly television, do however concentrate, justifiably it is supposed, on the most attractive aspects of a football match, usually the scoring of goals, and therefore encourage the tendency to present 'instant' soccer. The popular programmes like *Match of the Day* and the various Independent Television equivalents do, by their content, continue to emphasise that goals are the most important items for inclusion in a transmission. The goals scored in any match are the subject of 'action replays' and, not satisfied with that, special features are constructed around the goal material, such as 'Goal of the Month' or 'Goal of the Season', providing the opportunity for further repetition and concentration on the subject. Indeed, goals recorded on television are nearly always presented to the accompaniment of excited and feverish commentary, and one is left to wonder how the commentators can possibly avoid the onset of apoplexy!

It is evident that goal-scoring in soccer is the most entertaining (and exploited) feature of the game. Goals can sometimes be so scarce that every score has to be savoured and retrospectively relished to the ultimate degree. Some goals are not always worthy of the attention given to them, but like everything else in life, when a commodity is in short supply, even the poorest quality will have its value enhanced. If the highlights of a goalless match are broadcast, and the result is known before the programme is screened, even the keenest supporter has less desire to watch. Many people who never attend a football match enjoy watching the sport on television, but this does lead them to an appreciation of the game in the 'instant' sense, judged on the goal standard.

At the professional level, especially in the First Division of the Football League, goals have always been, and still are on average, very scarce. Throughout the League's history of almost a century, the number of goals scored in any season has on average ranged between only 2.6 and 3.8 per match, the total effort of both teams. If you were a football fan in the twenties, thirties, or late fifties, you would on average have witnessed only one goal more in every period of 90 minutes football than those spectators who attended matches in other decades, including the present one. So, even if a return was made to the higher goal standard, it could hardly be described as creating an abundance!

The number of players who *have* scored an abundance of goals in first class soccer are few and far between, and even they are subject to relative assessments. Nevertheless, an individual who reaches a high peak in the goal-scoring business, no matter in what period of football history he may have played, warrants special acclaim and gets it, usually at the time he is producing the goal profits. If his achievements include some of the most outstanding ever recorded in the history of the sport, it can be said that he has made a valuable and lasting contribution to the game, deserving to be remembered.

William Ralph Dean was a prolific scorer of goals and his average per match is second to none in English football. He also made a qualitative contribution to his profession, long before the 'instant' philosophy pervaded our society. Unfortunately for posterity, his accomplishments cannot be recalled with the aid of video tape and can only be highlighted through the medium of the written word. Regrettably, the writing of a biography of this man is likely to fall short when set against the highly successful things he actually did during his football career. It can be argued that the sport in which Dean was engaged made a specially valid contribution to saving a demoralised and economically deprived society from complete depression during the 1920s and 1930s. The distinguished service he gave to that sport in that situation is worthy of recall.

It is possible to argue that a biography of this man only has the purpose only of entertaining the fervent follower of football. Dean's career was, however, one of great sporting significance, extending to the wider historical context. Does sport deserve such wider acclaim in the history books? In order to fully appreciate Dean's football achievements it may be worth examining sport and its relevance to life in general, to consider the validity of its contribution to any civilising process in human development. A great many people are of the opinion that sport plays an important part in our lives and believe that soccer is the greatest game ever conceived by man. Dean was, and by name still is, an important symbol of the sport. With the help of men like Dean, sport – football in particular – has created an artistic form of its own, cultivating a sense of well-being in communities, sometimes where other more accepted art forms failed, thereby becoming a contributory factor to the civilised development of mankind.

The feats of sportsmen and sportswomen are often condemned to be nothing more than cold figures in the record books, statistics which can indeed be fascinating in themselves. But achievements tend to be recalled as images of mathematical formulae, ignoring much of their nature and character, and the inspiration that lay behind them; or the deeper significance of an outstanding contribution to sporting activity; or the consequential influence, for good or otherwise, such performances can have on a community. This is, perhaps, understandable. Outstanding artists, composers, painters, sculptors, and writers leave something tangible for posterity to enjoy, not only to derive pleasure from their creative works, but also to subject generations of people to intellectual influences and consequently broaden their horizons, which in the long term progressively helps to promote the quality of life.

Great men in the arts and sciences have their names enshrined in the saga of civilisation. Shakespeare, Michelangelo, Beethoven, and Newton are incomparable and immortal. It may be an impertinence to introduce such names into a story about a sportsman, who although making an extraordinary contribution in his field of human activity, was working in an area considered to be of lesser importance. But surely sport cannot continue to be regarded as of so little significance? Such pursuits, with their wide and powerful beckoning, have engaged the attention of people either as participants or spectators from time immemorial and therefore ought not to be brushed aside as having no relevance to the civilising process.

Some abusive and detrimental features of sporting activities have emerged from time to time and it is easy to focus on such examples to blur attempts to look upon sport as having any civilising influence. Like all other activity in the arts, sport, benefiting from the cultivation provided by normal evolutionary processes, has become more sophisticated and demanding of skill, enterprise, and intellect. Indeed it commands massive interest on such a worldwide scale that it justifies recognition as an integral part of society's development. From the time when sport was sponsored by monarchs to the present day when governments see the need for a Minister of Sport, there is presented a clear illustration of the vital and increasing importance of this basic human outlet.

The last hundred years have witnessed an unprecedented development in all forms of sporting activity. A more educated public, participating or watching, derives more enjoyment and is influenced for good or otherwise from the wider dimension of modern sporting events. Despite the inevitable abuses, induced by the very nature of some sporting activities with their intense competitiveness, both contestants and spectators by and large sustain a passionate desire to see fair play. It is one field of human involvement where genuine achievement cannot be founded on corruption (as happens in so many other areas of life) although situations do from time to time occur where this is alleged. Improved communications, together with a variety of scientific aids and learning techniques, has given the realm of sport the attraction of such intense interest that it might be regarded as disproportionate to its importance in the totality of human activity.

Sport, projected through the modern Olympics, has transformed what were once national games into international events, and they are now embraced by the world population as their own, completely ignoring national origins even to the point of disputing the nature of their evolution. But, like aircraft, television, or radio, who cares how or where they were invented or discovered? They now belong to all the peoples of the earth for better or worse. The number and variety of sporting pursuits is endless. But it may be significant that most of the major sports to receive world-wide acclaim and adoption seem to have originated in Britain. Of all the games in this category, none has made a greater impact on the peoples of the world than that of Association Football.

Of course, golf, tennis, and cricket are all played and performed at international level, and as they are some of the most popular of games, attract a fanatical following of both participants and spectators. Compared to Association Football, however, their universal appeal is perhaps something less. Although the number who actually play soccer, (a game which engages 22 players) is high, as a spectator sport it undoubtedly attracts more followers than any other. In less than a hundred years the development of Association Football has been phenomenal. In 1929 it was recorded that there were 40,000 football clubs in England and Wales, with a total of one million members.

The driving force behind this great development in football was the introduction of the English Football League. Arguably, the founding of this institution was the most important innovation in the history of sport. For the first time a number of football teams were organised to compete on a league basis. Spectator interest was stimulated to an incredible extent. The fluctuations in the positions of competing teams provided by the winning of points within the league tables inspired players and aroused public interest in an astonishing manner. Prior to the establishment of the League, spectators at football matches were measured in hundreds. The competition provided by the League immediately attracted thousands and later tens of thousands to regularly watch the games.

Twelve English clubs were selected to form the League and the first matches were played in September 1888. Within three years the number of teams had been increased to fourteen, but by 1898, ten years later, two divisions, each consisting of eighteen clubs, were in existence. Mr W. McGregor of the Aston Villa Club was the founder of the League, and his scheme of providing competitiveness in football by a league system was eventually copied and applied to nearly every other sport. McGregor's plan not only helped football, but probably revolutionised a whole range of sporting activities in a way never before imagined. Football teams represented famous towns and cities, a feature which lent a great deal of enchantment to the matches, stimulating not only the players but inducing a passionate interest from spectators. With such a widening interest, the sport became a vital part of the social life of the community and inevitably created an industry covering all aspects of the game.

Professionalism was introduced and was at first very much frowned upon. Indeed, the Football Association refused to sanction the inclusion of professionals in matches played under its rules. This stand was supported by many clubs for the very good reason that they could not afford to engage and pay full-time players. Their main argument was that if professionals were allowed, it would create unfair advantages for those clubs rich enough to employ them. However, there seemed to be no way of stopping the growth of professionalism, clubs adopting all kinds of devious methods in an attempt to conceal the fact that they were making payments to players.

The Football Association recognised that in spite of the ban on professionalism, violations of the rules would continue, so the Association finally surrendered, deciding in 1885 to legalise the employment of professionals, just three years prior to the founding of the Football League. This proved to be a progressive step and one of immense value to the development of the game. Team and individual skills improved, mainly through the increasing competitiveness derived from the league system, and of course the greater facilities from the financial gains sustained by an ever-expanding paying spectator interest.

The founding of the Football League undoubtedly created the conditions under which was cultivated a unique competitive team game, setting the high standards which have given Association Football its great eminence in the realm of sport. From this emanated the broadly-based talents of those who played the game under the auspices of the League. Out of this emerged a variety of individual skills on which the whole future of the game was built, and ever since have remained fundamental. In a similar way the Renaissance did this for Art, providing the fertile ground to produce the high ratio of exceptional men whose talents have been coveted by successive generations.

The cultivation and ultimate maturity of soccer covered a period of about fifty years. The Art (if it may be so called) of Association Football spread throughout the world and England remained its centre. The sport attracted millions, and on such a scale it ceased to be regarded as some minor recreational diversion. The famous episode of the 1914-18 war, when British and German troops, much against the will of the High Commands, spontaneously stopped killing each other to hold an unofficial truce and indulge in an international game of football, is surely symbolic of the influence the sport had achieved.

During the first fifty years of the Football League, until the time preceding the Second World War, the development of the game was based more on individual skill than team skills. This could have been a reflection of the general attitude of a society which proudly defended the individualism of *laissez faire*, the decline of which is often regarded as a source of regret. Although mass production was growing in the economic sense, the retention of individual crafts and skills in industry remained a matter of pride and society clung to an ambitious spirit of belief in the value of individual expression for most areas of human activity. Sport, and football in particular (although a team game) was encouraged to follow this philosophy and players performed intuitively, apparently without indulging in the excessive selfishness which it might be assumed such an approach would be likely to induce.

Indeed, the behaviour of spectators in those days was less susceptible to the mass hysteria which causes so many problems with today's football crowds. It is also important to note that attendances in former days were generally much higher than today. Perhaps there is something significant about this. Football followed a flexible pattern of play in the team sense with none of the complex pre-match planning, a predominant feature of soccer in the 1970s, in which individualism is much repressed by the team methods imposed by modern management.

All that remains on which to judge the standards of attainment during the first fifty years or so of Association Football are really the record books. Visual records of sporting events during that period were strictly limited, and compared with what can be done today, those early pictures must be regarded as of little consequence. In the purely individual sports like athletics the record books may provide authentic evidence of achievement. But in team games, individual performances in setting a standard for comparative attainment are more difficult to assess. Football, for example, produced many individuals who are greatly admired in retrospect, mainly on the basis of abstract judgments.

In the absence of figures which could readily identify the successful player (the scoring of goals or making a number of international appearances) judgment has had to be made on the basis of opinions and vague memories. It must be accepted

7

that in team games individuals who score the points hold positive proof of successful application to their game. For instance, although cricket is a team game, a batsman who scores a record number of runs or a bowler who takes a record number of wickets cannot be judged otherwise than outstanding, particularly if such ability is sustained over a long period of active engagement in the sport. This principle applies to individual scoring in the team games of rugby, hockey, baseball, and not least, Association Football.

Due to the rapid development experienced in all forms of sport, established records are constantly being broken. With improved techniques and equipment continually being designed to aid such purposes, present-day competitors hold distinct advantages over their predecessors. Comparisons of this nature could have the effect of tempering some of the glory attached to current records of achievement in sport. It is always a subject for debate. In this context, of course, nothing can be proven absolutely, but the fact remains that few records remain unbroken for long in the modern progression of sporting activities. Indeed the question is how many sports, particularly those subjected to intense development and wide application, can lay claim to any important individual record being held for much more than a decade?

One of the longest-standing records held for any sport was that achieved by Babe Ruth, the famous American baseball player who scored a record 714 home runs during a career which stretched for more than 20 years from 1914 to 1935, and involved him playing in 2502 games. The record was unbeaten until 1974, when Hank Aaron managed to surpass Babe Ruth's total after playing 2967 games. So Ruth still retained his record of runs per game, Aaron taking over 400 more games to emulate Ruth's amazing achievement. Incidentally, Babe Ruth scored a record 60 home runs in a season, a feat which remains unsurpassed. In this respect he has something in common with Dean. Ruth scored his record 60 runs in 1927 – a year that Dean will remember!

If Association Football can be regarded as the most popular sport in the world it would be logical to assume that records of individual achievement in that particular sport would be more likely to be overtaken than in any other. But the most outstanding individual goal-scoring record in football remains unchallenged and has done so for almost 50 years. In 1927-28, William Ralph Dean scored 60 goals in Division One of the English Football League.

The evaluation of any contribution to sporting activity has to be measured by standards set within the highest class. The game of soccer reached a high peak in England in the twenties (following the establishment of four divisions in the Football League) setting a standard second to none in the world. By its competitiveness, Division One had the best clubs and therefore the finest players in the whole range of the sport. Individual feats within such high standards must be regarded as world class.

In the game of soccer, successful team performance cannot be achieved without scoring goals. Goals in football are as vital as runs in cricket. The whole purpose of the game is to score goals, preferably in greater numbers than anyone else. The club possessed of a player who can score the goals is indeed fortunate, and the search for players of any consistency in this respect continues unabated to the present day, not only in the Football League but in every country where football is played.

Since the early 1950s the style, pattern, and approach to the game of soccer has been subject to radical but not necessarily beneficial influences. The team formations adopted by first-class clubs are now varied from one match to another, and 4-2-4 or 3-3-4 are commonplace descriptions of play patterns for the ten players (apart from the goalkeeper) traditionally known as full-backs, half-backs, and forwards. Nevertheless, the basic role of a team in a football match has not changed. That is to score goals and prevent their opponents from scoring. The size of the goals, the dimensions of the pitch and its various markings, and the accessories like corner flags all remain unaltered.

The rules of the game have not fundamentally changed since the off-side law was modified in 1925. But football, now a massive industry, is susceptible to being conned by the gimmickry of the commercial world. It is therefore brain-washed by new jargons put out by so-called sophisticated and expert sporting commentators following the style of commercialised American consumer advertising. And so much of it is meaningless gobbldegook to the layman. Football is a natural game, and cannot be changed in the way the army of administrators and commentators would have us believe. It still demands fundamental individual skills to be blended and adapted to a vast permutation of conditions which are the potential of any football match. Tactics there may be, but not to be computerised and applied to a game of soccer as though it were some kind of business office project.

Perhaps the most basic position in a football side is that of the goalkeeper. His role remains precisely the same as it ever was. Arguably all the other ten positions in a team have been subject to a variety of subtle changes in play patterns. There is one position, however, which requires exceptional skill and is perhaps the most crucial in any football team. That is the 'centre-forward'. The game has produced dozens of outstanding goalkeepers, full-backs, half-backs and other forwards. But the number of centre-forwards who can be placed in this category are extremely few and far between. It is the one position in a football team, as its title implies, that is the arrowhead of attack. If he has the talent and ability to perform his role successfully, which means scoring goals, a centre-forward will usually gather most of the glory.

A centre-forward, however, attracts the attention of opposing players to such an extent that his job is exceptionally demanding. That is a good reason why perhaps so few players in the history of the game have been able to sustain the skill and application to establish themselves as outstanding centre-forwards. With so few to choose from, it should be an easy task to select the really outstanding centre-forward, one who played at the top, and by his record of achievement, viewed in an overall and balanced perspective, taking account of time and the relative values of the football pattern, can be judged to be the most exceptional. It is debatable whether all historians of the sport will agree, but the evidence points to only one individual to occupy that honoured place. That is William Ralph 'Dixie' Dean, the former Everton and England centre-forward, whose football career ended in 1939. His all-round consistency and markmanship has not been surpassed even after a period of 40 years. His records are now legendary, not only in Britain but beyond. The biography of such a man cannot avoid being eulogistic, and for this, no apologies are tendered.

In 1976, Joe Mercer, the former England star and one of Dean's closest admirers, said of him, 'You know, Bill Dean never believed in team tactics. I remember once, in 1936 I think, Everton arranged a tactical talk, the outcome of which was that for the first time the team would play a third back, a position introduced by Arsenal in the thirties, in the next game to be played at Middlesbrough. The result was that Everton were thrashed by six goals to nil! Perhaps Dixie thought that proved his point!'

Many of the points made in this biography on the merits of

pre-war and post-war football reflect Dean's personal philosophy on the subject. Dean still believes that genuine accomplishment in soccer derives more from the successful blending of the player's individual skills than from the over-organised team tactics which dictate play in modern football. He asserts that preconceived match plans embodied in the so-called sophisticated team methods of today inhibit flexibility and free development. Such features, he says, are as vital to soccer as to nature itself. Indeed, he considers that modern methods, unless they are modified, will inevitably produce the mediocrity of the ersatz which pervades modern life – from fish fingers to football! Dean himself is an immortalised example of how individual skill can prosper. However, discussion on the comparative merits of one approach or the other will continue unabated for a long time yet. Polemics are the essence of sustained interest in sport, and soccer is no exception, so perhaps Dean's biography, in one way or another, may at least make a contribution to that end.

2 It's True What They Say...

PICK UP ANY BOOK on soccer records and Dixie Dean's name is there. Laurie Mumford, in his book *Centreforwards, the Great Ones,* opens appropriately with a short biography of William Ralph 'Dixie' Dean. He surely indicates that of them all, Dean tops the bill. Among some of the tributes to the Everton star he says:

> The record books are splattered with Dean's scoring feats and his name has become a legend in the annals of the game. Although decades have passed since he last wore the blue of Everton, it is doubtful whether there is a soccer follower anywhere who has not thrilled to the story of his feats, for he was a King among footballers – a man it was impossible to overlook.
>
> See the teams run out on the field and Dean could be recognised instantly. He had the looks, the build, and the carriage that made him stand out, not merely among other players but in a crowd too.
>
> It was not that Dean was particularly tall (he was 5 ft 10½ in) but he moved like a born athlete and power seemed to radiate from every muscle and sinew. This man had the build of a Bruce Woodcock and the speed of Derek Ibbotson.

During that period, top clubs had a huge playing staff of anything up to 40 professionals. There was immense competition for places in the first team. The world outside was much harsher than today, even allowing for the high unemployment at the time of writing. Although footballers received £8 per week, their summer wage was only £6. Nevertheless, it is a fact of life that such periods of adversity frequently harvest a greater crop of men and women with exceptional talent than do times of prosperity. Indeed, in most areas of human activity this has been a consistent and pervading feature of human development. In the field of sport, particularly football, it was a time of outstanding individual skills. That Dean was such a super star of the period must have some relevance when judging what an exceptionally good player he was.

Dean played eleven full seasons in Division One of the Football League, all with Everton, during which time he played 362 League games and scored 310 goals, which in itself remains a record for any player. In addition, he played 37 games in Division Two, scoring 39 goals. Dean's 60 goals in one season in Division One and 37 hat tricks in his career still stand as records to this day. Many of his other achievements in goal scoring also remain unbroken.

He was without doubt the super star (although the word had not then been coined) footballer of the late twenties and thirties. Despite the comparatively limited communications of those days, the name Dixie Dean was known to millions, including many people who had no particular interest in sport. He has been immortalised in the soccer world as a result of his phenomenal goal-scoring records. It is highly unlikely that his achievements will ever be surpassed. In view of his unique contribution, it seems incredible that the story of his career has never previously been told.

As one of the most outstanding sportsmen of our time, Dixie Dean's story is obviously worth placing on record. In his case the only records held are those reports and various articles which appeared in newspapers and sporting periodicals, in profusion at the height of his fame, and subsequently in commemorative form during the years following. The fact that the story of his football life, which came to a conclusion nearly 40 years ago, has never been told in any comprehensive fashion is perhaps due to the inherent modesty of the man. Here is a footballing phenomenon whose story ought to be of interest, not only to sport, but in the wider historical context, yet he made no previous effort to provide for his biography. Dean's achievements may not be as important as the discovery of penicillin, but nevertheless they are of interest in measuring the capacity and potential of human endeavour. Dean's activities, although totally involved in sport, ought not to be ignored. Sport, particularly football, is an activity which, however indirectly, makes a contribution to human progress. Those who hold a unique place in its development deserve to be remembered as a factor in the whole civilising process. It was once put to Bill Shankly, the famous manager of Liverpool F.C., that some people look upon football as a matter of life and death. His reply came; 'Be assured it is much more serious than that.'

On his record alone there is little doubt that Dixie Dean must rank as the greatest centre-forward of all time. Devotees of football may justifiably argue that records can be deceptive, and that is a fair approach, but if they examine other evidence, which supplements Dean's records, it would reveal a background of unique dedication and skill; humanity and humility; dignity and modesty; providing sincere sporting (in the real meaning of the word) values, which were his make-up and character, in order to sustain the remarkable achievements which were his.

Few footballers, even with outstanding ability, fail to retaliate to the provocations that inevitably come their way on the field of play. Dean's sense of sportsmanship and good humour sustained him in all those situations and throughout his career he was never booked by a referee or sent off in a game. He suffered many serious injuries whilst playing in top class football but consistently came bouncing back without any of his high sporting qualities tarnished in the least. His style and approach to the game is sufficiently creditable to warrant being looked upon as a fine example of sportsmanship, not only to football, but to the whole of the sporting world.

It is of some import in this context to consider the whole of the football cycle, the peaks and troughs which have occurred throughout its early development and beyond, and whether Dean's amazingly fruitful career was concurrent with an exceptionally good period or not. It can be argued quite strongly that it was. After all, it was a time when the game was at a peak, reaching a maturity, and embracing a more meaningful standard of professionalism, not subject to the commercial pressures of the modern game, which if applied to any sport inevitably pollute the spirit of true sportsmanship. His record was, on balance, achieved in a situation as creditable as could be found anywhere in the history of the game or possibly at any time in the future.

Since the end of the Second World War society has come round to expressing its appreciation of sportsmen in a more tangible way than ever before, with state honours and financial benefits never previously imagined. Footballers have received their fair share of this more reasonable and benevolent attitude to sport. Indeed, the book market has been flooded with biography and autobiography, covering many a footballer's fame and fortune, some of which has been the outcome of short and relatively not very impressive careers. It has to be said there can be no denying the achievements of 'Dixie' Dean. Had he been able to apply his prowess to the football scene of today, not only would his fame have been established, but also his fortune. The story of a man with such unique talent would undoubtedly have been monitored by the mass media and exploited very successfully through commercial channels for ravenous consumption by a soccer-hungry public. A comprehensive survey of his unique record has never before been compiled, an omission due mainly to the modesty of the man who, having made an exceptional contribution to the game of football, (one which would stretch the vanity of most mortals), never kept a detailed personal record, or adopted any approach that wasn't characterised by self-effacement.

Sir Matt Busby, in his book *Soccer at the Top*, has this to say about William Ralph Dean:

Who could ever have seen Bill Dean and not seen greatness? My first sight of him was when I arrived in Manchester to join City as a boy of seventeen. He was playing for Everton against Manchester United at Old Trafford. He confirmed what I had heard. He scored a hat trick. So this was English football. So this was Dixie Dean. Oh dear!

To play against Dixie Dean was at once a delight and a nightmare. He was a perfect specimen of an athlete, beautifully proportioned, with immense strength, adept on the ground but with extraordinary skill in the air. However close you watched him, his timing in the air was such that he was coming down before you got anywhere near him, and he hit that ball with his head as hard and as accurately as most players could kick it. Defences were close to panic when corners came over. And though he scored a huge tally of goals with headers he was an incredibly unselfish and amazingly accurate layer-off of chances for others. He was resilient in face of the big, tough centre-halves of his day – and I cannot think of one centre-half today to match up with that lot, though it was often the unstoppable force against the immovable object – and he was a thorough sportsman.

Dixie scored a record 60 League goals in the season 1927-28 in 39 games, plus three FA Cup goals and 19 in representative games, for a total of 82. There cannot be another Dixie Dean any more than there can be another anybody else. If there could be, the new Dixie would still score a great pile of goals. He would out-jump, out-time, out-head any defender or any number they could pack into the area. As a header of the ball only Denis Law and, less often, since he was more at the back than the front, Jack Charlton have come within a mile of Dixie.

J. T. Howcroft, the famous referee, wrote:

I have seen England's centre (Dean) in many moods, not only scoring goals, but playing perfect football, of the kind that has not been seen in this country since the days of G. O. Smith. I have known all the cracks for the last thirty years, but never one like Dixie Dean for anticipation and cleverness in all his work.

To quote Joe Mercer:

Dixie was unique, probably the greatest scoring machine the game has ever known, or ever will know. He hadn't a negative thought in his head; he never showed any nerves or any tension, he always believed his team would win and he never, never stopped scoring goals. In the air he could achieve anything and everything – gliding, deflecting, nodding it down or, as he did mostly, scoring. On the ground he had two good feet, never needed a back lift and would regularly poke in goals with his toe end. Most of all, he was a terrific competitor, perfect for the job in physique and temperament. Merseyside will never forget Dixie because the man manufactured new legends almost every week, tales that are still told and re-told whenever football is discussed. What is forgotten is that his scoring feats were a potent influence on the game. Every opposing team had to wrestle with the problem of how to stop Dixie but very few succeeded. It has been said that as many as four or five defenders were deputed to check him yet all they succeeded in doing was to watch him win the ball in the air and direct it to one or other of his capable colleagues. He was a flamboyant personality and made every match a big occasion. He was good with the public and marvellous with kids, and, on top of all this, a great captain. No one played it better on or off parade than Dixie. In 12 seasons he scored 349 goals for Everton and his 60 goals in 1927-28 is the Everest of goalscoring.

In the context of Dean's unique achievements, the foregoing comments are intended to emphasise the significance of his individual contribution in this important area of human activity. Dean was a working class boy who overcame many difficulties (of a kind not generally experienced today) to gain distinction.

Can sport be regarded as a significant factor in promoting civilised development? If it is, why shouldn't the names of those who have engaged in sporting pursuits, and made outstanding individual contributions, be enshrined in the wider civilised historical context which normally extends to sustaining the memory of those serving the arts and sciences? Perhaps it is sacrilegious to suggest that the sporting 'greats' deserve a hallowed niche carved out alongside the immortals from all the other important fields of human endeavour. In the modern world sporting activity has become an integral part of life. Exceptional individual achievement in sport may ultimately be subject to a changing historical perspective leading perhaps to a more appreciative evaluation of sporting attainment in the analysis of civilised progress.

3 A Star is Born

MR AND MRS DEAN had been married for fifteen years and with four children, all girls, a natural anxiety governed their anticipations about the sex of the next child, due to be born in January 1907. Would it be the son they desired so much? Not that they didn't cherish all the girls. The Deans were a close and affectionate group but it was the most normal thing in the world to expect the blessing of at least one boy. In those Edwardian times large families were not uncommon, but as society was dominated by the male sex, not to have a son induced an inferiority, a kind of lack of security even within the working class, to which the Dean family proudly belonged.

The Deans were not to be disappointed. On January 22 1907, Mrs Dean gave birth to a bouncing baby boy, a boy who was to more than make up for the male famine in the family by continuing to bounce in a most remarkable way throughout his life; and in a predominantly masculine fashion that few others have been able to match in the world of sport either before or since. The boy was christened William Ralph and although his forenames were destined never to be particularly well-known, his surname became linked with a nickname to form an alliterative title as famous as any in sporting history. 'Dixie Dean' became a household name coined by people everywhere, even by those who had no interest in sport. 'Give it to Dixie' was a catch-phrase that swept the country and beyond. You could address a letter to 'Dixie Dean, England' and it would be delivered to him without any trouble. Of course, this name became famous only because of the phenomenal prowess achieved by the man. He gave the name a magic and immortal sound which has echoed throughout soccer history. It was indeed an extraordinary lad that Mrs Dean brought into the world.

William Ralph's father was a native of Chester and an engine driver with the former Great Western Railway. Before marriage his wife was in domestic employment, the destiny of so many working class girls during the nineteenth century. She served a well-to-do family in Rock Ferry near Birkenhead, a town famous for shipbuilding, situated on the banks of the

Mersey. Chester was 15 miles away and Mr Dean, in order to be near his future wife, transferred to engine driving on the Wirral Railway and came to live in Birkenhead. Had he not done so, Merseyside or indeed England may not have boasted such an outstanding footballing son. Mr and Mrs Dean remained in Birkenhead for the rest of their lives, both reaching the age of 90. Such longevity may have some bearing on the extraordinary constitution inherited by their son, which was to sustain him so essentially in his football career.

In those early days, career aspirations for the sons of working class parents were synonymous with the search for security and the popular occupational symbols conceived were reflected in the minds of most fathers and sons. The job of an engine driver seemed an exciting prospect in the mind of any small boy, rich or poor. During Edwardian times it was a highly respected occupation, and of course it still is, but railways held a position of importance in those days which may never be recaptured. It was safe to assume that the only son of an engine driver (one who had in fact driven a Royal train) would be imbued with the idea of following in his father's footsteps. After all, most small boys, perhaps even today, nurture such hopes at one time or other in their boyhood. It was indeed to become William Ralph's first opening when he left school and joined the staff of the Wirral Railway as an apprentice fitter in the engine shop. At school, however, he was to develop talents in another direction which fortunately for the sporting world were recognised in advance of any he may have acquired in support of the railways.

William Ralph Dean, known as Bill in his school-days and to his special friends today – developed a football ability which was first given official recognition when he was twelve years of age. He was selected to play for Birkenhead Schoolboys in the centre-forward position. Before that he had led what might be called a chequered childhood, the result of his obsession with football. Being the only boy in a family of five sisters, four of whom were older than him, he followed a courageously independent course during his early days at school, pursuing a line of initiative and enterprise – one which many adults in similar circumstances would like to follow, but recoil from so doing for a variety of reasons. He was determined to play football whenever the opportunity arose, and if it didn't he would set out to create one. At the age of eleven he left home to enter a Borstal school as a *voluntary* inmate because he says the school provided such excellent facilities for playing football!

A Birkenhead institution for delinquents called the Albert Industrial School was run by a Scotsman who, needless to say, was something of a football fanatic. The young Dean was invited to play for the Institution's team at centre-forward alongside boys of whom some were sixteen years of age. This he did and was then persuaded by a soccer-mad school band-major to live in, even to the extent of having his name included on the roll call. He has vivid memories of the alphabetical list and recalls a boy named Carter, a surname immediately preceding his own. Carter was in the school band and showed promise as a musician.

Many years later Dean, at the height of his football career, was invited by Sir George Robey, the famous actor and comedian, to visit the Aldwych Theatre in London to attend a farewell party. Dean and George were firm friends and as they were talking backstage a voice called 'Hello Bill!'. Dean turned, and recognised the man who had addressed him as none other than Carter, the boyhood friend and inmate of the Industrial school. Carter was a member of the Aldwych Theatre orchestra. Dixie recalls with pride that Carter subsequently formed his own band and became quite a successful musician.

It is with some amusement that Dean reminisces about the Industrial school background, of the relationships he developed with the boys of the school, and how he had to hide the fact that he had not committed any act of delinquency to gain admission. Other boys continually asked him the obvious question 'What are you in for, Bill?' So, he says, he had to make up a 'cock and bull' story. He decided on the 'cock' and always told them he was in for stealing poultry. He could scarcely tell them he was only there for football, although Dean does not say how and when his imposter's role was ultimately exposed. At the same time he was also playing for his real school (the one he was compelled to attend under the education laws) and doing very well. During this period he seemed to be fully occupied in playing football, and scoring goals on an incredible scale, even by schoolboy standards.

At the outbreak of the First World War William Ralph was seven years of age. Football was the great attraction for all working class youngsters, and the war did nothing to detract from their enthusiasm for the game, except, perhaps, that many were to become retarded in their physical development by food shortages. Playing football demanded a high degree of physical stamina, particularly if lads entered the more competitive areas of the game at inter-school and town level. Physically, Dean was fortunate that he was blessed with a well-proportioned body, a decided advantage for the sports activities in which he excelled, which were not confined to the game of football.

The height of hard times during the First World War was in 1917, when the country suffered from a most critical food and man-power shortage. Boys of William Ralph's tender age sought and obtained jobs which they undertook outside school hours and this could also have put a great strain on their physical development. Even so, young William got himself a job as an assistant to a milkman, which meant him being out of bed at 4 a.m. each morning, seven days a week, to help harness the horse and off to a farm 4 miles away on the other side of the Wirral peninsular. There he helped to pick up the churns of milk, load them on the cart and return to Birkenhead to effect delivery. He finished his rounds at 8 am. to be welcomed at home with what he describes as a 'dripping butty' for his breakfast and then off to school. At that early age he was giving proof of his extraordinary physical constitution, which was to subsequently help sustain a phenomenal sporting career.

During this time he played football incessantly. Schools in those days were frequently closed. They suffered from the drain on human and material resources which that terrible war inflicted on the nation at large. Indeed, children were allowed in some circumstances to terminate schooling at the age of thirteen and such dispensations were not uncommon. Truancy was fairly rife. The young Dean was no exception. He recalls how he carefully prepared his own private exit in the school fence to escape to a secluded hideout for the purpose of indulging in football practice.

When questioned about what inspired him to give effect to this obsession with football, Dean asserts there were no individuals that made any impact on him either in his tender years or even later on in life. This seemed exceptional. After all, most successful people confess to admiring someone whose skills or standards exercised a degree of influence in their particular field of endeavour. Not to experience such influences is more rare perhaps in young boys, all of whom seem to generate a hero worship of some kind, however shallow it may seem in retrospect. When reminiscing about his early life, Dixie may mislead you on this particular point.

When pressed about his youthful susceptibilities to such influences during his football development, he responds that there was only one he can remember. He starts by mentioning a church not far from his childhood home. Was it the Vicar who lent him some encouragement and support? No, it was 'Wes Hall', he replies, and one might be forgiven for associating the name with another sport. But 'Wes Hall' was none other than the description given to the Wesley Hall chapel, a building designed to provide the young Dean with an aid to practice which was to help develop his skill for heading a football, a skill that has not been emulated by any footballer before or since. The building had a long low roof on which a football could be placed, and as it rolled back to the adjacent passageway it could be headed back by a small boy and the exercise repeated along the whole length of the roof without the ball touching the ground – if the boy was good enough!

As a result of those intense exercises, the young Dean became quick and developed the amazing reflexes which he applied to his own fine art of heading. The hours of undisturbed practice at the back of the small church hall were to help make him, in the game of soccer, the undisputed master. 'Wes Hall' is a name to remember, and one which can be said to have carried great influence far beyond its religious significance. Those who may have known the story and saw the great man at the height of his fame would be forgiven for presuming that some divine link had been established. Millions described Dean's outstanding heading ability as 'out of this world'. He insists, however, that practice was only incidental, heading a football has to be a gift, he asserts.

The only other influence of any significance in his youth that Dixie will admit to, is the name of a certain football club which played at a spot across the Mersey, in a district of Liverpool. His father, who apparently did not realise the great potential of his only son, was a supporter of Everton, the First Division club which attracted spectators (and still does) from a wide area of Merseyside. Only once did father take his son to see that great team. It was the last season prior to the suspension of all League matches for the period of the First World War. The season 1914-15 was completed with Everton winning the First Division championship. Mr Dean took his son along to one match (Dean can't remember the name of the opposing side) and it was there, at the age of eight, that the lad vowed he would become a professional footballer, and the only club he intended to join would be Everton.

As a paying spectator (actually his father paid for him) he claims he did not watch another professional football match.

That was the only occasion on which as a schoolboy he saw a First Division game. As it turned out Everton was the only First Division club that he actually played for professionally during the whole of his distinguished career. The absence of outside influence on his game has, perhaps, deeper significance. His genius no doubt came from the originality of his performance in the game and outside influences may well have corrupted the natural gifts he so clearly possessed. Even as a child he enjoyed his independence of thought and play, fully determined to go his own way in developing his art. It was ten years before he was to see Goodison Park (home ground of Everton) again, and then as a player, to become the most famous ever to don the colours of that great club.

Dean often talks about his childhood experiences at the Laird Street School in Birkenhead (the school he attended at five years of age and left at fourteen) and describes them as being full of boyish incident. Like most other lads he says he was frequently disciplined over some minor prank or misdemeanour. In some cases charges were made and punishment administered by the Headmaster during the school assembly, held each morning in the main hall of the school. It was not uncommon for the name of William Ralph Dean to be called out and he had to march out to face his punishment. Stepping up to the platform on one such occasion the young Dean was really perplexed, because he was unable to recall any recent misbehaviour, so it was indeed with some trepidation that he confronted the Head with the whole school standing and staring in the silent anticipation of a 'what's he up for this time?' situation.

The Headmaster looked at Dean and said 'William Ralph Dean, the whole school is proud of you.' The boy was so astonished that he immediately thought the Head was making a sarcastic introduction to a charge of indiscipline against him. Dean bowed his head and waited for the worst. But the Headmaster went on, 'William, I have the great pleasure of presenting to you this medal, which commemorates your selection and appearance for the Birkenhead Schoolboys football team. You have brought honour to the school and all the pupils and teachers congratulate you.'

The young Dean looked round countenanced with relief and delight grasping the medal with a suppressed excitement and pride. A memorable moment for him. Today Dean looks back to that occasion and asserts, 'Really, that was the most important event of my life. That medal takes pride of place in the honours list of my football achievements.'

By the time Dean was 26 years of age he had won every honour in the game. All the medals, representing those honours, were until his retirement scattered about his home in boxes or envelopes in sideboard drawers. Under pressure from friends he agreed that the medals be set in a wooden plaque with appropriate identifying inscriptions. In a single spot, at the top of the plaque, is set the Birkenhead Schoolboys medal, the one he was presented with by the Headmaster at that school assembly way back in 1919. One might ask why Dean never played for England Schoolboys. He says he was selected for an England trial but was unable to attend because of injury. But in the aftermath of war the organisation supporting schoolboy football was restricted and consequently must have by-passed a great amount of talent. And once a boy had reached the age of 14 in those days he was ineligible for national schoolboy soccer.

Throughout its history football has suffered from what is a seemingly perpetual problem – the scarcity of good centre-forwards. It would be natural for those few who proved themselves to be outstandingly competent in this position to adopt a superior attitude and become arrogant in the process. For Dean, as a boy asserting himself in that position, he might be expected, in the light of his exceptional achievements, to have assumed a lack of humility and become a spoiled character, a decline often the result of premature success. Such a reaction was alien to him. He strode through everything during his youthful period with a complete sense of nonchalance about his talent. This was an attitude he retained throughout an even more successful adult career, and became a quality admired as much as the skills he displayed on the field. No doubt many young footballers can claim prolific goal-scoring feats in school soccer. Not many could record the kind of achievements credited to the young Dean. He was in demand to play not only for school teams but at the same time with sides representing grown men.

When Dean was given his first trial for Birkenhead school-boys (at outside-right!) his team, the Probables, defeated the Possibles by eight goals, six of them scored by him. On that day his school side had a fixture which was timed to start when the trial match finished. So Dean, bearing this in mind, borrowed a cycle and when the trial match was over dashed off to play in the school match and there scored a further six goals! However, his day's stint had not yet been completed! Football to the young man was a three-shift exercise and he was working them all in one day. His football appetite was insatiable.

He was also engaged to play for a local Church team, Moreton Bible Class, a side fielding many grown-ups, the youngest (apart from Dean) being a sixteen-year-old. The chaps who selected the Bible class team were not aware of Dean's earlier exploits that day. Had they been they might have hesitated to include him in their side, concluding that no-one, even such an outstanding player as Dean, particularly one so young, could be expected to play three matches in one day. It sounds a tall story, but the result was that he scored another six goals for the Bible Class (a team playing in a league boasting a reasonable standard for local football), completing a bag of eighteen goals in three matches in one day!

It has been mentioned that Dean's father had taken him to a First Division football match on one occasion only. Mr Dean's hours of work did not give him the freedom to attend many League games. Whilst it is supposed that he had some idea of his son's potential, he had no thoughts of encouraging the boy to take up the game professionally. William Ralph was left very much to himself to follow his own interests. Of course Christmas and birthdays posed no problems to his parents when selecting presents. It was always some kind of football accessory that he received. With so many sisters it was perhaps natural for him to pursue his own interests in an isolated fashion. Although football was a team game, Dean confesses to becoming something of a lonely type. He liked to be on his own and frequently spent hours alone concentrating and practising with a football, minus friends or interruptions.

Following his selection for the town schools' team, Dean's father, proud of his boy's achievement, made the sort of promises that most fathers would make to their sons in similar circumstances. Of course it depends on whether or not such promises can be fulfilled. If you had a son with the potential of the young Dean you could not treat a promise (to give him a shilling for every goal he scored) in a light-hearted manner. Wages in those days were low and to shell out six bob to a twelve-year-old every time he played in a football match could prove a disastrous course, ending in possible insolvency for the family.

The one occasion his father made that kind of a contract with his son related to a Birkenhead schools fixture against Liverpool Boys, a strong team that could challenge most junior sides in the country. Liverpool won the match 5-0. Dean, playing centre-forward in a one-sided game, found himself operating in defence for the greater part of the match. In one goalmouth incident he put through his own goal. When he arrived home after the match, his father, with some trepidation, put his hand in his pocket and asked William Ralph how much he owed him, at the rate of one shilling per goal. 'I only scored one today so you owe me a shilling,' the boy replied. When his father read the result in the local newspaper, he had a strong desire to punish his son for lying. The boy's defence was that his father had made no reservations about how and for whom he scored the goals. There was no doubt a goal had been credited to Liverpool – an own goal scored by Dean – and that was that! Father let him off, but decided in the family interest that he would not provide any further financial incentives for his son to score goals!

Many stories circulated about the prowess of the young Dean. At the age of twelve he possessed the power of an adult in kicking a football. The legends he created as a result of his precociousness in the sport were forerunners of those he was to establish later on in his career. On one occasion, playing for Birkenhead schoolboys against Bootle boys, a match won 5-1 by Birkenhead, with Dean scoring four goals, the Bootle goalkeeper was injured in attempting to save a shot from the young centre-forward. Dean's shooting with either foot was really exceptional and had to be seen to be believed.

A contemporary of Dean, who was a schoolboy spectator at the Bootle match, still relates the story. Dean gathered the ball in the penalty area and the Bootle goalkeeper scarcely had time to advance when Dean shot. The goalkeeper bent forward to block a hard low drive, and the ball struck him on the forearm. He dropped to the ground obviously stunned by the power of the shot. It was then discovered that the young goalkeeper's arm had been fractured! It may have been considered an unfair advantage to play such as boy as Dean with schoolboys, but it had to be done. The advantage may even have been viewed similarly by the adults he often played against! In the not-too-distant future many a defence in the First Division would be expressing similar sentiments!

Other troubles befell him as a result of his youthful obsession with football. Another sister was born to the Dean family and young William had to take his turn in taking the baby out in the pram. On one occasion, Dean recalls, he took the baby up to Bidston Hill, a pleasant green area of Birkenhead about a mile away from where the Deans lived. A group of boys were engaged in a game of football near the spot where young Dean was parading the baby. He was invited to join in the game – an offer he could not resist. The pram containing the baby was utilised as a goal post. Coats, sticks, and the usual makeshift articles were used to provide the other posts or to mark out the pitch for the match. The game went on until it was almost too dark to play. The boys finally left for home, including the young Dean. When he arrived home the first reaction from his mother was to enquire anxiously about the baby. The boy had left her, still in the pram, somewhere on Bidston Hill! He ran out of the house, and ran faster, he says, than he ever ran in his life to return to the scene of the game. With great relief he found the pram exactly where he had left it, the baby asleep inside, safe and sound! It was a lesson he never forgot, and the situation was never repeated – his parents saw to that.

Dean's reputation as a schoolboy footballer grew enormously. His regular appearances at centre-forward with the Birkenhead schools' side created a great demand for his services from a number of local clubs, many of which were fielding teams of adults and playing in highly competitive leagues. In those days the spectator attraction of this kind of football was much greater than exists today. It was not exceptional to find anything up to a thousand people gathering to watch such matches. The financial support came from a collection box passed around. Great rivalry was generated between clubs representing different areas of a township, with supporters quite passionate about the success or otherwise of their particular football heroes. Some finals in knock-out competitions were often arranged to be played on a League club ground and would attract a crowd of up to five thousand or even more.

In such a football environment it was quite exceptional for a schoolboy to be even considered as a candidate to play for any of those clubs. On some occasions Dean would play as many as four matches in one day! Not all, of course, for the adult teams. Nevertheless he did play and would invariably be amongst the goals. This kind of experience groomed him for the successful career which he was destined to make for himself and the unique experience that he was to bring to English football.

Football was, of course, the sport he was most interested in, but there were other sports he got into, by joining a club which catered for other activities besides football, thus enabling him to prove his qualities as an all-rounder. On one such occasion at the age of 12, as a member of the Boys Brigade (which he had actually joined only for the football opportunities it offered) he was asked to represent the unit at an athletic meeting. He did so and won the 80, 100, and 200 yards sprints, as well as the high and long jump events!

It was during this early period in his life that he took an interest in golf. At first this was inspired more by a desire to earn some additional pocket money. Not far from his home was a fairly exclusive golf club 'The Wirral Ladies Golf Club', to which he became attached as a caddy at the age of twelve. The fact that it was a women's club cannot be interpreted as being of any significance, Dean says. There was only a schoolboy interest in earning a few coppers and learning about a sport involving co-ordination of mind and body – a great ball game! The caddying job presented him with many opportunities he would not otherwise have had to practise the game of golf. As an engine driver's son, particularly in those days, he could scarcely have afforded to take up the sport seriously, but in the circumstances he lost no opportunity to develop his game. Dean was a natural in the sense that he possessed, even as a boy, all the physical and mental attributes which enabled him to acquire a high standard of skill at any ball game. It is of interest to know that his grip of a golf club was unorthodox. Although a right-handed player, he gripped the club left hand below right and this, he says, proved very successful.

By the time Dean was 15 years of age his golf handicap was down to two strokes. Such progress was indeed a sign that he might well have played the game professionally and possibly have achieved as much success at golf as he eventually gained on the soccer field. However, he now insists that he could not have had a happier life than the one he followed, despite the fact that if he had taken up golf he would have escaped all those major injuries sustained during his football career. By succeeding in football, however, Dean was provided with opportunities to play golf a good deal. By the age of 20 he was a scratch player and was successful in a number of tournaments arranged for professional footballers. Indeed, he once won the Wirral Amateur Golf Championship and still holds the trophy he was awarded to prove it.

When Dean reached the age of fourteen in 1921, it was a time when opportunities were extremely limited for any boy with potential in sport. If you were good, the only way to be recognised was to move into the privileged classes and perhaps attend university. Dean came from a family of ordinary working folk, and his potential, although duly appreciated by local people, was obscured from national recognition by the limitations imposed by the attitudes which existed at that particular period. If a boy was to succeed in sport he had to persevere and win through purely on his own merit, which even then had to be exceptional. The only two sports clearly open to ordinary folk were football and boxing. Very few working class boys with talent at sport got to the top in any other field. Top class athletics, cricket, tennis, and rugby required facilities generally denied to the mass of people.

William Ralph Dean left school at the age of fourteen in January 1921. It was a Friday, and as soon as he arrived home his mother took him straight down to the shopping area of Birkenhead to have him fitted out for a denim boiler suit. The boy was to start work the following day in the engine shop at the Wirral Railway, where his father worked as an engine driver. Although he was only fourteen the boy had to do shift work, including night duties. Any thought of him becoming a professional footballer did not arise in the minds of his parents. There in the engine shop he assisted in the repair and maintenance of steam engines. He did, however, manage to get some football practice when he was on night work, which, he says, he opted for on a regular basis. The practice was not with a football and he certainly didn't get the opportunity to indulge in any heading experience.

The Wirral Railway engine shops were plagued with rats, and during the night the rodents made their appearance in dozens, so Dean recalls. Rodent operators, if there were any in those days, were not very successful, so the lad helped in the one way that he knew best. As the rats ran across the floor, he would move almost as quickly and take a running kick at the chosen target and send the rat spinning through the air to land against the wall or engine or whatever, where it would finish stone dead with a broken back. Dean claims his score was at least two or three each night, but he has no record of the number of hat tricks he achieved during that period. Anyone who saw Dixie Dean on the football field would know how he could hit a ball with either foot and will readily accept that those rats never had a chance!

As an employee of the Wirral Railway he was naturally in the field for selection to play for the football team of that name which at the time was playing in the West Cheshire League. The reserve teams of one or two Third Division clubs of the Football League played in the same league, including Tranmere Rovers. So Dean found himself performing in a higher class of football, with professionals, when he was just fourteen years of age. In today's football that may not be unusual, boys generally being more mature in physique and playing with all the advantages created by modern equipment, with lighter boots and plastic footballs. But in 1921, for a mere boy of fourteen years to play with grown men was remarkable, particularly if the youngster occupied the centre-forward position. The greatest success of the Wirral Railway team was to reach the Cheshire Senior Cup Final, only to be beaten 1-0 by Tranmere Rovers.

At this time a club called Pensby, playing in the Wirral Combination, persuaded Dean to join, and he says he became very attached to it because everybody treated him so well. The club gave him 2s 6d per week expenses, which, he emphasises, was a lot of money to a boy of his age. He had to travel about eight miles from his home to the ground. In those days this presented many difficulties. If he missed the bus, he would often run all the way in order to get there in time. The Pensby Club liked him and he had a great affection for the team. That season the club won the championship of the Wirral Combination with Dean one of the stars. However, at the same time he continued to work for the Wirral Railway and play for its football team.

Dean often refers to 'Old Doc Martlew' whom he says was Chairman of the Railway. The 'Doc's' two sons were directors of the New Brighton Football Club, which at that time was in the Third Division of the Football League. The directors invited the young Dean to play for their club, but, he says, he refused on the grounds that he was not ready for League football. In any case, he adds, he was determined not to play for any other team but Everton, remembering the vow he made when his father had taken him to the only League match he had ever seen in his life. So Dean continued to play with Pensby, until he was nearly sixteen years of age.

4 Turning Professional

DEAN STAYED WITH the Pensby Club for a couple of seasons and then one day when he was not quite sixteen years old a scout representing Tranmere Rovers approached him and said the Third Division club was interested in signing him on as an amateur. The young William Ralph was really only interested in joining one club and that was Everton, but he was eventually persuaded by the Tranmere scout, a man named 'Dump' Lee, to sign, thus revoking his earlier vow. In signing for Tranmere, Dean imposed one condition and that was for some compensation to be given to the Pensby club, if only, Dean decreed, it was in the form of a new 'strip' for his old team-mates. An assurance was given that this would be done. Dean recriminates that the promise was broken and his old club received nothing. This was the first of a number of breaches of faith he experienced whilst with the Tranmere club.

In those days Rovers were considered to be in a reasonable position financially. Gates were of the order of ten thousand and more at each home game. Dean played several times as an amateur for the reserve side but when he became of age, at sixteen, he signed professional forms and began making appearances in the first team. In the 1923-24 season he had two games without scoring. In the following season he made his presence felt and played more regularly in League matches. But Dean alleges that Bert Cooke, the Tranmere secretary, was only interested in arranging a deal to transfer him to another club – at a big fee.

Ashington, a town in Northumberland not far from Newcastle-on-Tyne, is an area which has produced some great footballers, the most famous of which are the Charlton brothers, Bobby and Jack, who both regularly played for England in the sixties and seventies. In the early twenties, Ashington played in the Third Division (North) of the Football League. The Tranmere Rovers side to play Ashington in an away fixture included the young Dean at centre-forward. The team travelled from Merseyside on the Friday evening before the match but it was not until the Saturday morning that Bert Cooke, the Tranmere secretary, called Dean to invite him to accompany him on a visit to the famous St James' Park ground, home of Newcastle United.

No other member of the Rovers team was included in the invitation. Dean, rather puzzled, accepted and went along, totally unaware of the real purpose of the visit. During the journey Cooke told him that arrangements had been made for him to meet a number of very important people in the football world. Dean, still somewhat preplexed, arrived at the ground to be introduced to a number of well-dressed gentlemen who turned out to be representatives not only of Newcastle, but also of Aston Villa, Arsenal, and Birmingham football clubs. Dean says Cooke had certainly cooked something up! In turn each representative attempted to persuade Dean to join his club.

Dean was rather astonished to learn he had earned a reputation which created a demand from such famous clubs. To be recognised in this way overwhelmed him. He was only 17 years of age and aware that he could not make an immediate decision. He told them all he would have to consult his parents. He still hankered for the opportunity to play for Everton. Although he had not kept to his childhood vow in this respect, he felt justified in modifying his wishes and was determined at least not to play for any other First Division club. So all the offers were subsequently rejected and Dean continued to play for Tranmere.

For some reason the incident at Ashington has always rankled Dean. He says that the Tranmere secretary proved he had no other interest in him but to exploit his value and make money out of a transfer deal. From an early age Dean hated anything that smacked of wheeling and dealing in football, or in anything else for that matter. His character had developed to be fair and honest about every aspect of the life he now led. On the football field this attitude produced the highest standards of sportsmanlike behaviour, and all this refreshing openness stayed with him throughout his career.

Dean's two games with the Tranmere first team in the 1923-24 season had brought him no goals but in the following season he began to establish a pattern of scoring which continued throughout his footballing life. From September 1924 to March 1925 he played 27 matches for Tranmere and scored 27 goals. At 17 years of age he not only demonstrated his remarkable skills with a football but also an outstanding personality and a flamboyance which produced an entertaining relationship with the spectators, a rapport which endeared him to them and never went sour. And there were huge crowds in those days, not only at Tranmere but at many other Third Division grounds, and Dean's flair was widely appreciated and enormously increased his popularity throughout the country.

His temperament was such that he never displayed any nerves or tension and, whatever the provocation, was never guilty of retaliation. As a centre-forward he held the most vulnerable position in that respect, his opponents frequently deputing four or five defenders to mark him, creating situations which would surely tax the patience of any player. Dean, however, had the ability to overcome such tactics, possessing as he did unique skills which he could exploit to advantage for the benefit of his team-mates.

Many of the older supporters of Tranmere will recall the pre-match arrangements introduced to keep supporters waiting outside the ground informed of the names of the home team playing that day. Crowds would be gathered on an open space opposite the Prenton Park site. A large board on which the names of the team had been inscribed was carried round the front of the first line of potential spectators by a young man who more often than not staggered along under its weight. He seemed anxious to complete his task quickly in order to deposit the board back in the office from which he had set out. Consequently, he did not circulate among the crowd as fully as he was supposed to do. Shouts from the waiting spectators were constant, appealing to those who could see the board to let them know the team selection.

'Is he down to play?' was the cry. A stranger might wonder who the crowd referred to. The name of course was 'Dixie' and if 'Dean' appeared on the board it would be the signal for the crowd to surge forward and take their place in the queue at the turnstiles, full of pleasurable anticipation that value for money would be obtained that Saturday afternoon! If his name did not appear on the board, a goodly portion of the crowd would depart in disappointment just as would occur outside a theatre when it is announced that the star of the show cannot appear.

Incidentally, the ground at Prenton Park, although holding 20,000 spectators, was in a rather dilapidated condition in those days. Corrugated iron sheets formed the enclosure, and the terraces were pure earth, sloping down to the pitch within a yard of the touchline. There was, however, a small wooden stand for the privileged few who could afford to pay to sit and watch the games. Football crowds in those days would endure anything. They put up with all the elements, there being very little cover, but no doubt they thought it was all worthwhile when they could watch someone like the great Dixie Dean.

Dean's first major injury, one of the many he was to suffer during his football career, occurred in a match against Rochdale at Prenton Park. The game was half-way through the second half and Tranmere were leading 2-0, both goals having been scored by Dean. The Rochdale centre-half, whom it was said had passed his better playing days, accosted the young centre-forward and issued a stern warning. 'Tha'll geet no moor bluddy goals, young fella-me-lad, ah'll seeth't!' Dean took little notice of his remarks and went on to play his normal game. A few minutes later however, when Dean gathered the ball in the penalty area and was looking dangerous in front of goal, the Rochdale centre-half, obviously out to show he did not issue idle warnings, kicked Dean in the genitals so viciously that the lad went down and out.

Dean, recalling the incident, says, 'I went down as though I was poleaxed,' and adds ruefully, 'what a tipster that bloke was!' Indeed, when the other players gathered round him, concerned as to the nature and extent of his injury, one player put his hand down Dean's shorts at the front to apply the only aid he knew – that of attempting to ease the pain by rubbing. Dean, in a rather agonising voice, made a desperate appeal, 'Never mind rubbing 'em – count them!' The result was, Dean asserts, that he actually lost a stone, emphasising it was not a loss in weight!

Dean was rushed off to hospital, where he was examined and informed he would have to undergo an operation, but not before the swelling in the groin had gone down. He describes the lump as being so enormous that he had to warn the doctor to evacuate the hospital for fear of an explosion. Dean enjoys telling this particular story. People always react by asking many questions, curious to know the biological details. Dean laughs and laughs at their disbelief when he tells people he was not really affected in any respect. Of course he can afford to joke about it now, but at the time he had to miss a game or two, he says, and that was serious. He soon recovered and resumed his place in the Rovers team. His capacity to recover quickly from many serious injuries, which he subsequently sustained, proved to be almost as unique as his soccer skills.

When he signed professional forms to play for Tranmere, Dean gave up his job with the Wirral Railway. The club paid him £4 5s 0d per week – the standard wage for Third Division players at that time. It seemed a reasonable income for a boy in those days, but there was no security attached to a footballer's continued employment, either to cover loss of form or injury. A player could be seriously injured and his career ended without any means of compensation. The players union suffered from a great deal of apathy, and did little to improve pay and conditions. Indeed, in 1921 the maximum wage was cut from £9 to £8 after the union had submitted a claim for a £10 minimum! Some clubs in fact would not allow their players to join the players' union, including, so it is reported, Everton. Everton was proud of its benevolent attitude, and saw no need for its players to join such organisations as unions.

The youthful Dean was quite happy to play football full time, and the amount of wages paid was not the main attraction. In fact he says he would have played for nothing! But as a professional he had to live, and with a bonus of £1 for a win and 10s. for a draw he did very well. Of course there were other aspects to be considered in assessing the football business of those days. If a club set out to entertain 10,000 spectators, and received £600 or £700, the players (the entertainers) between them were entitled, one would think, to a greater share than the £50 wages bill paid by the management.

There were occasions when a Third Division side actually fielded only ten players in some matches! The wages bill would then be less! Indeed, when Tranmere played Southport in a qualifying round of the FA Cup in 1923, the Rovers team was one man short from the start. But as no substitutes were allowed in those days, apparently nothing could be done about it, the team playing with only ten men throughout the game.

Although training sessions were compulsory in Third Division football, nothing like today's strict discipline was observed. There were no managers to administer training disciplines of any co-ordinated pattern. Training consisted of running exercises and ball practice. No serious attention was given to the adoption of tactics or team methods for Third Division soccer. Players performed intuitively, but despite the apparent disadvantages there is no doubt that this led to individual skills being more freely exercised, making a valuable contribution to the game and perhaps raising the level of entertainment for spectators.

Sport has retained a reasonable following of spectators blessed with a good sense of humour. This has sometimes rubbed off on the players or participants and on Merseyside in particular is a consistent feature of the soccer scene. Dean illustrated this with a story about an event which occurred whilst he was playing with Tranmere Rovers. During a match at Prenton Park, the outside right of an opposing team was being barracked unmercifully by the crowd. 'What a crap winger. An outside right with two left feet. What a load of rubbish! . . . etc., etc. The player, racing down the wing with the ball at his feet, could stand it no longer. He suddenly stopped, turned towards the crowd and kicked the ball out of touch, directly at the mass of jeering faces, shouting, 'What the hell do you expect for four pound ten a week, Sam Chedgzoy?' The barracking ceased and good humour was restored.

This less organised soccer environment of Third Division games suited Dean, enabling him to develop, uninhibited, his natural skills which were applied in a positive fashion with a style and flair perhaps never to be seen again. It is possible that had he been subject to the over-organised management techniques of the modern game, his natural skills would have been so stifled that his phenomenal output may never have been realised. On the other hand, anyone who knew his character might say that such genius as he possessed could not be restrained under any circumstances.

Tranmere Rovers Football Club was founded in 1883. The club became a member of the Cheshire League, later joining the Central League until 1921, when it then became a founder member of the Third Division (North) of the Football League. When Dean joined Tranmere in 1923 the club was struggling to maintain its position in the Third Division, but it was nevertheless able to attract a large number of loyal supporters. For example, in 1924 a record 15,000 spectators attended a match at Prenton Park when Rovers played the famous Wolverhampton Wanderers, a team which at that time spent a solitary year in the Third Division. But although that gate was exceptional, Tranmere regularly played before ten to twelve thousand spectators during the period right up to the beginning of the Second World War.

Tranmere cannot boast of achieving many honours in the League, and although the club did win promotion to the Second Division in 1938 it returned to the Third the following season. The club can however, claim to have made a rare contribution to English football. Every soccer enthusiast knows that a centre-forward of class is the scarcest commodity in the game. Yet Tranmere Rovers gave the world of soccer two of the greatest in the history of the sport. Both were born and bred within a short distance of Prenton Park, Tranmere's ground in the town of Birkenhead. Those players were Dixie Dean and 'Pongo' Waring.

It may not be generally known that the goal-scoring feats of Dean and Waring include the records of being the first and second for the highest number of goals in a season in the First Division of the Football League. It would appear that neither of the records will ever be broken. Dean's 60 goals in 1927-28 may be better known, but Waring scored 49 in 1930-31 with Aston Villa, which remains the second highest to Dean. Both were international players, appearing for England on a number of occasions at centre-forward. Another outstanding player from the Tranmere nursery, who distinguished himself during the Dean-Waring period, was Ellis Rimmer, a Birkenhead schoolboy who subsequently played for Sheffield Wednesday and England.

During the 1924-25 season many First Division clubs showed an ever increasing interest in the young centre-forward, nicknamed 'Dixie', who was scoring regularly for that obscure club, Tranmere Rovers. Few people realised where the club was situated. Many today are not aware that the club is from that hot bed of soccer fever, Merseyside. In those days of Dean's youth the name Tranmere was even more foreign to the rest of the country. Everton, the local First Division club, could afford to keep a regular eye on the progress of the young genius playing at Tranmere. And Everton were determined to have him on their books before long.

One day in the early spring of 1925, March 16 to be precise, Dean arrived home in the afternoon, having just spent a few hours sitting through a matinee at the local cinema, a popular indulgence of professional footballers at that time, training sessions being confined to mornings with the rest of the day free to do as they pleased. Dean's mother greeted him with the news that a visitor had been to the house who was a representative of some football club. His mother, not being too well acquainted with the names of football teams, scratched her head and tried to think of the name the man had given. 'I think he said it was Everton – is there a team of that name?' she pondered.

Dean could not contain his excitement at the news. He asked his mother for more reassurance on the matter. His mother replied that he should find out for himself, the man had said he would be waiting for him at the Woodside Hotel, about two miles away from the Dean home. Without further ado, the young man ran out of the house and made his way, poste haste, to the hotel. Sure enough, when he arrived, there was Tom McIntosh, the Everton secretary, waiting to discuss transfer terms and sign the young Dean to play for that famous club. Dean did not hesitate. He duly signed to make his boyhood dream come true!

In retrospect, when Dean recalls the event, it is not without some bitterness he tells of the part played by Mr Bert Cooke, the Tranmere secretary, in the conduct of the transfer. Apparently, Dean will never forget what he regards as a great injustice imposed on him by Cooke over the terms of that transfer deal. Cooke had promised Dean that he would receive 10% of the fee paid by Everton to Tranmere. When Everton paid the £3000 to the Tranmere club, Cooke sent for Dean and handed him a cheque for £30. Dean's immediate reaction was to hand it back to Cooke and inform him of the mistake. 'You've left a nought off this haven't you, Mr Cooke?' Dean said, pointing to the figures on the cheque. Cooke shook his head and told Dean that the League would not allow 10% to be paid.

The young man was not satisfied and appealed to his new club to help, but he was told that it was Tranmere's business, not that of Everton. Dean was advised to seek an interview with the President of the Football League, Mr Tom McKenna. So Dean followed the advice but was informed by the League that having signed for Everton there was nothing that could be done for him, but had he raised the issue before he signed, some protection might have been afforded to him in the matter. So Dean still nurses some ill feeling about the incident. The main reason, he asserts, was that he had promised his parents most of the money he had expected to receive and Cooke's broken promises naturally embittered him. Dean alleges that other players from Tranmere, who were subsequently involved in big transfer deals, suffered similar experiences at the hands of Cooke during that pre-war period. Dean gave the £30 to his mother, who donated it to the Birkenhead General Hospital, where 50 years later Dean was admitted for the amputation of his right leg.

Dean has many criticisms of the way football clubs were run in his day, particularly as a result of his early experiences at Tranmere, but he has none whatever for the Everton club which he regards as second to none in the world. Yet he had every reason, when he finally left Everton, to be sour about the treatment he got from that club. Dean had an almost blind loyalty to the Goodison Park club which in a way was very commendable. Third Division clubs in the twenties, no doubt having to find their feet in an entirely new world, made many mistakes as a result. But Dean says the administration at Tranmere was vested mainly in a board of directors, who were appointed, by and large, on the basis of their social and financial status in the community. He waxes somewhat cynically on the subject, saying that the directors had no real knowledge of the game. There were some, he asserts, who thought the club played rugby football, yet such men carried great influence in the selection of the team!

There is the story of one club director who regularly attended matches and on one such occasion, after watching a poor display, visited the dressing room at the interval determined to give his team advice on the tactics he thought should be adopted in the second half of the game. He approached one player and explained the advantages of switching his position to the middle of the field, to watch his distribution of the ball, to delay any passes until he was tackled etc., etc. The player he was addressing went on sucking a lemon whilst the director prattled on. Then the player threw the peel away, wiped his mouth with the back of his hand, spat out a pip or two, and commented, 'It's no good you telling me all that, Sir.'

'Come, come, man,' the director insisted. 'Take notice of me and we shall win this game.'

'But, Sir, your plan has nothing to do with me,' protested the player.

'Why not, may I ask,' puffed the director.

'Because, Sir, I'm the bloody goalkeeper and have been for the past five seasons,' snapped the player as he moved to join the team, by then leaving the dressing room to start the second half.

In another case the secretary of a club promised his players the best possible wages within the rules. 'I'll pay you £8 per week during the season and £6 per week in the summer,' he announced. Subsequently the centre-forward discovered that the centre-half would be paid £8 per week during the off season.

'Why is he receiving the top wage, all the year round?' demanded the centre-forward.

The secretary beamed and replied, 'Ah, but he is a much better player than you!'

'Maybe,' retorted the centre-forward, 'but not in the bloody summer, he isn't!'

There were, Dean will argue, many instances of maladministration at all levels in football, much of it even at international level. Trial matches, ostensibly arranged for selecting an international team, were arranged to be played, in some cases, six weeks before the side was required. The remoteness of the top management to the men who actually produced the goods in football was to some extent a reflection of the general attitudes of society which then existed. The class system, in the commercial, industrial, and social world, extended in a variety of ways over the whole sporting scene, even to a working class game like football. Soccer however, never reached the debasements, which it is understood took place in the world of Cricket, where it has been said separate entrances and exits were provided at some grounds for amateurs and professionals to enter and leave the field of play. Discrimination in sport is apparently not something new!

When Dean signed for Everton he had completed 27 games during the season and had scored 27 goals, but he had proved himself not only possessed of the ability to score, but also to play intelligent and skilful football. No doubt Tranmere was proud to have nursed such an exciting prospect as the young Dean, but one is led to believe the club was much more interested in the financial value of the lad. Admittedly, although a sport, football was also a business and a harsh one at that, and Tranmere could not be blamed for a mercenary approach. Like most situations in life however, it is the people, in this case the spectators and supporters of Tranmere, who recognised and appreciated Dean's great talent in a genuine sporting sense. Much more so, it would appear, than those who administered the club.

The *Liverpool Echo*, the Merseyside evening newspaper, has always devoted itself to reporting in full all aspects of local football interest. Its sports writers have to be competent in their task in an area where soccer forms a predominant part of the life of the local community. Nowhere is football followed with more passionate interest. A former sports reporter with the *Liverpool Echo* (who wrote under the pseudonym of 'Stork') had this to say when summarising Dean's achievements:

There was not a greater personality in the game than Dean. Everywhere he went he was beseiged. 'Give it to Dixie!' was the slogan at Tranmere Rovers. It followed him throughout the length and breadth of the country and even at continental matches it was to be heard in broken English. In his Tranmere Rovers' days Dean was the most sought-after man in football. I was reporting the Rovers' games in those days and hardly a week went by but there was a representative from one of the big clubs to give him a look over. One director, however, said he wouldn't have Dean at any price! One said I was crackers about him. I was and did he not justify my opinion of him to the full?'

It is gratifying to know that at least one sports writer at that time made an accurate forecast of the potential of the young footballer. The Tranmere supporters also had no doubt of Dean's value and potential. They were the supporters responsible for giving Dean the nickname 'Dixie', a title which he at first resented, always insisting on 'Bill' when friends and acquaintances addressed him. The reason perhaps was that at that time he felt 'Dixie' had connotations with colour, the problems connected with the southern states of America, and therefore contained the inference that he was of that origin, or half caste.

Dean was blessed with a mop of jet black curly hair, an obvious characteristic of coloured people, and this may have led to the association of the nickname. Tranmere supporters had no intention of giving offence to their idol, the name stuck, and as Dean progressed to entertain and delight his admirers, 'Dixie' seemed an appropriate title, which as people got used to it, bore no relationship to anything other than a superstar footballer. Not that the name could be offensive in any way, but in those days a great deal of ignorance and prejudice was prevalent on such matters, and people were generally more sensitive about them.

Indeed, Dean became so popular in the twenties and thirties that the nickname 'Dixie' came to be bestowed on countless numbers of males who happened to possess the surname 'Dean'. They found themselves automatically addressed as 'Dixie' whether they liked it or not. The nickname continues to be widely applied, even to this day, but many are not aware of its origin in being exclusively linked to the name of Dean the footballer. In fact Dean and his nickname can be described as a rare achievement. No doubt generations to come will forever associate the name 'Dixie' with Dean – all started by a group of Tranmere Rovers' supporters in 1924! However, without the fame and honour William Ralph Dean brought to it, the title 'Dixie' would have little significance in the heritage of such peculiarly British appellations. George Bernard Shaw by his literary attainments caused the introduction of the word 'Shavian' into the English language. 'Dixie' is of comparable characterisation in the world of football parlance, the credit for which must go to the man who first bore the name and established it so firmly and proudly in the annals of soccer history.

Dean played his last game for Tranmere on March 14 1925 at Darlington, scoring his side's only goal in a 2-1 defeat. It is of interest to peruse the League Division III (North) table at the close of that day's fixtures. Tranmere were next to bottom and had scored 44 goals, 27 of those having been collected by the wonder boy, Dixie Dean.

The League – Division III (North) – March 15 1925

	P	W	L	D	F	A	Pts
Darlington	32	20	5	7	66	24	47
Bradford	33	15	8	10	70	34	40
Nelson	29	18	7	4	55	32	40
Southport	31	16	8	7	45	27	39
New Brighton	31	16	9	6	62	42	38
Rochdale	32	16	10	6	60	44	38
Ashington	34	13	12	9	62	67	35
Lincoln C.	33	14	12	7	41	46	35
Crewe Alex.	33	11	11	11	45	57	33
Chesterfield	31	13	12	6	44	31	32
Halifax T.	32	11	12	9	40	41	31
Doncaster R.	33	12	16	6	44	53	30
Barrow	31	12	13	6	42	51	30
Accrington Stanley	32	11	14	7	51	60	29
Wigan	32	9	13	10	45	54	28
Walsall	33	10	15	8	34	44	28
Grimsby T.	32	10	15	7	38	46	27
Hartlepool	31	9	13	9	36	47	27
Durham C.	31	8	12	11	34	57	27
Wrexham	33	9	17	7	34	52	25
Tranmere R.	30	10	16	4	44	49	24
Rotherham U.	31	5	19	7	32	66	17

Comment on Dean's transfer was fairly extensive in the local press and the 'World of Sport' column in the *Liverpool Daily Post* was particularly accurate in assessing the potential of the young Dean. It referred to the lad's strong constitution and, having scored a lot of goals for Tranmere, 'he had a lot more in his locker'. On those two points the writer perhaps didn't realise how accurate a forecast he was making. He also said it was to be hoped that fans would not make a God of the boy and ruin his development. Well, the fans did just that, but it certainly didn't affect Dean's progress. The fee paid by Everton was £3000 – reputed to be the highest ever for a boy of such tender years. The press at that time were not sure whether he was 17 or 18 years of age!

5 Everton Football Club

THE STORY OF WILLIAM RALPH DEAN cannot be told without making particular reference to the club he served for the major part of his career and with which he achieved so much glory. Needless to say, it was with the famous Everton club that he combined his talents to contribute so much to the history of the game of soccer. Everton and Dixie Dean are synonymous. Dean's football skills may well have been irrepressible, whatever team he joined, but the fact is that his attainments with the club entitle Everton to embrace his immortal records as part of its proud history.

Of course there is more to Everton than Dean (and he would be the first to say so) which would still make the club one of the most important and respected in British football. With Dean as a major contributor to its history Everton can claim an overall record to match that of a great many top football clubs. Indeed, there are very few clubs in the wider context of soccer history to emulate Everton's fine record.

In the 'All Time League Tables' 1888 to 1975, published in the sixth edition of *Rothmans Football Yearbook*, Everton, who admittedly have spent seven more seasons in the First Division than any other club in the land, head the table with a total of 2966 points – almost three hundred points ahead of their nearest rivals. With a maximum of only 84 points available in the First Division each year, it will be many years before Everton are overhauled, and seemingly only relegation would seriously threaten their position at the top. Whilst you can compile statistics to support almost any theory, Everton's 72 years in the First Division, and their record total of 4643 goals, stand as testimony to a great club.*

---

*Facts stated are correct up to the end of the 1974-75 season. If one includes the 1975-76 statistics – the latest full season records available at the time of going to press – Everton have spent 73 years in Division One, scoring 4703 goals, and on April 7 1976 they beat Stoke City at Goodison Park by 2-1 to become the first club in the history of the First Division to score 3000 points. It is an ironic coincidence that during the season when Everton passed the 3000-barrier, they scored a total of 60 goals – and Dean once scored 60 all on his own!

When Dean joined Everton in March 1925 the club had been in existence for 47 years. Founded in 1878 by a group of young men who attended a Methodist Chapel, the club was first known as St Domingo FC and played at a ground in Stanley Park, Liverpool. A year later the team changed its title to Everton, the name given to a district of the City of Liverpool. It is interesting to note that the ground the club took over in those early days is now the home of their great rivals Liverpool FC at Anfield. Everton's first match was against Bootle St John and took place on December 23 1879. For that match the Everton team formation was two full backs, two half backs, and six forwards – a sure sign of attacking football! Modern teams have indulged in a variety of formations, but not, it would seem, one so novel as that fielded in 1879.

As one of the original twelve clubs which founded the Football League, Everton can claim to be as long established as any top club in the world. Another credit which it can be proud of is that it was the last of the original twelve to be relegated from the First Division, and that occurred after forty years in the higher sphere. When the club did go down in 1929-30, they came bouncing back winning the Second Division championship after one season and then the First Division championship the following season. The next year the club won the FA Cup to achieve a unique hat trick of success, with Dean making a remarkable contribution in the attainment of those honours.

The club gained a reputation for applying a grace and artistry to the game of soccer which has been sustained since the early days. Despite the ups and downs of the football scene, Everton's capacity to produce play of a high standard has scarcely ever lagged. Steve Bloomer, England international and an immortal in football history wrote in 1928:

> We owe a great deal to Everton. No matter where they play, and no matter whether they are well or badly placed in the League table, they always manage to serve up football of the highest scientific order. Everton always worship at the shrine of craft and science and never do forget the standard of play they set out to achieve.

Dean, of course, subsequently beat Steve Bloomer's career record of 352 goals, but whereas Bloomer took 22 seasons, Dean scored that number in just over 13. Dean had scored his 352 goals in 388 games, a fantastic achievement.

Everton also hold, as a club, a great tradition for goal-scoring, and it is fitting that it is in the position to claim the honour of having had a centre-forward of the calibre of Dixie

Dean. In the first ten seasons of the Football League from 1888 to 1898 Everton had scored a total of 324 goals, second only to Aston Villa with 326. It is a strange coincidence that both clubs have since played the men who hold the two highest goal-scoring records, as individuals, for a season in the First Division – Dean with 60 and Pongo Waring with 49. Both were born within a mile of each other in the town of Birkenhead, and both started their professional careers with Tranmere Rovers.

The Goodison Park club holds the distinction of being one of the few clubs to score more than 100 goals in a season on three occasions. When Dean scored his record-breaking 60 goals in 1927-28 it was out of a team total of 102. In 1930-31 Everton scored 121 goals and followed this with 116 in 1931-32. Those are the only occasions Everton have scored more than 100 goals in a season and in aggregate total 339, of which Dean scored 144. When modern football has reached the stage of forecasting that 60 goals would be the most anyone could expect the First Division champions to score in a season, Everton's and Dixie Dean's achievements may well, in retrospect, be more greatly appreciated.

The Everton club can boast of having been First Division champions on seven occasions. – In 1890-91, 1914-15, 1927-28, 1931-32, 1938-39, 1962-63, and 1969-70. The club has been First Division runners-up six times, and has won the FA Cup three times, being runners-up on a similar number of occasions. Throughout its history Everton has had an exceptional share of international players, many of outstanding merit. Only seven years after the Football League was formed, Everton had twelve international players on its books. The standard has been maintained ever since.

It is nearly one hundred years since the club was founded, and during the whole of the period hundreds of their players have gained the distinction of being capped for their countries. To mention all would be impossible, but not to mention any would be to ignore an important part of the club's history. In the early part of the century the most distinguished players were John Sharp and Harry Makepeace, who not only played football for England but also cricket. Contemporaries of Dean are mentioned elsewhere, but since Dean's day there has been Lawton, Ball, Bingham, Collins, Eglington, Farrell, T. G. Jones, Labone, Newton, Parker, Pickering, West, Royle, Wilson, Wright, and last but not least, Alec Young.

Another name synonymous with the Everton club is Sam

Chedgzoy. Sometimes described as a man with a name which sounds like a sneeze, he was one of the most famous of the Everton internationals during the period after the First World War. He played outside right for his club and for England and was a great sporting character who has a claim to fame in addition to his particular football talents. Sam was a participant in an experiment to expose a deficiency in the laws governing League football in 1923. The rules allowed a goal to be scored direct from a corner kick, but omitted to specify that the taker of the kick could not play the ball twice.

A Liverpool sports reporter, Ernest Edwards, offered Chedgzoy £2 to conduct the experiment of taking a corner by dribbling the ball towards the goal. Sam accepted the challenge and in a First Division match played at Goodison Park in 1923 the home team forced a corner. Sam placed the ball at the flag and then startled one and all by dribbling the ball towards goal. The referee was so astonished that he dropped his whistle, quickly recovered, and nearly blew it out of his mouth running towards Sam to admonish him about daring to attempt to take corners in such a manner. Sam stood his ground and told the referee that he should read the rules which most certainly allowed corners to be taken that way.

At half-time Sam persuaded the referee to check the rules about corner kicks and at the end of the game it was conceded that Sam was right. As a result the rules were changed to specify that the taker of a corner kick could only play the ball once and could not play it again before another player had touched it. Sam made soccer history and joined the ranks of many who before and since have had to resort to breaking the law to expose its deficiencies! Everton can claim this incident to be an interesting slice of its history. Sam played for England eight times, twice after the corner-taking episode.

In the field of administration, including training and the welfare of its players, Everton have set standards which are the envy of many professional clubs. The ground at Goodison Park is one of the best in the country, a position it has held for nearly the whole of the present century. Even in 1928 Everton possessed three fine stands, with an overall ground capacity of about 80,000. In 1975 the ground held 56,000 spectators with stands to seat 25,000. The latest stand to be constructed cost £1 million in 1971 and provides seating for 10,000.

It is interesting to note that in 1907 a double-decker stand was built at Goodison which cost £13,000. In 1909 another double-decker stand, with offices and players' quarters, was built at a cost of £28,000. In 1926 a further double-decker stand was constructed which cost £30,000 – an enormous sum in those days. The Everton training grounds, situated at Bellefield in the suburbs of Liverpool, cover several acres and provide indoor facilities of every conceivable nature, and are probably second to none in Europe.

It is not perhaps generally known that the Everton club was a pioneer in the use of goal nets. In the early twenties the club was the first to print programmes of matches which provided details of the visiting players and other items of information to increase the interest of spectators at home games. Prior to this, spectators had no idea of the background or otherwise of the performers, and such a programme leaflet added much to the enjoyment the crowd could obtain from every match. Another innovation, and subsequently adopted by every other club, was the arrangement whereby the half-time and full-time results of other League matches were made known during the game. This was done by means of a telegraph board set up at Goodison Park.

Everton was the first club to provide a benefit match for long-serving players and established a guarantee of £500. No doubt this was one of the reasons why the club thought it was unnecessary for its players to join the union. In 1929 it was at Goodison Park that a referee first experimented with the idea of controlling a football match from the sidelines. Indeed, Everton can justifiably boast of being an enterprising and progressive League club.

The club has not only been fortunate in engaging players of outstanding ability – internationals by the dozen – but has also been blessed with a number of excellent administrators, the most famous of which was W. C. Cuff, who was Chairman during the twenties and thirties. He was one of the most formidable characters in the history of football in Britain, and his sound administrative approach reinforced the base on which Everton continued to flourish. Perhaps his most important decision was when he persuaded the secretary of the club, Tom McIntosh, to sign Dixie Dean in 1925.

Subsequently, Cuff was elected President of the Football League and his reign in that capacity has been described as paternal but determined. He is credited with showing exceptional foresight during his chairmanship of the Everton club at a time when football had become an extremely tough business. Perhaps his proposal, made in 1936, may prove, if it is ever accepted, how far-sighted he was. He said then that football should return to the old offside law (which was changed in 1925) and stop the developing defensive tactics of 'W' formations or 'third-back' methods. Dean has often recorded his admiration for 'Old Cuff'. He says Cuff had a shrewd business mind and succeeded in negotiating property transactions for the club, advantages which it continues to benefit from today.

The traditions of Everton, a club which in a few years' time will celebrate its centenary, are an excellent example for sporting administration everywhere. The glories in those traditions have been sustained by a consistently large band of loyal supporters, one generation following another. The club is an important part of the history of the great port of Liverpool. Everton draws its support from Merseyside and its environs, an area in which there exists an intensely concentrated passion for the game of soccer, as great, possibly, as could be found anywhere in the world. This heritage of support can claim to be the foundation on which Everton's proud traditions have been maintained.

During the course of all those years of high class football, Everton supporters have given deserving acclaim to many of its players. With all due respect to such heroes, the one who will never be forgotten and on whom there will be general agreement as symbolic of the whole procession of eminent men around whom the club's reputation has been built, is the name and the man William Ralph 'Dixie' Dean. Dean's vow to join the Everton club was not misplaced either in the interest of the club or that of himself. No better mutual contribution between a football club and a player was ever achieved. The names of Everton and Dean will be perpetually synonymous.

When the centenary of the Everton club is celebrated in 1978-79 the names of many of their great players of the past will be mentioned and enshrined in the history of Everton and Merseyside football. Supporters will debate the merits of various players who have worn the club colours in the past in much the same way as is done when discussing the talents or otherwise of the current team. That's what soccer is mostly about. Spectator interest derives from discussion, argument or comment on the past, present, and future merits of their team, generating as much interest as is provided from actually watching the matches.

Everton supporters, even those who never saw the famous Dean play, will, out of loyalty and pride, boast to rival fans of his amazing records, records which in their view are an integral part of the Everton club's historical assets to be readily proclaimed to the world. They will of course mention other famous names of the past and the present who brought credit to Goodison, their country, or perhaps the game in general. All will vary in their views as to the merits of the players. To mention some particular heroes, to be recalled with pride, will not mean that any who may be excluded are regarded as making an insignificant contribution to the club's history.

Naturally in a story about Dixie Dean, apart from the subject himself, it is his contemporaries that will gain the most mention. During that conspicuous period of glory between the wars, when Dean was at the centre of it all, Everton found players of exceptional ability who served to complement those successful teams. Dean is the first to admit that without them his achievements and those of the club could scarcely have been gained. All the men, intuitively, in the absence of any specific directions, ably combined to make a marvellous contribution to the game.

Many of Dean's colleagues carved their own elevated places in soccer history, and will be specially remembered when the anniversary takes place. Tom McIntosh, the secretary who signed Dean, and trainer Harry Cooke, both of whom Dean deeply admired, were the outstanding non-playing members between the wars. The 1928 championship team of Kelly, Hart, Davies, O'Donnell, Virr, Critchley, Cresswell, Martin, Weldon, Troup and Dean will be recalled with much affection.

In addition there were a number of players whom Dean thought highly of and who cannot be overlooked. Some of them have since died. A number have become famous on the business side of football. Names to savour and recall with great relish will be Chedgzoy, Stein, Stevenson, Coulter, Mercer, T. G. Jones, Sagar, Cook, Britton, Dunn, Geldard, Cunliffe, and Lawton as well as many others. All made vitally important contributions to produce years of glorious football that supporters, and even opponents, enjoyed whilst Dean was with the Everton club.

In the pre-war days each home game at Goodison Park was graced by the presence of a local brass band, which played a programme of music before kick-off and at half-time, much to the enjoyment of the spectators. The programme of music to be played was given due notice in the local press on the eve of the match. There is not much demand for such entertainment these days. Now it is usually canned music that serves to introduce the games, providing a kind of canned atmosphere which compares unfavourably with the old days. Indeed,

Everton have now adopted the theme tune of a BBC television programme, *Z Cars* as its 'signature tune' and this is played before each game, when the team takes the field.

The Everton club commemorated its 50th anniversary in a celebration gathering of about 700 people in the Philharmonic Hall, Liverpool, in April 1929. The distinguished guests included the Earl of Derby, and Dixie Dean was in attendance, together with players who were members of the Everton team which won the 1892 championship of the Football League. The names may not mean much today – Holt, Crelly, Chadwick, and Geary. But if Everton celebrate in 1979 and Dean, with some of his contemporaries, are there, the link with the 50th anniversary would be established to cover one hundred magnificent years.

It would be appropriate if Everton could achieve some particular success like winning the championship or the Cup or both in season 1978-79. The spirit of W. R. Dean still rides with them. Perhaps the inspiration will have some effect and produce a suitable cup of success to mark a hundred years of historic endeavour by the Everton Football Club.

Dean was renowned for his sense of humour. It is commonly accepted that in any human enterprise, retaining a light heart is a quality almost as important as that of competence. Of course, one is not much good without the other. They are complementary virtues. Dean, although he grew to feel part of a family when he was at Everton, giving the club his undivided loyalty, was always ready to joke against both himself and the club. On the rare occasions when Everton go through a bad patch he will tell a story which in a humorous way sums up the dilemma or the misfortune. One such story he has told on many occasions.

An Everton director was one day strolling along Upper Parliament Street in Liverpool when he came across a coloured boy playing football. The boy was on his own kicking and heading a ball with remarkable skill against a large area of brick wall. The Everton director watched with utter amazement and fascination, and was so impressed with the boy's evident talent he approached him and said, 'How would you like to play for Everton, my boy? I am a director of the club and I could easily arrange for you to sign up to play for the First team.'

'Not bloody likely,' the boy replied, 'It's bad enough being black in this city!'

But whatever the club's misfortunes have been, in regard to

actual results, it has always held to a high standard of play. W. C. Cuff, the former Everton chairman, was reported in the *Liverpool Daily Post* in February 1946 as saying:

> Throughout its history Everton has been noted for the high quality of its football. It has always been the unwritten policy of the board, handed down from one generation of directors to another, that only the classical and stylish type of player should be signed. The kick-and-rush type has never appealed to them.

The rivalry between Everton and Liverpool is perpetual and stories circulate, as they have done throughout the years, which can be reversed by either supporters to illustrate the merits of their respective teams.

Dean is always ready to tell such a story. 'Did you hear about the Everton fan who used to take his dog to the derby games?', he will ask. 'When Everton scored, the dog would indulge in an amazing performance of acrobatics. A Liverpool fan who observed this asked the Everton supporter what the dog would do if Liverpool scored. "I wouldn't know," the Evertonian replied, "I've only been bringing him to these matches for the past ten years!" '

In this story about Dean much of what is written relates to the Everton club, so it is relevant to criticise the club's apparent failure to keep adequate records of its history. It is understood that Everton is no exception in this respect, other League clubs being similarly remiss. In compiling Dean's story, no assistance has been given by the club because the present administration possess few records of the past, and, it would appear, even less about the greatest player who ever donned its colours. What will happen when Everton commemorates the centenary of its founding is anybody's guess. As with this story, much reliance on the local press, *The Liverpool Echo* and *The Liverpool Daily Post,* for historical information and facts will be the club's only course perhaps, that is if it intends to mark the occasion with some kind of printed record of its magnificent successes, and of course its failures, over the last century.

The Everton Football Club will have plenty to boast about when it celebrates its centenary. It can claim to have made as great an all-round contribution to the game of soccer as any club in the long history of the sport, a sport which is probably the most popular in the world today. Everton will have no prouder claim than that its most famous player was Dixie Dean, who for thirteen of those hundred years served professional football as eminently as any individual who ever played the game.

6 Dean's Colleagues

OVER A PERIOD OF THIRTEEN YEARS at Everton, Dean played alongside a great number of outstanding professionals, all of whom gave him the wonderful support which was a major contribution to his amazing individual achievements. Dean calculates that during this time at Goodison Park Everton's first team turnover of players must have been in the region of nearly one hundred. Dean's memory of those players is clearer of some than others. Here he comments on those names he has thoughts about and offers his apologies to any he may leave out. The list is not in order of preference, or indeed merit, but follows a chronological sequence as far as he can remember. The names will conjure happy memories of the glory which covered the great Everton sides during the sporting and peaceful soccer scene of the late twenties and thirties. The words are Dean's.

Sam Chedgzoy was a Merseysider from Ellesmere Port. Sam was a regular outside right when I joined Everton in 1925. A wonderful character and like a father to me. Sam and I used to indulge in special practice to work out tactics of wing-to-centre moves. He was a great ball player and won eight international caps. He retired to Canada and died there.

Bobby Irvine was a great inside forward and Irishman in the mould of Georgie Best. Played regularly for Everton and Ireland. He was well established when I joined the Goodison Club.

Alec Troup – what an amazing little man he was. Alec was so cool when he produced the centre for me to nod the one that gave me the 60-goal record. He had given me a lot of those goals. Wee Alec brimmed over with courage and skill. Do you know, that man was only 5 ft 5 in, and had a weak collar bone which had to be strapped up for every game he played. One of the best wingers ever, and he scored a lot of goals too. He and I had an almost perfect liaison. I have to thank Alec as much if not more than anybody else for helping me to score goals. He was playing for Scotland before I joined Everton.

Warney Cresswell was a dour Geordie and an amazingly calm, unhurried kind of lackadaisical character. No better full-back ever played. Got nine international caps but should have had more. Good reader of the game – never had to exert himself because he had such wonderful anticipation. On the social side, he rarely took his hand out of his pocket – it always stayed there – except when he was holding his pipe or supping a pint of beer. If four of us went into a pub he would be last to pay. And when he had supped three pints he would then point out that the beer wasn't very good and suggest going to another pub, in the hope that we'd forget it was his turn to pay! Warney never bought a newspaper, even to read about himself — he always waited to pick up someone else's. A great chap though!

Albert Virr was a good half-back in the 1928 championship side – a local boy who not long afterwards was badly injured and went out of the game altogether. I believe he became a school teacher, working in Liverpool somewhere.

Bill Coggins was a young goalkeeper who came to us from the West Country in 1929, and although he played only for a few seasons he served Everton well. Had a good sense of humour – you had to have in those days. When he first arrived I told him that he must conform to the Everton standards of dress when travelling to away games, which was a bowler hat and plus four suit. Bill was an innocent country lad and fell for it. There was a riot when he turned up at Lime Street Station in that get-up, which incidentally was brand new! Poor lad had borrowed the money to buy the bowler and plus fours! He took it all very well, however.

George Martin was a very good inside forward – scored a few goals in the 1928 side. Never got the kudos he deserved, clever ball player.

Ted Critchley took over from Sam Chedgzoy at outside right and helped me to score those 60 goals in 1927-28. He knew how to centre a ball, and we harmonised well. In 1933, as Captain, I had to agree to leave him out of the cup final side. That was a difficult decision, and of course I was very sorry for Ted, who had scored the vital goal in the semi-final to send us to Wembley. A great player from Stockport.

Jimmy Dunn – a great friend as well as team-mate. He and I had some fun together both on and off the field. He was always contriving some practical joke to play. One of the famous 'Blue Devils of Scotland' team in the thirties. A very tricky ball player. He headed a goal in the 1933 cup final and immediately collapsed, unconscious – he didn't know until he recovered that he had scored! I kept in touch with Jimmy right up to the time he died of cancer. A very sad end for a wonderful character.

Hunter Hart was a famous name in Everton's records. Centre-half of the side in that glorious championship season of 1927-28. He dominated the middle of the park, and played well in any half-back position. A very good captain at one time, and commanded much respect from the players.

Cliff Britton was one of the finest half-backs in the history of the game. He joined Everton in 1930 and didn't look strong enough to play in top class football. Old Cuff saw his potential and made sure the club helped to improve Cliff's physique, and by 1932 he was a regular in the first team. A great artist who laid off quite a few goals for me. Played for England many times, and when he retired from playing came back to Everton as manager.

Albert Geldard was a very fast outside right. Could score goals too! Some say the game is faster today – you should have seen Geldard! Tommy Lawton said Albert could catch pigeons. Geldard replaced Critchley in the 1933 cup final side, and this caused some controversy at the time. We won the cup and the decision was proved right. Albert was capped for England four times.

Charlie Gee was a good strong centre-half. I played with Charlie in his first international for England against Spain. I wagered Charlie £6 we would beat Spain by more than 5 goals – we won 7-1 and he lost the £6 fee he received for the match. On one occasion Everton provided both centre-halves in an England v. Wales match. Charlie was one, Tommy Griffiths the other.

Tom Griffiths was a great centre-half – a regular for Wales in the late twenties and early thirties. He was only with Everton for a couple of seasons.

Billy Cook – a storming full back with a powerful kick, and a good ball player. Took many penalties. Played in the 1933 cup final team to become one of the few players to win a Scottish and FA Cup-winners medal. A bit vigorous, Billy, but a great asset.

Tosh Johnson and I got on well together. He was inside-left in our goal-hungry forward line of 1930-31 when we recorded cricket scores in some matches. Tosh won a cup medal in 1933 and then went over to the opposition camp at Anfield just afterwards.

Jackie Coulter was an Irish international winger who, with Alec Stevenson, formed the famous left-wing partnership for Everton in the mid-thirties. He knew the way to goal, and I remember he scored three in the legendary cup replay with Sunderland.

Alec Stevenson was an inside-forward of rare skill, a very tricky ball player who read the game brilliantly. Alec, only 5 ft 3 in, would leave towering opponents wrong-footed and helpless with his dribbling skill. He could head a ball, too. A jovial sense of humour and, like Jimmy Dunn, a practical joker – you were always afraid of being a victim when he was around.

Jock Thomson – I nearly overlooked him. He was in the side that achieved the triple success between 1931 and 1933. An intelligent half-back – played well in the 1933 cup final. After I left Everton, Jock became captain and led the side to the 1939 championship of Division One.

Jimmy Stein – a Scotsman and an outside-left with talent. He was a regular in the side that won Everton the hat trick of success in 1931-1933. He scored the first and important goal in the 1933 cup final. In 1931 our forward line was the scourge of opposing defences. Jimmy scored the first goal when we set up an all-time record against Charlton, each forward scoring, to get five within the space of 17 minutes.

Tommy White was, in my opinion, the most versatile footballer ever. Tommy was a perfect club man and could play successfully in any position. He was an inside forward who later took up the regular centre-half berth. But then he deputised for me at centre-forward on many occasions and scored a lot of goals – often three and four at a time. A marvellous chap and a natural footballer who, regrettably, was only capped twice for England.

Ben Williams was full-back and captain of the Second Division championship side in 1931. A real sportsman for Wales, playing for his country many times. He was a good boxer and could have made his living at that. I believe he went back into business in Wales when he retired.

Nat Cunliffe was a great inside-forward who scored a lot of goals. When I was off the field (changing my shorts that had been ripped to pieces) at Sunderland in 1935 Nat scored the goal that earned us the famous cup replay. A clever player, who eventually played for England.

Ted Sagar. In my job I always hated goalkeepers, even though many were my friends off the field. One goalkeeper I loved on the field was Ted, because he was on my side. A great 'keeper, who I understand played a record number of games for Everton – 460-odd. A team feels very secure when you have someone like Ted in goal. He was one of the greatest – he was there when we won the cup 3-0. Goalkeeping is a bit of a lonely job on the field, and Ted seemed to follow this line off the field – he always left for home after training and matches – he didn't mix much. But what a marvellous custodian for Everton!

Jack O'Donnell must be mentioned. He was in the 1927-28 side at full-back with Warney. A good strong player, who filled in so well as the counterpart to Cresswell.

Joe Mercer – what can I say about him? Everything has been said. He's still part of the game. Well, Joe was one of the greatest players of all time. A brilliant tackler, always giving his all, and demonstrating an excellent football brain. When he first arrived at Everton in the early thirties he came into the dressing room, and appeared a little overawed by the occasion. He was a skinny lad who had come from junior football – a Merseysider from Ellesmere Port. I looked him up and down and thought, blimey, his legs wouldn't last him one day on a postman's round! But, my, what a footballer he turned out to be. A great brain and tremendous courage. He needed it with that physique. With Cliff Britton and Joe, Everton had the best wing-halves in the country. The selectors thought so too, for both played together for England. I don't know whether Joe ever forgave me for missing a penalty once in a cup-tie against Tottenham, a miss which resulted in Everton going out of the Cup. Joe is today back on Merseyside. We have always been good friends.

Tommy Lawton was my successor at Everton. I met him at the station in Liverpool when he arrived as a young boy of 17 from Burnley. He impressed me right away. Just the right build for a centre-forward. I told him he was joining a great club. He turned out to be a natural footballer and a gentleman of a player. Tommy often came to me for advice and he always took notice. Often, after training, he and I used to play head tennis, which I like to think helped him to perfect his headwork for scoring goals. In fact we appeared in a number of matches together with Tommy playing at inside-forward. When I left in 1938 he was top scorer in the League with 28 goals and then scored 34 in the 1938-39 season to become top scorer again. We all know what a great player he became. I liked Tommy very much. He played for England many times both before and after the war.

Harry Cooke was a great friend. I owe a good deal to that man. He nursed some of my injuries more successfully than the doctors. He was the club trainer. I always said there were only two trainers of any value in the whole country – Cooke and

Boyd-Rochfort!

Dean concludes, 'All the players I've mentioned were excellent footballers, any one of whom would be successful in the modern game. What strikes me in looking back is the high proportion of mixed nationalities among the players who served Everton in my time. This perhaps contributed a great deal to the Blues' success – all the men, whatever nationality, showed a team spirit and followed this intuitively without being directed into it. Remember we had no manager then.'

7 Division One
-Early Days

To BE INVOLVED in a big transfer deal in 1925 must have been a heady experience for any young footballer, but it is probably fair to say that it did not carry the same impact on Dean personally as it does on his counterpart in the football business of the seventies. Not that such transfers in the twenties failed to attract a great deal of publicity. There was however, much less ballyhoo and commercial exploitation. Dean's quiet, unassuming self-confidence helped him to resist the inevitable conceit which often develops, to varying degrees, in some highly priced players and consequently adversely affects their performance. Dean's keen yet nonchalant approach assisted no end in his habilitation to top-class football. Although he had a great respect for Everton – to play for the club was after all a childhood dream come true – he was in no way overawed by the prospect, a virtue he was to demonstrate consistently in many other situations throughout his life.

In that sphere of football most players had to observe certain disciplines but seemingly these made little or no intrusion of the kind which could undermine the skills or talents of individuals. In the main, a footballer was recognised as a positional player, either a full-back, half-back or forward, right, left, or centre, but integration on any broader scale for team patterns of play was not developed so much as it has been since. Each player was regarded more as an individual holding down a position in the team, with his performance assessed in that context, which was used as part of the criteria for his selection in the team. And team selection was not the exclusive responsibility of a manager, because managers as we know them did not exist in those days. Selection of the team was apparently a shared responsibility among a variety of club administrators, not all of whom could be said to be well-qualified for such purposes.

However, just five days after signing for Everton the young Dean was selected to play at centre-forward in a Division One match, an away game at Highbury, against the famous London side, Arsenal. The Everton team travelled by train to London on the Friday evening and according to Dean was mainly occupied in playing cards and the players talked and gossiped about everything but the match to be played on the Saturday. Dean received no specific instructions on team tactics. This match was to be his first experience of what was after all the highest class of football played anywhere in Europe and on a ground situated in what was then the world's leading capital city. Enough to create some nerves even in the most mature men who found themselves facing such an unknown quantity. Although only 18 years of age, he was regarded as a highly valued footballer, recognised as possessing the necessary individual skills to fill the centre-forward berth, and that was that.

It seems that Dean did not even expect to be advised on his footballing role, despite the fact that others recognised this was for him a strange situation. He anticipated that his debut for Everton would be assessed purely on his individual performance although account would have to be taken of how he managed to fit this in and blend with the play of his colleagues. Possibly his work was judged like that of a skilled carpenter on joining a firm of cabinet makers; the pieces of timber he fashioned would be expected to fit into the parts made by others and be assembled to complete the construction of an acceptable item of furniture. Not, perhaps, the best analogy, but it is important to note that at that time team games in sport reflected this kind of individualism, which in a curious way often enhanced team performance.

At the time Dean signed for Everton, the club was going through a particularly bad patch. Indeed, when he made his debut against Arsenal, Everton were third from bottom of the First Division, facing the prospect of relegation. Arsenal were not doing much better, but they nevertheless won the game 2-1. Reports of the match said that Dean played fairly well but had little support. Dean himself states that he did in fact score a goal which was disallowed, despite the general consensus of opinion, even among his opponents, that it was a good goal. The following week he made his first appearance at Goodison Park, where Everton had a home game against Aston Villa. In this match Dean scored his first goal for his new club, the first of the 349 he was to score in 399 League games for Everton. However, lack of cohesion, which plagued the Everton team at that time, tended to obscure the realisation of Dean's potential. He was excluded from the first eleven in the next match.

Dean returned to the team a fortnight later. No doubt his selection was due to a good performance with the reserves, combined also with the fact that Everton were getting desperately close to relegation and trying out many players in a panic situation. He played in the first team for the remainder of that dismal season. The club finished seventeenth in the League table, only just escaping the drop to the Second Division. Dean had played in only seven games and had scored but two goals. However, added to his total with Tranmere, his season's bag was 29 goals in 34 games. Everton, it is interesting to note, scored a total of only 40 goals in the 42 League games for the season 1924-25 and had 60 goals against them. When some people look back on those days they are often deluded in their assessments, believing that prolific goal-scoring went on in every department of the game. Everton's matches registered only 100 goals during that season and one would hardly consider an average of 2.5 per match (the total contribution of both teams) indicative of goal abundance! Perhaps it was the outstanding individual performances, like those of Dean, that influenced the theory that goals were never difficult to get in those pre-war days.

During the summer of 1925 Dean maintained his dedication to physical fitness. He played tennis, golf, and some cricket, and looked forward to his first full season in First Division football. He realised his place was not assured in the Everton team, and even though he was one of the most expensive footballers in the land, it provided no guarantee. Those in the club who contributed opinions on team selection no doubt bore in mind that Dean had to be nursed. The lack of team success during the previous season did not augur well for the period ahead. Everton were, of course, a wealthy club and could afford to have a large number of full-time professionals. This was reassuring, but scarcely the only requirement for fulfilling desired achievement. And so it proved.

The club will look back on the 1925-26 season as a not very successful one, except perhaps to say that it was the period when the young Dean undoubtedly proved his potential. It was, after all, his first full season in the higher class of football. At the end of April 1926 Everton finished in the middle of the table having played 42, won 12, lost 12, drawn 18 and goals for 72, against 70. Points 42. During that season no fewer than 27 players had been tried in an effort to progress to greater success.

For Everton the outstanding attainment was the clear knowledge that they now possessed a great centre-forward, the scarcest commodity in the game. When the 1925-26 season opened Dean was not an immediate selection for the first team. He played in the reserves against Bradford City Reserves at Goodison Park. Dean scored a remarkable total of seven goals in that match and with Everton still in a depressed situation even the most cautious administration could not ignore such a performance by him and simply had to recognise his claim to a first team place. So Dean was given his opportunity and played in 38 league games during the season, finishing with 32 goals out of the 72 the team scored in 42 matches. At that time 32 goals was within striking distance of the First Division record of 38 held by Bert Freeman of Everton. The cry of football fans – 'Give it to Dixie! – was already gathering momentum in the soccer world. Not only was the young Dean being praised for his ability to score goals, but the skill and enthusiasm he displayed in every department of the game was greatly admired. His unique art of heading the ball was producing an exceptional number of goals, a source of power any football team would not hesitate to exploit.

It is this area that Dean refers to when he commends the natural skills of the two wingers who served the team and who sustained the development of the heading technique in which he excelled. Sam Chedgzoy, outside right, was one of the few men who combined with Dean to actually work out moves involving wing and centre-forward play. When the Hungarians in the fifties and sixties exploited their tactic of the winger pulling the ball back to centre following a dashing run on the right, with the centre-forward running from a deep position to make contact, hitting the ball on the volley, surprising defenders by the speed of the manoeuvre and often producing a brilliant goal, football fans were full of praise for a tactic which brought about such exciting and superlative play. Dean and Chedgzoy operated this move with the ball in the air. Dean could read the intended projection of the ball in advance, by watching Chedgzoy's feet, and knew exactly where the centre, pulled back in the air, would drop. And running from a deep position Dean would connect with his head, even from twenty yards out, and the ball would often enter the net like a rocket, leaving the defence and the goalkeeper helpless.

Alec Troup, on the left, could place the ball to hang in the centre in a different way, knowing Dean's ability to out-jump most defenders and glide the ball with his head either to a colleague or into the net, and this proved just as efficient as the move from the right. During that first season Dean rapidly became the most dangerous centre-forward in the First

Division, and as he went on could only get better. Sam and Alec had provided much of the foundation for his success.

In retrospect, Everton's position at the end of the 1925-26 season may not be regarded as such a deplorable failure as was felt by the club at the time. It was obvious from the goals for and against figures that the major faults to be righted were in the defence. The forwards had proved themselves a prodigious force. To score 72 goals and (apart from Dean's magnificent 32) for Alec Troup and Sam Chedgzoy to bag six each as wingers was a great source of satisfaction. Everton looked forward with some optimism to the opening of the 1926-27 season. However, before that even commenced an event was to occur which would dampen many of the club's hopes. Their greatest find, the centre-forward on whom most of Everton's aspirations were pitched, was to be involved in a most serious accident sustaining personal injuries which could so easily have ended his career – an event which could have adversely affected the whole future of the club. If the accident to Dean had turned out differently, Everton may not today have been in a position to boast of such a proud and glorious history.

8 Serious Accident

ON SUNDAY JUNE 10 1926 the young Dean called for Evelyn Jones, a girl friend, to accompany him for a spin on his motorcycle. Miss Jones was also his partner when he played tennis, a sport which occupied him a lot during the summer break from football. And at tennis, as with most other sports he pursued, Dean was no slouch. At nineteen years of age he was in the peak of physical condition and very conscious of maintaining his fitness with a dedication symptomatic of his obsession with soccer. Dean also played club cricket and golf, the latter sport as an accomplished scratch player. Motorcycling was an additional joy. In those days such machines were not as sophisticated as they are today, but nevertheless could be exciting to ride and perhaps demanded much more skill than some of today's models. The destination that fateful Sunday was North Wales, so easily accessible from his home in Birkenhead, across the Wirral peninsular via Queens Ferry and along the road to the popular seaside resorts of Rhyl, Llandudno, and the rest, and no more than 50 miles from home. Little did he realise what a traumatic event that Sunday excursion would turn out to be. Everything went fine until he and his passenger had travelled well into the Welsh countryside.

The year 1926 was not turning out to be a happy one to remember. The General Strike in May had torn the country apart economically, and although on this June day the strike had been over for some weeks, the effects were still felt and few people enjoyed any measure of prosperity. They were hard times. Even to own a motorcycle put you in the privileged class, and although Dean was not wealthy, he was in the position to enjoy such pleasures, and, of course, the dangers. Crash helmets were not in vogue, the roads scarcely overflowing with traffic. But during the summer, particularly at weekends, a relatively large number of vehicles hogged the highways, and roads at the time perhaps were not so well designed or maintained to cope with heavy traffic as they are today. A high ratio of accidents did occur, and motorcycles were involved in a fair share of them. Expensive footballers like Dean were apparently allowed to indulge in such leisure-time hazards, and that perhaps is how it always should be, although some clubs no doubt did impose some restrictions on their highly valued players.

Proceeding along the St Asaph road on that fine Sunday, Dean and his pillion passenger observed a motor cycle combination (a popular form of transport in 1926) darting in and out of the traffic coming towards them. The combination came out to pass and Dean's solo machine hit it head-on, violently unseating both himself and his passenger. That is all that Dean can remember. The newspaper reports say that Dean and two male occupants of the motor cycle combination were picked up unconscious and taken on the back of a lorry to the Lluesty Infirmary, a hospital-cum-workhouse (a type of institution commonplace in the twenties) which was situated near Holywell. All three were found to be seriously injured. The girl was taken by car to the same hospital but her injuries were not so serious and she was discharged the following day.

It was established that Dean had his jawbone broken in two places and also a suspected fracture of the skull. These reports were naturally of concern to football fans everywhere. Much speculation went on about the prospect of Dean ever playing football again, or whether indeed he would recover at all. As a player renowned for his heading ability, even if he resumed playing, how would he be able to score goals in the manner he had been so well equipped to do? Dean was unconscious for the best part of 36 hours. The infirmary did not possess X-Ray equipment and over a week passed before he could be removed to a hospital in Liverpool to discover the extent of the injuries to his skull. Dr Baxter, the Everton club doctor, made several visits to the hospital and forecast that Dean would never play football again. That the doctor was proved wrong was a relief to all in the world of football.

Most people were not aware of the extraordinary constitution Dean possessed, and received with some astonishment the news of his remarkable recovery. In addition to the broken jawbone it was revealed that he had a fractured skull. Metal plates were inserted to aid the healing of the broken bones in his jaws. It is interesting to note that when he resumed his football activities and continued to excel in his heading skills, fans latched on to the myth that he was assisted by the metal plates which they wrongly assumed remained permanently in his head. The plates were removed when the bones had set, well before he returned to play football. How plates in his jaws could possibly improve his heading of a football is, of course, nonsense, but the story serves to illustrate how rumours develop and the way in which people can be deceived.

Dean was up and about weeks before he was discharged from the hospital. Being a naturally active person, he offered his services to the nursing staff. His pleas for a job to do were finally answered. To his surprise one of his tasks was to transport the corpses to and from the mortuary! Then one day his doctor discovered him climbing an apple tree in the hospital garden helping to pick fruit for the kitchen staff. Sir Robert Davis, the famous bone specialist, who noticed Dean was moving from branch to branch with great agility, remarked 'If you are fit enough to do that, you can get back to Everton as soon as you like!' Delightfully, Dean scampered down and after thanking Sir Robert rushed off to make ready to return to his beloved Everton and football.

One of the first things he thought of when he returned home was to find a motorcycle and ride it to re-establish his confidence. This was consistent with his character. He had never lacked this quality in anything he ever did. But the accident had been a major event in his life, and may well have shattered the strongest of men. He seemed to successfully and consistently overcome any possibility of losing his enormous confidence. He was anxious to get back into traning and play football again. He had no doubt about his ability to do so, but his team-mates, and those who controlled the Everton club, naturally held many fears for his future.

However, fifteen weeks after the accident, Dean was included in the Everton Reserves team to play at Huddersfield against Huddersfield Town Reserves on October 9 1926. The crowd gave him a great welcome but were clearly apprehensive. Many of his admirers anxiously felt that if he was called on to head a ball, he would immediately collapse, or some tragedy would occur which would prevent him ever playing again. Early in the game a centre came over and his black curly head connected, crashing the ball goalwards. He was still on his feet. The crowd road 'His head! His head!' and pointed to their own heads in delight. The relief was evident by continued chants of 'He's alright, He's alright.' He had resumed play without any apparent effects from his effort, and completed the match without fuss.

Dean was declared fit to be included in the first team on October 26 against Leeds United at Leeds and scored in what was Everton's first away win that season. He was back in business, and would be, with a vengeance, for the remainder of the season. His recovery was complete and he continued to head many goals with his old consummate skill. No wonder spectators concluded that he must have been aided by the addition of a steel plate in his head! He could head the ball goalwards from twenty yards with as much power as some players could project it with their feet. His goalscoring skills were not restricted to controlling the ball in the air. He could shoot with either foot from up to forty yards and leave a goalkeeper helpless.

For the rest of the season he played in 27 games and scored 21 goals. By the end of April 1927 he had an aggregate of 55 goals from 72 League games with Everton, all scored in the First Division. He had played in his first international and during April 1927 was England's hero in a memorable match against Scotland at Hampden Park where England defeated the Scots on Scottish soil for the first time in 23 years, all this following a serious accident of the kind which many other sportsmen may never have recovered from. When Dean talks about this episode in his life he comments rather philosophically, 'Having broken bones can help. Those parts of my jaw and skull which were fractured and healed are much stronger as a result.' A curious way of looking at it, but it was the kind of philosophy which was to sustain him throughout his hazardous career. When one thinks of the adversities he had to face in the soccer game, such an outlook was to some extent essential for his survival.

A Scotsman who was a young spectator at that 1927 England v Scotland match says it was the only occasion an English footballer was ever given a standing ovation at Hampden Park, and Dean was the man. At that time Scotland had the reputation of producing the best footballers in the world, not without some justification. The Scottish League had a centre-forward named McGrory, who played for Celtic and actually scored more goals than Dean! However, without detracting from McGrory's performance it has to be recognised there was scarcely any comparison between the Scottish League and the English First Division. Most of Scotland's best footballers were with English clubs and played in the English League. Scotland had two clubs – Celtic and Rangers – which dominated the Scottish League for decades. The opposition to these clubs was generally regarded as of the second or third division standard in the English Leagues. Therefore McGrory's records, although commendable, are not considered comparable with Dean's attainments in the English First Division. McGrory's career record shows he had an average of 1.004 goals per match. Dean had a League average of .867 goals per match, but overall an average of .93 goals per match. Hughie Gallagher's average was .712 and Steve Bloomer, the great English international player, an average of .586 goals per match. Dean's average is the highest ever recorded in the English Football League, and stands to this day.

At the end of his first season in top class football in May 1926 Dean had made himself famous by scoring 32 goals in First Division matches. His name was talked about as much as any other in the soccer world. As a promising newcomer his potential was the subject of wild and optimistic speculation. In addition to his well-rated skills, he was blessed with an outstanding personality; and perhaps of some significance to his popularity rating he was known by a name (Dixie Dean) that could scarcely have been better conceived by the Hollywood experts engaged to create pseudonyms for actors that were so shaped in syllables and sound as to roll off the tongue and sublimate the public mind, the purpose of which was to make stars of some performers – often those without talent. Of course Dean had talent, together with many other attributes, but combined with such an easily identifiable title as 'Dixie Dean' he was accepted as a tailor-made star.

When that terrible accident occurred, the public was delivered a shattering blow – it was a broken promise to the future of soccer.– as music lovers might feel on hearing the news that a favourite concert pianist had crushed his fingers in an accident. Apart from the personal suffering of the young footballer, the public disappointment that it would never witness the blossoming of such great potential was profoundly felt. Not for one moment was it thought that Dean's potential could possibly ever materialise. That it did, following such appalling injuries, is surely one of the most amazing recovery episodes in sporting history.

9 Sixty Glorious Goals

DEAN PLAYED PROFESSIONAL FOOTBALL for about 16 years. He first signed for Tranmere Rovers in 1923. In 1925 he was transferred to Everton, with whom he remained for exactly 13 years. He played all his top class soccer with that team. The highlight of his whole career, indeed for football in general, was the season 1927-28, during which he scored one hundred goals, including sixty in League games, to establish not only an all-time record but immortality. The story of that season, during which he produced a never-to-be-forgotten glut of goals, emerges as a fiction writer's fantasy – one perhaps that few writers would dare to compile because, even as an imaginative story, it would lack any measure of reality.

The old adage is that truth is stranger than fiction, and this has never been better illustrated than by Dean's story of an incomparable eight months of football. Many a soccer star with an eventful and glorious career behind him will draw on his memories with pride, and no doubt pay particular attention to one period or another. But in all the history of football there is perhaps no other comparable achievement for an individual player to have experienced than that of Dixie Dean during the 1927-28 season.

Players have been members of football teams that won both the Cup and League in one season and members of those sides have at the same time been capped for their countries, but never can any individual but Dean have been embroiled in such a dramatic, breath-taking series of exciting personal events within a football season, culminating in a finale which can only be described as incredible. Looked at from the football scene of today the story assumes a kind of mythological base, which football historians would like to invent to give the game a background flair. It is a story which will probably never be re-enacted.

Everton opened the 1927-28 season with a home game against Sheffield United at Goodison Park, which Everton won 4-0. The scorers were Troup, Weldon, Forshaw, and Dean. Dean was described as thrustful, difficult to subdue, and effervescent, but his goal only came after 75 minutes. On that same day Hughie Gallacher, whom Dean himself admires as the best centre-forward of his day, was scoring a hat-trick against Huddersfield Town, a team which was to dominate both League and Cup during the rest of the season. It was hard to appreciate that less than twelve months before, Dean had been lying in hospital in a critical condition, his life hanging in the balance and here he was, the most lively and enthusiastic player on the field. No-one watching would have thought he had even suffered from a headache in his life, let alone a broken skull. All his old heading and shooting power was there in abundance. But neither he nor anyone else imagined that the goal he scored was to be the first of the most glorious goal-scoring spree in the history of soccer.

In their second game of the season, Everton played Middlesbrough, a side newly-promoted from the Second Division. This was an interesting clash because Middlesbrough fielded George Camsell at centre-forward – the player who in the previous season had set up a League record of 59 goals. Although achieved in the Second Division, it was a magnificent performance and was something no-one imagined could never be surpassed in any Division of League football, least of all the First Division! Camsell was regarded as a great rival, because Dean had already set an exceptionally high standard in his first two seasons with Everton in the top sphere. Middlesbrough won the match 4-2, with Camsell having a field day. He scored all four of his side's goals, giving an all-round scintillating exhibition of centre-forward play. The reports of the game, however, did not ignore Dean's performance, emphasising that it was of international standard and that his heading, dribbling, and shooting were superb. Dean scored one of Everton's two goals but he had to admit that it was his rival's day. Everton played their third match at Burnden Park against Bolton Wanderers, a powerful force in the First Division in those days, and drew 1-1. Dean scored and saved his side a point. Reports indulged in all the superlatives about Dean's performance, going so far as to describe it as being of 'positive brilliance'.

In the next fixture, against Birmingham at Goodison Park, Everton went nap, winning the match 5-2 before a crowd of 38,000. Dean scored two goals and Alec Troup, Everton's outside left, also put two in the net. One of Alec's goals was scored with his head, and this was an occasion to celebrate. Alec was but 5 ft 5 in tall and was still suffering from that weak collar bone, which had to be strapped up for every game. He played in the days when wingers were supposed to keep to the area of the field indicated by their position on the team sheet. But as with most recollections of the past, misconceptions abound, not least on the subject of wing play. Outside-forwards scored many goals from the tactic of cutting in, and Alec was capable of doing so. Alec could not only score goals, but was also a unique provider for the master of goal-scoring, creating with Dean an unforgettable combination during that particular season. Alec had the ability to give the ball plenty of air, and to vary the process, skilfully projecting it with his feet almost as effectively as a spin bowler could manipulate a cricket ball with his hand. And, like a top class batsman in cricket who anticipates the flight of the ball, Dean knew almost exactly where it would hang in the air and he was nearly always in position to strike it with his head, confusing the defenders who could not. Ted Critchley, successor to Sam Chedgzoy at outside-right, provided crosses from his wing that could be read in a similar way by Dean, thus creating another great combination. The forward line, which also included Forshaw and Weldon, formed an efficient quintet rarely playing out of tune.

The advertising media in newspapers at that time were clearly exploiting the achievements of Dixie Dean. Cartoons and caricatures were featured in all the sports pages of the press. Advertisements for cigarettes appeared regularly containing a drawing of Dean in football action but without any reference to his name because he was so easily identified with the sporting public and indeed by many who had no interest in sport. Dixie says he received no financial reward for any commercial exploitation of his sporting achievements in this way. During that particular season 'Players Please' advertisements regularly featured a caricature of Dean without commitment. One wonders what would happen today with sponsorship so prevalant in the sporting field. The only benefit Dean says he gained in this respect was a £50 cheque from 'J. Wix & Co.' plus some free cartons of cigarettes, which he mostly gave away. Warney Cresswell, the famous Everton and England full-back to whom Dixie gave many a carton of the cigarettes, used to crush the tobacco from them and smoke it in his pipe!

The cricket season continued then, as now, into the early part of September, and whilst Everton were preparing for their fifth game of the football season to be played on the 14th of that month at home against Bolton, the newspapers were reporting that Harold Larwood, the fast bowler, had just taken his 100th wicket and Wally Hammond, another immortal of English cricket, had chalked up 2916 runs. What a period for sport in general! And here was Dean in the game against Bolton scoring again in a 2-2 draw. He had scored in every one of the five games so far and the tributes about his play were unceasing in their admiration. The Everton team were even accused of too much finesse, and in the Bolton match they apparently should have had a crop of goals.

The next game, against Newcastle United at St James's Park, was played before 50,000 spectators – a figure no doubt enhanced by the fact that Dean was on view, not to mention Hughie Gallacher (the Newcastle centre-forward and Scots wizard) who was reported to have waged a war of words with the referee throughout the game. The match was drawn 2-2, with Dean scoring both goals for Everton. O'Donnell, Everton's full-back, had missed a penalty and comment was that if Dean had taken it he would have recorded a hat-trick and Everton would have gained two points. At this stage of the season Newcastle were topping the League table. Dean was maintaining his consistency, and had not failed to score in any of the matches so far.

On September 21 Dean was selected to play for the Football League against the Irish League. In a one-sided match the Football League won 9-1, but it was an extraordinary game, because there were no goals in the second half! In the first half, there was a goal every five minutes, with Dean scoring four of them. Incidentally, it was a time when immortals in sport had their names cropping up consistently. The next day – September 22 1927 – Gene Tunney fought Jack Dempsey in Chicago for the heavyweight boxing championship of the world. Tunney not only won, but took a prize of £200,000, which in the modern inflationary days may not appear outlandish. But in those days the sum must have been regarded as an immense fortune. Contrast this to Dean's £8 per week! In the football scene he was as great a star as Tunney was in the boxing world but there wasn't a cat in hell's chance of Dean making one tenth of Tunney's prize, even if he gave 100 consecutive star-studded champion performances. When Dean played before 150,000 spectators at Hampden Park, his reward for a 90 minute display of energy and exceptional skill was a mere £6 – or a medal. The players had to make a choice!

The next game (in what was becoming a memorable season for Everton and particularly Dean) was against Huddersfield Town. Here was a team, consisting of nine international players, and one of the most talented teams in the country, who were to lead the First Division for most of the season. The match was drawn 2-2 and Dean scored both Everton goals. His display was described as classic, and his heading superb. Such consistency indicated that, barring accidents, he would have a very successful season, which augured well for his club.

It was about this time that Dean entered into an arrangement with a local bookmaker that on the basis of a £2 stake he would receive odds of evens for one goal scored in any one match in the 1927-28 season, 5-2 for two goals, and 10-1 for three goals. The bookmaker was Billy Cave, friend of another bookie named Freddie Tarbuck, father of Jimmy, the well known comedian. Billy was a Liverpudlian, a fanatical Liverpool supporter, and one who was obviously moved by emotional rather than rational motives to enter into such a gamble. Freddie, supporting Dean, also took on the bet, but the way Dean was consistently scoring caused Billy to become rather apprehensive about the whole thing. By Christmas 1927 Cave was appealing to Dean to revoke the contract. Naturally Dixie wasn't having any of that! He was supplementing his income by his own efforts, and Freddie Tarbuck wasn't doing so badly either!

Down to London for the next match against Tottenham Hotspur where Everton won 3-1. Dean scored two goals and reports in the papers referred once again to his genius. He had now scored in every game so far in the season, but he was to cap all in the next match against Manchester United at Goodison. Everton won 5-2 and Dean scored all five of his team's goals! United adopted off-side tactics throughout the game, but Dean's masterly activity thwarted everything that United tried against him. In nine games he had a total of 17 goals. If the match against the Irish League is taken into account he already had 21 goals from 10 appearances. Sports writers were raving in their admiration of his skills. He was described as a beautiful natural footballer and sportsman, delighting crowds and thrilling followers everywhere – even those who could only derive their enjoyment by reading about his exploits on the football field. The effect on gates was tremendous, and home or away attendances were greatly improved by the news that he would be playing.

The next match had to be a sell-out. It was the 55th Derby game between Everton and Liverpool. With Everton and Dean in great form, the locals looked forward to a match of intense interest and excitement and, of course, what every football crowd wants – goals, glorious goals. Everton possessed the greatest virtuoso of them all to provide such delicacies. Dean wanted to succeed in a derby game more than any other. The rivalry between Liverpool and Everton was intense. Elisha Scott, the Liverpool goalkeeper, (the best, Dean says, he has ever seen) always received a package the night before a derby game. It contained a bottle of aspirin together with a note signed, 'Bill Dean'. The message said: 'Get a good sleep tonight – I'll be there tomorrow!' Alas, as with so many sporting occasions conceived out of such promise, the outcome was disappointing. The match ended in a 1-1 draw, with Alec Troup scoring Everton's only goal, and Edmed, Liverpool's outside-right, scoring his team's goal. So much for the story that wingers rarely got goals! Liverpool's great centre-half, 'Parson' Jackson, successfully kept Dean under control.

It was Jackson's day, and Dixie was the first to admit it. Jackson studied for the church and was later ordained as a Minister. It was said that sometimes in 'Liverton' matches his presence restrained the strong words normally used in the light-hearted dialogue which continued throughout the game between Elisha and Dixie. The legends which developed from the intense but friendly rivalry between Scott and Dean are still referred to today. The classic story is that if Dixie met Elisha in the street and nodded his head in acknowledgement Elisha would instinctively dive into the road and narrowly escape being run over! With so many characters and good footballers around for that derby game it was no wonder that 64,000 turned up. The receipts were £4000. The spectators, it would seem, got good value for their money in those days.

An interesting report appeared in the local newspaper in October 1927. The headline 'Will Liverpool have a Dean?' would, on Merseyside, quite naturally be interpreted in a football sense. No research has been made as to the real significance of the question but it would appear that an ecclesiastical body was considering such an appointment. The appointment was in fact subsequently made, because now Liverpool does indeed possess a Dean of the Church. At the time however, Evertonians emphatically rejected such a suggestion. Everton had the only Dean that mattered. The question was considered impertinent, and how could any other team lay claim to such a thing, least of all Liverpool! They had their 'Parson' Jackson – wasn't that enough?

Dean was called on to play for England against Ireland in Belfast and was therefore absent from the Everton team to meet West Ham at Goodison Park on October 22. Elisha Scott, his friend and rival, was in goal for Ireland. The occasion was one on which, according to Dean, more excitement was created just prior to the kick-off than in the game itself. The English players were indulging in some ball practice, shooting in, as was the usual custom before any football match, when suddenly another form of shooting broke out within the ground. What sounded like either rifle or pistol shots rang out. The players stopped in their tracks to listen. Hufton, the West Ham goalkeeper who was playing for England that day, suddenly collapsed. The players thought he might have been wounded but when they ran to pick him up he was found to be suffering from shock brought on by the rifle shooting, and it took some minutes for him to recover. It seems that things have not changed so much today! However, the game, although considerably delayed, got under way. England lost 0-2 and gave a pretty poor show. The reports said that Dean might have had a few goals but the England wingers, particularly Joe Hulme on the right, kept cutting across to the other side of the field, and this upset the forward line, denying Dixie many chances. Everton, meanwhile, were having a field day at Goodison Park. West Ham were beaten 7-0. Everton had proved that perhaps they were no one-man team! However, it has to be said that the Hammers were without their regular goalkeeper, Hufton, who was on duty in Belfast. So, for two matches running, Dean had not found the net. Supporters were thinking perhaps he had run out of steam, or luck, or whatever. Football crowds were as fickle then as they are now.

Dean returned for the next match at Portsmouth and proved he was back in business with a brilliant hat-trick in Everton's 3-0 win. An interesting game, with Dean exploiting the deep centre-forward play. This tactic, introduced by the Hungarians 20 years later and subsequently renewed in English football, was hailed as something entirely new! The reports of the Everton v Portsmouth match say that Dean, reading the offside methods exploited by his opponents, fell back to a position behind the half-way line, and although very closely watched, his speed and skill enabled him to race through and score three times. His genius for reading a game of football was becoming more and more appreciated. The next match, against Leicester at Goodison, brought him another hat-trick in a 7-1 win. Everton had now scored 44 goals from 13 games and Dean had bagged 23 of them – more than half his side's total! And it has to be noted that in one game in which Everton scored seven goals, Dean was absent.

Everton, in their next match, had another convincing away win, 3-0 against Derby County. Dean scored two of the goals but the report of the game argued that he had tended to dribble too much and 'play draughts' with the ball, whatever that was supposed to mean. Followers of football saw in him a fascinating goal-scoring machine and no doubt disliked any form of dilly-dallying. It was goals they wanted, and Dean's capacity to provide these in quantity tended to make them shun the other quality aspects of his play. Having had their appetites whetted, fans wanted cake and nothing but cake. But Dean was not only a virtuoso of goal-scoring, he was an intelligent player and entitled to perform in a game as he interpreted it. Percy M. Young, in his book *Football on Merseyside* had this to say of Dean.

> Dixie Dean was a player of affecting loyalty, practising his skill with the same determination whether for a winning or losing side. He had, as centre-forwards must have, courage. As a player Dean combined power with grace, intuition, and intellect. His shots were both vicious and accurate but he was a brilliant header of the ball. Dean was a shrewd tactician and master of positional play, which meant that like all great stylists he was in the right place at the right time. The tumults of the years of depression stood still while Everton won the championship, the championship of Division Two, and the English Cup.

All eyes (despite the economic depression) were now focused on Dean, wondering whether or not his amazing consistency in scoring goals could be maintained. Of course he was not only scoring goals but was at the same time demonstrating all his other fascinating qualities, so rarely bestowed on an individual footballer. He was rapidly gaining that status which inevitably made him attractive to the social strata, and all the temptations which could so easily affect his performance. At the age of twenty he might have been more vulnerable, but he resisted many of these influences and retained a level head. The strain which those in the public eye can encounter did not affect him, nor did it interfere with his dedication to maintaining his physical fitness. He was regularly invited to social functions throughout Merseyside and elsewhere. Each match became increasingly tougher, but he kept on proving his extraordinary constitution and, whatever the odds, faced all situations with a remarkable lack of tension. His feet never left the ground, metaphorically speaking of course! He always paid tribute to his colleagues in the Everton team who gave him such wonderful support. Nonetheless, they in turn were obviously inspired by Dean's own performances.

Having said all that, the next game, which was against Sunderland at Goodison Park, gave the team's confidence a severe jolt. Sunderland won 1-0, Everton's display being described as poor and decidedly off-form. It was clear from the reports, however, that Dean's prolific goal-scoring feats were inducing opponents to adopt a variety of tactics designed to suppress his talents. In this particular game Dean was throughout surrounded by several Sunderland players crowding and jostling him in the extreme. The Everton team failed to take advantage of the situation. Dean's genius for using the experience he had gained in successive matches was to ensure that whatever measures future opponents might indulge in, he would ultimately counter them.

A revived Everton team met Bury at Gigg Lane in the next match, and won 3-2. Bury were well placed in the League and widely considered to be strong challengers for the Division One championship. The Bury team included one or two international players and in those days the club was always a formidable force in the First Division. By scoring three goals Everton brought their total to 51 for the season so far. Dean got two in this match, and had a personal total of 27 goals in 15 games, and his dribbling and shooting continued to attract high praise in the Press. The season entered December, and Everton's match on the first Saturday in the month was at home to Sheffield United, and ended in a tame 0-0 draw. Dean faced the crude tactics of being bustled out by a cluster of opponents continually surrounding him throughout the game, but his colleagues once again did not exploit the advantages the situation offered. Perhaps they were dreaming of a white Christmas or one of the trips to America that were being advertised in the local press at that time by the Cunard Steamship Company, at a charge of only £37 return!

On December 10 Everton played Aston Villa away, and before a 40,000 crowd, won 3-2. The spectators had full entertainment value with Dean in buoyant mood scoring a brilliant hat-trick. It is interesting to note that the newspapers announced prior to the match that Everton's team would travel on the 9.40 a.m. train from Liverpool Lime Street on the morning of the fixture. It is equally interesting to note that crowd behaviour was excellent. No reports of hooliganism or otherwise. And yet following the Oxford v Cambridge Rugby fixture which took place at Twickenham on December 14 1927 the newspapers were full of reports about hundreds of undergraduate fans of the rugby match storming the West End of London wrecking theatres and terrorising the audiences, as bad as, if not worse than, the low levels reached in modern soccer hooliganism.

The weather was becoming more seasonal and it was reported that all Europe was ice-bound. Everton faced Burnley at home on December 17 and won 4-1 with Dean failing to score, although he was described as Everton's most dangerous forward. Following this game Everton were leading the First Division by five points, having totalled 28 from 19 games. Cardiff City were in second place with 23. Then Everton faced a Christmas programme of three matches, and with the relatively inferior travel arrangements of those days it was decidedly a much more intense itinerary in many ways than it is today. There were three games to play within four days.

A study of the First Division League table on December 19 1927 is of interest.

	P	W	D	L	F	A	Pts
Everton	19	11	6	2	57	20	28
Cardiff City	19	8	7	4	36	36	23
Huddersfield Town	18	9	4	5	43	31	22
Newcastle United	19	9	4	6	40	34	22
Leicester City	20	8	6	6	38	34	22
Tottenham Hotspur	19	9	4	6	37	34	22
Blackburn Rovers	20	7	8	6	27	29	22
Middlesbrough	19	7	6	6	40	41	20
Liverpool	19	6	7	6	45	33	19
Arsenal	18	7	5	6	37	37	19
Manchester United	20	8	3	9	36	37	19
West Ham United	18	9	1	8	38	41	19
Bury	19	9	1	9	35	42	19
Aston Villa	19	7	4	8	38	34	18
Bolton Wanderers	18	6	5	7	29	26	17
Sunderland	19	6	5	8	38	36	17
Burnley	19	8	1	10	36	46	17
Sheffield Wednesday	19	4	7	8	34	39	15
Birmingham City	19	4	7	8	31	40	15
Sheffield United	19	5	5	9	23	38	15
Derby County	18	4	5	9	23	47	13
Portsmouth	19	4	5	10	32	51	13

Everton had scored 57 goals from 19 games and Dean was credited with 30 – more than half of the total. George Camsell of Middlesbrough, promoted from the Second Division, had at that point in time scored 20 of his side's 45 goals. There were five teams on 22 points and it is interesting to note Blackburn Rovers so high in the table with only 27 goals from 20 games.

Everton travelled to London to play Arsenal in the next match and lost 3-2, Dean scoring one of the two goals. The team returned to Goodison Park to play Cardiff, a top-of-the-table match, on Boxing Day, and won 2-1 before 50,000 spectators. This match produced some disgraceful conduct from two of the players – actually sparring up to each other, a rare occurrence at that time. Dean, however, was not involved and the reports described his performance as brilliant, doing the work of three men, and refer to him even throwing-in the ball – a function normally designated to the half-backs in pre-war football. He was injured during the game and went off the field for a time, which caused a great deal of apprehension among the fans. In this match Dean scored both Everton goals, which made his total 33 from 21 games. People increasingly speculated that if he escaped serious injury and continued to score at this rate he would surely set up an all-time record.

The festive season's programme was not yet over and a return game away to Cardiff City had to be played the following day – December 27. The wintry conditions which prevailed obviously did not help to reduce risks of injury and combined with the fact that Cardiff were a hard and tough combination it was not a match to relish. Cardiff won this fixture 2-0. Fortunately, the game was played in a far better spirit than the one on Boxing Day. The Christmas goodwill had seeped through, but Everton came away without any Yuletide present except perhaps to be thankful that no injuries had been sustained. The fourth game within a week was played on New Year's Eve at Sheffield against Sheffield Wednesday. Everton won 2-1 and Dean was credited with both his side's goals. The team had travelled approximately 1000 miles by train, and played four matches within the week. Dean at this stage could claim a total of 90 goals from 95 league games with Everton. At the same time the club was leading Division One by four points.

Most people, however, were watching Dean's progress with increasing interest and thrilling to the excitement it generated. He was on the verge of toppling so many individual records, and speculation was rife. The pressures gained greater momentum, but the coolest person in all this was the great man himself. Man is the right description but in those days he was still considered to be a minor. After all, he was only 20 years of age and here he was probably the most mature and professional footballer in the world. He was on the threshold of making soccer history, causing palpitations to the hearts of football fans everywhere and much anguish for those teams yet to meet Everton during the remainder of what was to be an unforgettable season.

Of course sporting interest was not confined to soccer, although any other event would have to be a spectacular one to divert attention from Dean's current progress in the soccer world. On New Year's Day 1928 the MCC were touring South Africa and the redoubtable Hobbs and Sutcliffe, opening batsmen for England, were reported to have made a protest (during the course of a match) which was described as a colour problem. The headline in the papers – 'Colour Protest' – would, if it had appeared today, have been followed by an entirely different report than the one given under this head on January 1 1928. What the cricketers were complaining about then was the fact that the ball used in the match was black instead of red! A subtlety which escaped the minds of people in those days, but would be interpreted today as a protest about racialism and several other things as well! It is not relevant to Dean's story, but fifty years ago sport was sport, and supposed to enjoy complete isolation from all other activity, including politics, and no doubt did.

Nevertheless, football in Britain was a safety valve for the majority who were enduring (and were to continue to do so for some years) terrible economic depression of a kind that almost demoralised the nation beyond repair. For the masses, soccer was a means of escape and as in all situations of this nature if a hero is not created then it seems one has to be invented. In the football world Dean, by his outstanding performances, was the natural choice for this role. Nothing had to be invented about his prowess – it was there in abundance and was eagerly devoured as an acceptable stimulating diversion from the deprivations which masses of people suffered from at that time. 'Give it to Dixie' was their cry, but he in turn provided them with manna from his heavenly football sphere.

The New Year of 1928 promised much on the football front. Dean had scored two goals on New Year's day and the following day scored another two in the match against Blackburn Rovers at Ewood Park, before a crowd of 47,000. Blackburn defeated Everton 4-2 but Dean's aggregate of goals was now 37 for the season. He was one short of equalling B. C. Freeman's club record of 38 goals scored for Everton in the

1908 season. It looked certain that Dean would not only create a new club record but that he would also break the existing Division One total then held by Harper of Blackburn Rovers, who had scored 43 goals in the 1925-26 season.

A big crowd turned up at Goodison on January 7 to see Everton defeat Middlesbrough 3-1 and Dean bag two goals to break Freeman's record. This was, unfortunately, one of the rare occasions when two players were sent off, Weldon, of Everton, and McLelland, of Middlesborough, being despatched to the dressing room by the referee. In the next few weeks cup-ties were to dominate the football scene, causing a break in the exciting course of the goal-scoring race in which Dean was now involved. On January 14 Everton beat Preston 3-0 in the third round proper of the FA Cup, Dean getting one of the goals.

The period in which all this was going on was productive not only of sporting giants, but also men of great literary stature. People suffered adversity from which, paradoxically perhaps, men and women drew their inspiration, and genius was displayed in many fields. Dean himself, like millions of others, nurtured through wars and constant economic crises, suffered from a lack of academic opportunity. He confesses to having little or no formal education and his capacity to enjoy literature was restricted through the neglect of his early schooling. Yet during his life society was producing writers of great merit, some of whom may be regarded as immortal. Dean did not read very much, not even what they said about him in the papers. Yet he was, in the context of his particular occupation, described as one of the really intelligent men of the football profession. He could read a game of football better than most. The only future provided for him was football, and in the kind of adversity from which he and society suffered he demonstrated a genius which may have been helped by that particular period, one so fertile in producing a host of successful men from a variety of human activities.

For example, on January 16 1928 Thomas Hardy, the author and poet, was buried at Westminster and the pall bearers at his funeral were George Bernard Shaw, J. M. Barrie, Rudyard Kipling, and John Galsworthy, a concentration of great men which might be regarded as a literary symbol of the age. Football might be considered light years away from such civilised references, but standards of achievement were high in many areas of human endeavour, including the sporting world. At that time Dame Clara Butt, the international concert singer who was touring the provinces, was described as the 'Queen of Song' (which she obviously was) in posters advertising her appearance. But today many of her admirers would probably be offended by such commercial and popular connotations of reference to one whom they regard as a cultured and classical artist not to be associated with the light entertainment which that title implies!

Dean's appearances in the League, and his entertainment value for the massive following of football enthusiasts he now commanded, continued with a game at St Andrews against Birmingham in which Everton drew 2-2 before 40,000 spectators. Bobby Irvine scored both Everton goals and disappointed followers saw Dean consistently marked by two opponents throughout the game. But the reports say he was splendid and greatly assisted his side in gaining a point. Everton were drawn away in the next round of the FA Cup against Arsenal. The match was played at Highbury on January 28. The result was a 4-3 win for Arsenal, but Dean scored two of Everton's goals in what was an exciting and entertaining cup-tie. Everton, now released from cup-tie commitments, were able to concentrate on the League programme and Dean on his goal-scoring records.

The next League match was a tough one against Huddersfield Town, a team strongly challenging Everton for the leadership of Division One. It may surprise some to learn that in that period Huddersfield Town were one of the best footballing sides in the English League, and in the twenties won the Division One championship three times in succession. When the Yorkshire side welcomed Everton and Dixie Dean on February 4 at Huddersfield, 51,284 spectators turned up to see the home side thrash the Merseyside club 4-1. This win put Huddersfield only one point behind Everton, who continued to lead the Division. Once again some great wing play was demonstrated in this game by Alec Jackson. The famous Scottish international wizard of an outside-right scored a hat-trick and the other Huddersfield goal came from Smith on the other wing. Dean scored for Everton and thereby continued his onslaught on the Division One goal-scoring record.

During the next week Dean was selected to play for England in a trial match against 'The Rest' at Middlesbrough – a match played to consider team selection for the home international against Scotland at Wembley on March 31, six weeks hence! The fixture with Scotland was then the highlight of the international football calendar and inclusion in the side was keenly sought by players. England swamped 'The Rest' by winning 8-3 and with that score those who were not present automatically raised the question 'how many did Dean get?' The answer was five, and according to reports he might have had a dozen. It was said that each goal he scored was in a class by itself. The praise of his play was embarrassing. He was certain to appear for England at Wembley.

Following Dean's success in the midweek trial, Everton's home game on the Saturday against Tottenham was full of expectation. But, as invariably happens in these situations, severe disappointment can occur. Everton were thrashed 5-2, and worse, Dean failed to score. Winger Alec Troup scored both Everton goals. The reports were of a waterlogged pitch and little support for Dean. He was on the verge of breaking so many records that the crowds were beginning to lose patience if he failed to score.

The next Saturday was the occasion of the fifth round of the FA Cup and Everton, having been removed from the competition by Arsenal, had no game. So it was a little dismal for Everton fans. Leadership of the League was lost, and Dean had lapsed a little. It would soon be three whole weeks and he hadn't scored a single goal for Everton! His tally was 40 League goals, but the number of games in which he was likely to play in the remainder of the season was rapidly diminishing. And with more determined opponents out to stop him creating records at their expense, there was also the increasing hazard of sustaining a serious injury.

On February 11 1928 the news was announced that Tranmere Rovers had transferred Tom 'Pongo' Waring to Aston Villa for a big fee, not disclosed at the time but eventually given as £4700. Waring was a scarce commodity, a centre-forward of great skill and prolific scorer of goals, and came from the same background as Dean. Waring was a Birkenhead lad who became the only other footballer ever to be in striking distance of the 60-goal record Dean eventually established. Within days, another contemporary of Dean who had played in the same Birkenhead schoolboys team with him was transferred from Tranmere Rovers to Sheffield Wednesday for a similar fee to Waring. He was Ellis Rimmer, an outside-left who was to distinguish himself by being capped for England several times in the years ahead.

What more appropriate occasion than a derby game against Liverpool to mark Everton's revival from the doldrums of the previous few weeks! Dean always enjoyed doing well at

Anfield, and as Elisha Scott, Liverpool's Irish International goalkeeper, had been called to duty for his country on that day it was expected that Dixie would exploit the absence of his great adversary. Riley, who deputised for Scott in goal, was no mean substitute, and Dean could not expect to have it all his own way.

Saturday February 25 turned out to be a day to remember. Not only was the match between Liverpool and Everton one of the most thrilling of all derby games, but six goals were scored, a number only exceeded on one previous occasion in all the 56 played. The match ended in a 3-3 draw but Dean scored a hat-trick and equalled the First Division record of 43 goals held by Harper of Blackburn. It was surely a red (or blue) letter day for Dean.

Nothing pleased him more than to register goals against the 'Reds'. He made his usual acknowledgments to the Kop (then, as now, the end of the Anfield ground holding about 10,000 of the most partisan of Liverpool supporters) bowing gracefully in the manner of a Spanish matador, following each of the goals he scored. The response would normally not be enthusiastic, but the 'Kopites', although strongly partisan, are nothing if not appreciative of football achievement and when Dean equalled the Division One goal-scoring record in that memorable game they expressed their admiration no less than the other 50,000 spectators. Dixie now had 43 goals, and with only 13 League matches to play required 17 goals to break Camsell's record of 59.

As anticipated, Everton's remaining fixtures got tougher and their opponents seemed more determined than ever to stop Dean breaking Harper's record, never mind the one held by George Camsell. The next match against West Ham in London clearly demonstrated such intentions. The game was drawn 0-0 with Dean crowded out of the game, but according to all reports, never really suppressed. The reports described Dean as worrying his way through an 'avanlanche' of opponents. The result of this game meant that Dean had only a possibility of playing 12 more matches in which to score 17 goals. It was clear that he would miss at least one of those when he played for England against Scotland on March 31 and it was something of a tall order to expect him to net such a bag in a maximum of 11 games.

On the day of the West Ham v Everton game, Huddersfield reached the semi-final of the F.A Cup and were being tipped to achieve the elusive 'double' of FA Cup and Division One championship. However, the pursuit of two titles was to deny them both in the end. The attraction of football at that time was aptly illustrated by the fact that nearly 200,000 watched the four cup-ties on March 3 1928.

On March 6 the Football League made an historic gesture by sanctioning clubs to provide 'benefit' games for footballers. Two Everton players qualified, the condition being five years' service with the club. They were Alec Troup and a full-back named Raitt. Troup had scored 10 goals in 30 games and had supplied Dean with as many more. The season was reaching a critical stage, and speculation reigned over who was going to be relegated, and who would win the championship or the Cup. And attracting more interest than ever was the absorbing issue of whether Dean would create a goal-scoring record. As far as Everton and Dean were concerned the result of their next match appeared to dash all hopes for both club and player. Everton's designs on the championship faded and Dean had still not beaten Harper's record.

Against Manchester United on March 14 before a crowd of 30,000 Everton lost 0-1. The Division One table showed Huddersfield leading Everton by three points but the former having played a game less. The reports in the papers were full of pessimism. It was calculated to be the end of Everton's championship hopes, and as for Dean, although he was described as being in a class by himself and having played brilliantly, it was too much perhaps even for him to expect to break any of the records which had been forecast as being within his reach a few weeks before.

The next match at Leicester emphasised the validity of such forebodings, because Everton again lost 0-1. Now they had not scored a single goal in three games. In the Leicester match Dean was described as the only Everton forward of any note. He was injured, pulling a thigh muscle, and was off the field for some time, returning to play at outside-left for the remainder of the game. Nothing was going right and all the expectations for a rousing end to the season diminished rapidly. Everton were now trailing Huddersfield by four points and Dean had still failed to break the Division One scoring record. He had now only nine games in which to obtain 17 goals to break Camsell's Division two record. Bookmakers would give 1000-1 against Everton winning the championship and no doubt 10,000-1 against Dean attaining his target.

Another setback occurred. On March 10 Dean was selected to play for the English League side against the Scottish League and missed Everton's game with Portsmouth. Everton drew 0-0, which did not contribute much relief for their championship hopes. Dean scored two goals for the English League in a 6-2 win over their Scottish rivals. But those two goals would not count in his apparently vain attempt to set up a new goal standard for League matches. The position could not be more hopeless, either for him or his club. Only nine more League fixtures and the maximum that Dean could play in was seven. It was considered well nigh impossible to score 17 goals within such a programme, particularly when every game was a possible championship decider.

Fans even began to think he would be lucky to exceed Harper's record, for which he only required one more goal. Dean was, however, irrepressible, and if the Everton team could only recover its form there was nothing Dean couldn't do if he really wanted, and 17 goals could come, perhaps only from someone like him who was never affected by tension or the pressure that the existing situation obviously presented. He took it in his stride and all his unique qualities were there in abundance to master what must have been the most enormous odds any sportsman has ever had to face when attempting to beat a record. March 1928 had proved a disastrous month and Everton goals did not come until the 24th, the day they drew with Derby County 2-2, the match in which Dean actually broke the Division One record by two goals to make his total 45.

The next Saturday Dean was to play for England whilst Everton were meeting Sunderland at Roker Park. So he was faced with the prospect of performing the miracle of registering another 15 goals in seven remaining league games provided he escaped injury, a hazard which hovered overhead ready to swoop and destroy all the high hopes for the club, himself, and the millions of football fans everywhere who had thrilled to his progress in this fantastic goal race. Dean, however, was probably the only one in the soccer world not breathless with excitement at the prospect. He had lost some ground in the race, but the challenge was not beyond his capacity or his spirit. The situation was becoming a great deal more exhilarating for all concerned.

If March 1928 was disappointing for both Everton and Dean it marked a number of events in the world outside which no doubt attracted attention away from the exploits of footballers. The Grand National steeplechase was won by Tipperary Tim at 100-1 and the Lincolnshire Handicap by Dark Warrior at 33-1, making for a record spring double! In the political field the Bill to give women the vote at 21 was introduced by Parliament. This provided for about 5 million more voters on the electoral roll. During the month, the Reverend G. A. Studdard-Kennedy, a minister of the church who became famous as 'Woodbine Willie' serving as a padre in the trenches in the First World War, gave a sermon in St Nicholas Church, Liverpool on the subject of 'Sex and Christianity'. The reader might wonder what this has to do with the story of a footballer. But when talking about Dixie Dean and his achievements most people will consider that the age in which he lived was a far cry from the 1970s. Not so. The report in the paper about 'Woodbine Wille' and his sermon was headlined with a quote: 'The sex question had today come into Art to such an extent that people were nauseated by it'. The Reverend went to criticise the so-called degenerate behaviour of society in precisely similar terms as some of his counterparts do today! Sporting competition was as great then as it is in the 1970s!

Entertainment for the masses, and footballers, came from the live theatre and the silent cinema which had an enormous output. Indeed, the advertised theatre shows were often not so different from today. In 1928 *Peter Pan, Rose Marie, The Desert Song,* and *The Skin Game* were showing at provincial houses. The pubs were also apparently doing a roaring trade, indicated by the statistics announced on March 31 1928, which revealed that the nations's drink bill was £300 millions for the past year. And you could buy an awful lot of drink for that sum in those times! There were plenty of other forms of entertainment which provided temptations for those in the public eye, including footballers (particularly the stars) who were seduced by them in no different a manner than in modern times. Dean could have been just as susceptible, but his obsession with soccer kept him on a reasonably straight course. His unique constitution was his great physical asset. Even if he indulged in the wine women and song saga to any extent, it appeared not to affect him in the least.

Dean, whose League programme was interrupted by his appearance for England against Scotland at Wembley – a game which both he and the England team would no doubt wish to put out of their minds forever – was determined to return and give all to help his club in the championship race and if possible end the goal-scoring drought which had recently afflicted Everton. The 1-5 England defeat by Scotland was a crushing blow and could have had a tremendous psychological effect on all the home players, especially Dean, who, as a highly-rated individual, was looked on as a temporary failure and to some extent responsible for England gaining only a single goal in the match. The 'Blue Devils' dominated the game at Wembley and once again proved that wing play in the football of the late twenties was a force to be reckoned with.

Alec Jackson, the Scottish outside-right, scored a hat-trick just to prove the point. However, Dean forgot the matter altogether, and braced himself to tackle the seven remaining League games in Division One. And what a sensational episode it produced, something so dramatic, it tended to arouse suspicions that it had all been deliberately staged! A colossal and stupendous epic, to coin the then Hollywood film preview ballyhoo indulgences of the time. Almost as many people watched football as they did the cinema, but no rehearsals could be staged for soccer games, and no one could foresee at that time what was to come.

The Easter football programme loomed ahead, the results of which were usually regarded as an indicator as to where the end of season honours would be bestowed, and therefore the matches were regarded as crucial for teams engaged in championship or relegation areas in the League tables. Everton clearly retained hopes for the championship, but there were many ifs and buts about it. The results of their games played on Good Friday and Easter Saturday could not have been better. The team took on a new life. There were 60,000 spectators at Goodison Park to see them beat Blackburn Rovers 4-2, with Dean collecting two of the goals. Neighbours Liverpool beat Huddersfield Town on the following day, thus aiding Everton to take the lead in Division One on goal average. Everton drew their match with Bury on the Saturday and Dean got their only goal. He now had 48 goals with five matches to play.

On April 14 Everton visited Sheffield United and won 3-1, with Dean scoring twice, thus chalking up his half-century for the season. Fifty goals in 35 matches! Four more to play and ten goals wanted to beat Camsell's record. Any suggestion that he could achieve this was put down to wishful thinking. The pressures were becoming intense, and diminished the possibility of him reaching the 60-goal target. The team was obviously affected by it all, but Dean was quite blasé and seemed immune from the tensions, taking every game as it came as an entirely separate event. The next fixture was held in mid-week at Goodison Park, where Newcastle United were the visitors. Everton won 3-0 but Dean could only secure one goal. Still,

Everton were leading the division and had the advantage that two of the remaining three matches were at home.

The first of the trio of matches was against Aston Villa and attracted a great deal of interest because two of the most expensive centre-forwards would be on view, both Merseysiders, and with similar origins in the football world, namely Tranmere Rovers. The 60,000 who watched the game did not realise then that history would prove 'Pongo' Waring and 'Dixie' Dean to be the two highest-scoring players in a season in Division One – probably for all time. The Everton v Villa match proved to be absorbing and entertaining, with both centre-forwards demonstrating their skills and Dean taking the honours by collecting two goals to Waring's one in Everton's 4-2 win. Dean now had 53 goals and two matches to play. Seven goals were required to reach what was a seemingly impossible objective. On the day of the Villa match, Huddersfield town, Everton's nearest rivals for the championship, were being beaten by Blackburn Rovers 3-1 at Wembley in the FA Cup Final, thus destroying hopes of the 'double' which Huddersfield had so dearly cherished during the past few weeks.

Everton had to win the next away game against Burnley in order to remain in contention for the championship and of course Dean would have to indulge in some kind of a goal-scoring spree in the match to have any hope of breaking the record. If he managed to score one goal only then it would be beyond even Dean to register six in the final game of the season against Arsenal. With such a range of speculation, the two remaining fixtures were a sell-out in advance. Although Everton's chances of winning the championship relied much on Huddersfield failing to win their matches in hand, the odds were shorter on Everton reaching their goal than those on Dean attaining his. If Everton had had another half-dozen matches to play, the possibility of Dean scoring seven goals would still have been remote.

The match at Burnley was a most exciting affair. Everton won 5-3 and Dean scored four goals, all of them before half time! The result could not have been better. Everton now held the possibility of winning the championship and Dean held the distinct opportunity to complete a hat-trick in the final game. Of course, scoring goals in the First Division (even a single one in a match) was not something that could be made to order. A hat-trick was even more remote but Dean had shown in the Burnley match that he was on top form and he was the one man in the whole football world who had the confidence to do it.

The Burnley match was, however, something of a tragedy because Dean was injured, pulling a thigh muscle, and became a passenger for most of the second half. It is quite possible that had he not been injured he may have achieved the record 60 goals in this game, with the last match of the season to spare! Harry Cooke, the Everton trainer, was determined to have his idol fit for the fixture against Arsenal and he had just one week to do it. Dean had the patience and the constitution to respond to treatment, but the situation caused much doubt and apprehension. Harry Cooke decided to stay with Dean for the whole of the ensuing week, applying treatment continuously, and the only way he could do this was to take up residence with the player. Harry did the job successfully, and Deans' appreciation for the man knew no bounds. Harry Cooke was loved by all the Everton players, and Dean in particular was forever praising him. If Dean is ever asked about the people who helped him in his success, Harry Cooke is one name he mentions with great reverence, warmth and appreciation.

So the stage was set for one of the most exciting sporting events ever presented. The last match of the season, Everton on the brink of winning the championship, and the thrilling prospect of Dean creating the most phenomenal goal-scoring record in the history of soccer. Such prospects enthralled millions and led to wild speculation, from brimming confidence about the possibility, to scornful dismissal of such expectations of the miraculous. The situation had all the ingredients to satisfy the keenest exploiter of sporting promotions. If the event had been available in today's market someone would have made a million out of it. In those days of course the commercial strings were not manipulated so easily, but nevertheless the interest of millions could not be aroused more intensely on the sporting prospects of the great climax which the match against Arsenal contained.

For a whole week excitement simmered and boiled as the high degree of expectancy developed. Huddersfield Town's efforts collapsed during the week and Everton were declared champions before the match with Arsenal took place. Whatever happened, even if Everton lost the game with Arsenal, the First Division Championship Cup would be presented to Cresswell, the Goodison captain, by Mr J. McKenna, President of the Football League. Thus, some of the strain imposed on Everton was eased and concentration could be freely centred on providing Dean with the opportunities to gain his individual honour of a record number of goals and at the same time exceed the 100 mark in the season for the club. Everton's total before the game stood at 99. Dean had already scored 57 goals and this number would stand as a record for the first Division (14 more than the previous best of 43 by Harper of Blackburn) but Camsell, the Middlesbrough centre-forward, had scored 59 in the Second Division. And although on a point of merit there was no comparison in the two achievements, the 59 was there, and the numerical attraction of sinking the figure and substituting 60 or more was irresistible.

Dean had just turned 21 years of age and was indisputably the star footballer of the age. The hours before entering the arena for such an event as this final and crucial match of that season would have shattered the nerves of most men even of established maturity. Dean carried on normal activities, despite his injury, almost oblivious of the prospects. In view of the importance of the game which faced Dean, an illustration of his calm attitude was given by the fact that he accepted an invitation by a Roman Catholic Priest to open a local charity fête at Prescot on the evening before the match. Dean says that when he and a party of others (following the opening ceremony at the fête) went along to the Priest's house for a meal something happened which for the first time disturbed his equilibrium. The Priest, whom Dean recalls as Father Brown, called all to silence whilst a prayer was offered. Father Brown appealed to the Almighty to help Dean to score the goals necessary to break the record on the following day. Although Dixie is a Christian, he is not a Roman Catholic. But, he says, the event in the priest's house somehow affected his emotions far more than if he had been playing before 150,000 spectators at Hampden Park!

The day of the great game dawned. It was the main topic of conversation throughout the whole of Merseyside. The weather was ideal and the state of the pitch perfect. Profound sporting interest, latent in everyone, was greatly aroused. People who normally don't gamble have their gambling instincts stimulated on Grand National or Derby days. This particular sporting event had similar effects. Some who had never attended a football match in their lives held a curious interest in the vital game to be played that afternoon.

Would Dixie Dean add to his already well-filled cup of success and achieve the impossible? Nothing attracts like the magnet of seeing the miraculous. The only comparable sporting event to contain such a challenge was to come a quarter of a century later when Roger Bannister and his fellow athletes set out to beat the four-minute mile. Those who did not witness the event awaited anxiously to enjoy the genuine thrill the news of such phenomenal human achievement would bring. It was that kind of situation which prevailed on that Saturday afternoon – May 5 1928.

Soccer fans from the Merseyside area converged in their thousands on Goodison Park. Ferryboats and trains from across the Mersey plus the special football trams in Liverpool steamed, purred, and clanged along to convey fans from far and near. The crowds were all imbued with the mystic expectancy of a religious pilgrimage, set on bearing witness to some supernatural vision and bathe in its glory. There was no guarantee the spirit would appear, but the slimmest hope was sufficient attraction. Not to be there if it should happen would condemn devout football souls forever to purgatory, a penance Everton fans were determined not to suffer.

So every able-bodied supporter who could manage to get there *was* there, ready to put up with the thronging, jostling and other attendant inconveniences without complaint. Throughout all the marshalling and travel arrangements, no disturbances occurred, and there was a complete absence of any kind of hooliganism, despite the excitement and tension which the occasion inevitably created. Supporters willed and wished and prayed the miracle would happen. That 'Dixie' would capture those three goals and be credited with the nice round figure of 60 to establish an all-time record. There was no dispute about that, except perhaps among the Arsenal players and supporters.

The ground was packed with more than 60,000 spectators when the teams ran on to the pitch to be welcomed by tumultuous cheering, mostly and especially for the man of the moment. The referee, 'Lol' Harper, of Stourbridge, shook Dean by the hand. However there was another man for whom this match must be regarded as memorable. Charlie Buchan, the Arsenal forward who had graced the English football scene so well for many years, had announced his retirement from the game and this was to be his final appearance. It was perhaps unfortunate that his departure from the soccer stage had to be overshadowed by an event which diverted attention from him and which inevitably had to take prior importance. The crowd enjoyed the electric atmosphere of the occasion and the sense of privilege it conveyed. The red jerseys of Arsenal and the blue of Everton's strip all appeared brighter than usual. The green background of the pitch combined to add a sense of gaiety in contrast to the serious challenge and purpose which the game presented to a deliriously cheerful and expectant multitude.

The Arsenal team was as follows: Paterson; Parker, John, Baker, Butler, Blythe, Hulme, Buchan, Shaw, Brian, Peel. The Everton side was: Davies; Cresswell (Captain), O'Donnell, Kelly, Hart, Virr, Critchley, Martin, Dean, Weldon, Troup. The kick-off which the huge crowd of spectators had so patiently waited for was duly approved by the referee, but within minutes Everton hearts sank, ostensibly with all their hopes. Arsenal had scored. Shaw, Arsenal's centre-forward, hit a cannonball shot which would have done credit to 'Dixie' himself. Davies in the Everton goal fumbled the shot and allowed the ball to go through his legs. The early tension and excitement had no doubt affected him and this early reverse did no good either for Everton's or Dean's intentions at that moment of crisis.

The situation demanded immediate retaliation if the game's expectations were to be fulfilled. Dean realised this and right from the restart he was on his way goalwards sweeping through the Arsenal defence to score with a thunderous shot to chalk up Everton's 100th goal of the season. And of course his own 58th! Only two more wanted! Hearts and hopes were immediately restored to their pre-match elevation in the Everton camp. Dean was determined to reach his target. He was in top form and rampant throughout. Arsenal players, however, were resolved – so far as they were concerned, Dean would not score again.

The score remained at 1-1 until midway through the first half when Dean was unceremoniously bought down in the penalty area by an Arsenal defender. The referee pointed to the penalty spot. The crowd, with feverish exictement, roared 'Give it to Dixie!' and impatiently waited whilst it was being established that the great man would take the kick. Dean took the ball and placed it on the spot. Silence descended over the ground as though every single one of the 60,000 spectators had been temporarily transfixed, that all life had been extinguished by some supernatural force. An eerie silence, breathless yet electric in its intensity, inert like a fuse ready to be ignited. Dean ran up to take the kick. The fuse was burning and suddenly the vast arena exploded with a deafening roar. The ball was in the back of the net. The crowd shouted and screamed, delirious with ecstasy and delight. The miracle was on the horizon. The goal-scoring record had been equalled and now it was surely not beyond Dean to score another goal. But the Gunners were not taking it lying down. They pressed hard during the remainder of the first half and ultimately got their reward. O'Donnell, the Everton full-back, put through his own goal and the teams went into the dressing room with the score 2-2 at half time.

The crowd naturally thought the interval was far too long. They sensed somehow the miracle must happen. That elusive goal must come, but a lot of nails would be bitten in the meantime. The second half opened and Arsenal made it obvious that they would do their utmost to prevent Dean scoring that vital goal. A tight rein was kept on Dean throughout. Arsenal frequently adopted the off-side trap. Time was evaporating. There was only eight minutes to go, and still the goal, that diamond goal, did not come. The atmosphere was charged as though an electric current was continually passing at varying force through spectators and players alike. Everton players were concentrating in trying to feed Dean with the essential ball that would give him the goal that everybody (except Arsenal) wanted and prayed for him to get.

The tension reached fever pitch when five minutes from the end Everton were awarded a corner. Alec Troup, the diminutive Scot, placed the ball to take the corner kick. The crowd, tense with bated breath, wondered whether this could be it. Would Dean get that magnificent head of his to the ball? Alec sent over his speciality, a hanging centre and Dean was there. With a perfectly timed leap above the fourteen players in the goalmouth Dixie had nodded it past the Arsenal goalkeeper for his record 60th goal. The sound of the roar from the crowd must have reached a thousand decibels. The co-ordinate of voices was like a thunder-clap heard throughout the length and breadth of Merseyside. The crowd was jumping with joy and blessed with what must have been the most ecstatic delight ever bestowed on any sporting gathering in history. Dixie bowed his head modestly. The crescendo of the storm of idolatrous worship echoed around the ground for several minutes. The players of both teams ran to shake Dean by the hand or otherwise show their appreciation of his remarkable achievement. All, that is, except Charlie Buchan, who according to Dean showed no inclination to express any form of congratulation. Dean thought this was simply pique on the part of Buchan because his own farewell to football had been over-shadowed by the 60-goal event.

Only a few supporters ran on to the pitch to congratulate Dean, a significant feature of crowd behaviour in those days.

One supporter was seized by the referee who held him by the scruff of the neck and bundled him off the ground, much to the amusement of the crowd. The game continued but no one seemed to care what happened in the closing minutes. Arsenal, who throughout had played well, pressed hard and scored in the final seconds to make it a 3-3 draw, and all present were of the opinion that it was a fair result to a magnificent game.

The championship cup was duly presented to the Everton captain Warney Cresswell. However, Dean's achievement was the dominant theme. The modest way in which he minimised his success, insisting on his colleagues being entitled to a full share of the praise, was widely commented upon and described as 'one of the charms of the fraternisation'. Following the memorable game the news was conveyed to the world and praises poured upon Dean. Nevertheless the success story, one of such magnitude, was in fact treated by the media in a far lower profile in 1928 than it would be today. *The Times,* always a model of reserve, but generally factual and sound in its comments had this to say, which from such a source was praise indeed. '. . . that very brilliant player Dean is largely responsible for Everton winning the championship. A hard, eager player, Dean has had a lot of marking to put up with, but his strength and good humour have carried him through.' The game of soccer received less prominence in *The Times* than most other sporting activities.

The news of Dean's prodigious feat reached the United States and an agent from that country was immediately despatched to make Dean an attractive offer to play over there. The amount involved was no doubt high for those days. But Dean rejected the offer of £150 down and £20 per week, not because it wasn't enough but because he had no intention of leaving Everton at any price.

The 1927-28 season was still not at an end for Dean or Everton. A Swiss tour had been planned, commencing on May 9 with matches arranged between Everton and the Basle, Berne, Zurich, and Geneva clubs, the team returning to Liverpool on May 23. Dean's reputation was already established in Europe and crowds packed the Swiss grounds to see him and Everton win all four matches. Dean scored a total of five goals in the four games and brought his goal tally for that season to 100! In the First Division he had scored 60. In other matches, including the cup-ties and representative games plus internationals he scored 35, thus completing a century of goals in the highest class of football in the world in one slightly extended season. And surely never to be emulated!

The analysis of Dean's League performance for the season was that out of 39 games he had scored in 29 of them. They included one match in which he scored five, and in another four goals; five threes, fourteen twos, and eight singles made up the remainder. Dean's century of goals for season 1927-28 was amassed as follows:

	Games	Goals
Football League Division One	39	60
FA Cup	2	3
Inter-League	2	6
FA trial matches	2	8
FA Continental Tour and Internationals	5	9
Everton Tour	4	5
Blackpool Hospital Cup	1	5
Fleetwood disaster match	1	4
	56	100

The records show that of Dean's 60 League goals 40 were scored with his feet and 20 with his head.

The Everton Club, no doubt restricted by Football League rules, made no presentation (either monetary or otherwise) to Dean in respect of his great achievement in breaking the goal-scoring record. Nevertheless the Everton supporters, determined to commemorate the event, presented him with a large shield suitably inscribed. The shield was mounted with relief figures of solid silver surrounded by 29 silver medallions each containing an inscription of the name of the club against which he scored his crop of goals. These included five against Manchester United and six other hat-tricks, one to which he attaches special significance because it was scored against his old rivals Liverpool at Anfield. The shield is now Dean's proudest and most treasured possession.

During the course of this great and memorable season Dean attained his majority by becoming 21 years of age on January 22 1928. The townspeople of Birkenhead, where Dean was born and raised, marked the occasion by presenting him with an illuminated address, reputedly the first ever presented by the town to one of its sons. The inscription states it was awarded for 'Good sportsmanship, brilliant play, unfailing tact, and initiative as a leader'. How appropriate. With all those

Above: Heading the first of four goals against Sunderland at Goodison Park on Christmas Day 1926. *Below left:* Dean shakes hands with Arsenal's Alex James before a match at Highbury in August 1936. The stand in the background is still under construction, and the referee is Lol Harper. *Right:* Dean as a baseball player with coach Alan Robertson (left) and pitcher Alan Forrest.

Above: Dean walks out to take the kick-off in his testimonial match at Goodison in 1964. *Below:* Pictured at 'The Dublin Packet'.

Above left: Dean receives the congratulations of local fans after recovering from his motorbike accident in 1926. *Above right:* Dean playing golf—note the unorthodox left-below-right grip. *Below left:* Closely shadowed by Arsenal's Herbie Roberts—the original third back. *Below right:* Mr and Mrs Dixie Dean on their wedding day.

Above: Dean greets Steve Bloomer outside Lime Street station shortly before breaking Bloomer's scoring record. *Below:* Dean receives the FA Cup from the Duke and Duchess of York (later King George VI and Queen Elizabeth) at Wembley in 1933.

LEAGUE CHAMPIONS, 1928.

T. H. McINTOSH.   J. KELLY.   H. HART.   A. L. DAVIES.   J. O'DONNELL.   A. VIRR.   H. E. COOK

E. CRITCHLEY.   G. S. MARTIN.   W. R. DEAN.   W. CRESSWELL.   A. WELDON.   A. TROUP.

Above: The 1927–28 Everton League Championship team. *Below:* The only surviving photograph of Dean's 60th goal that season.

Above: A young Dixie Dean pictured with Sam Chedgzoy. *Below:* An example of Dean's heading power as he scores one of his four goals against Southport during Everton's 9–1 victory in an FA Cup-tie in 1931.

Mr. William Ralph Dean, 'Dixie',
EX TRANMERE - EVERTON - NOTTS COON.
living in Bebington
Cheshire.

Please help Mr. Postman.

Above: He could always be found—the postman had more than enough information here! *Below:* Dean celebrates with executives of the Whitbread brewery, who presented him with a tankard following the amputation of his right leg in 1976.

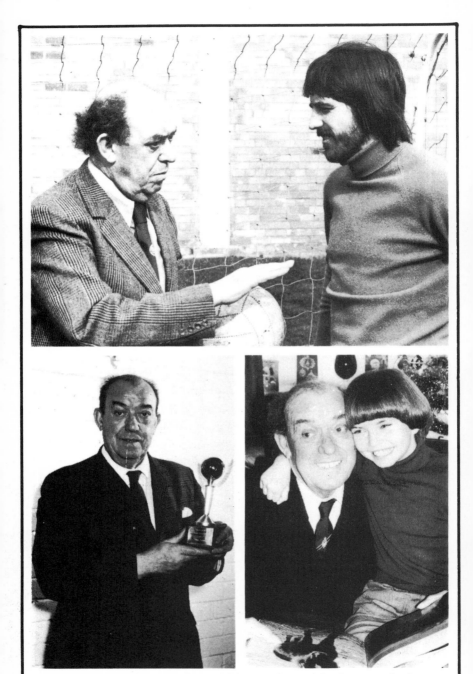

Above: Still involved, Dean gives advice to Bob Latchford, currently the most expensive striker in the country. *Below left:* Pictured with the Hall of Fame trophy presented to him in 1971. *Below right:* Happy in retirement with the apple of his eye—granddaughter Melanie.

qualities he achieved a unique record and immortality at the age of 21.

Following the return from the Swiss Tour in 1928, Dean was keenly sought after by the public and fêted wherever he went. Autograph hunters pursued him everywhere. He was always polite and willing to oblige. Elderly ladies who had never seen a football match and knew nothing about the sport would recognise him and pose the question 'You're Dixie Dean aren't you?' with an earnest request for his signature. Of course the young and handsome football star was also pursued by much younger ladies who would enjoy telling their friends that they had met the great man. Many rumours circulated about his love life. This was no doubt due to him being in the public eye. According to gossip, dozens of young women had been engaged to Dean. No doubt all stars of the entertainment world are subject to such gossip. However, Dean strongly denies he was involved in such ties except to the girl he married in 1931 when he was 24 years of age.

During the summer of 1928 at the age of 21 the world was his oyster. A hero in the sporting world, he accepted public acclaim with great modesty. Dean did not make a fortune or have the aid of modern communications like television to assist in spreading his fame. Nevertheless, wherever he went, at home or on the continent, thousands flocked to see him and even followed him in such numbers through the streets of Paris and Berne. Dean continued to maintain his fitness by playing tennis and golf, keeping mainly to the locality of Merseyside, although he liked to attend race meetings (gambling was, perhaps, his major weakness) and consequently mixed with many distinguished people connected with the sport, particularly during that star-studded period of his life.

In 1927-28 Dean scored 60 goals in League games for Everton, to establish an all time record for a season. George Camsell scored 59 League goals for Middlesbrough in the Second Division in 1926-27 making 41 appearances. Dean broke this record (by scoring one more than Camsell) in 39 appearances in the First Division. In 15 away games Dean scored 31 goals and 29 in 14 home matches. Here's how!

Sheffield Wednesday	H	1	Huddersfield	H	2
Middlesbrough	A	1	Tottenham Hotspur	A	2
Bolton Wanderers	A	1	Manchester United	H	5
Birmingham	H	2	Portsmouth	A	3
Bolton Wanderers	H	1	Leicester City	H	3
Newcastle United	A	2	Derby County	A	2

Bury	A 2		Derby County	H 2
Aston Villa	A 3		Blackburn Rovers	H 2
Arsenal	A 1		Bury	H 1
Cardiff City	H 2		Sheffield United	A 2
Sheffield Wednesday	A 2		Newcastle United	H 1
Blackburn Rovers	A 2		Aston Villa	H 2
Middlesbrough	H 2		Burnley	A 4
Huddersfield Town	A 1		Arsenal	H 3
Liverpool	A 3			

At the end of that magnificent season Everton not only became League Champions, but scored more goals than any other team and jointly with Bolton Wanderers had the least goals against.

Football League – Division One
Final Table 1927-28

	P	W	D	L	F	A	Pts
Everton	42	20	13	9	102	66	53
Huddersfield Town	42	22	7	13	91	68	51
Leicester City	42	18	12	12	96	72	48
Derby County	42	17	10	15	96	83	44
Bury	42	20	4	18	80	80	44
Cardiff City	42	17	10	15	70	80	44
Bolton Wanderers	42	16	11	15	81	66	43
Aston Villa	42	17	9	16	78	73	43
Newcastle United	42	15	13	14	79	81	43
Arsenal	42	13	15	14	82	86	41
Birmingham City	42	13	15	14	70	75	41
Blackburn Rovers	42	16	9	17	66	78	41
Sheffield United	42	15	10	17	79	86	40
Sheffield Wednesday	42	13	13	16	81	78	39
Sunderland	42	15	9	18	74	76	39
Liverpool	42	13	13	16	84	87	39
West Ham United	42	14	11	17	81	88	39
Manchester United	42	16	7	19	72	80	39
Burnley	42	16	7	19	82	98	39
Portsmouth	42	16	7	19	66	90	39
Tottenham Hotspur	42	15	8	19	74	86	38
Middlesbrough	42	11	15	16	81	88	37

A most interesting season. The club in fourth place had only five points more than the club in twentieth place. Only sixteen points separated the top and bottom clubs. As competitive a season as had ever been completed. Each team had scored an average of 1.9 goals per game, which made Dean's tally of 60 goals an individual average of 1.5 per game.

10 Attitudes and Experiences

DEAN'S CHARACTERISTIC working class attitude, whereby he retained his simple earthiness when mixing with some of the upper social strata was a constraint on him ever attempting to become a part of that set. He certainly enjoyed the social functions which at the height of his fame increasingly demanded his presence. Consequently with so many invitations he felt compelled to purchase evening dress, the sartorial trapping he regarded as the uniform of the upper crust, a class which he had no ambition to join. In those days the middle class had taken over and it was much more difficult to defy convention, so at least in one respect Dean succumbed and accordingly extended his wardrobe.

Celebrities like Dean were in great demand to bring lustre to a range of functions, dull or otherwise, many of which he attended, from the National Sporting Club to the local Police Ball. Dean never attempted to obscure his background, and claims, quite proudly, to have retained an honest and open approach which demonstrated that he held none of the pretentiousness to which most people in his circumstances would be generally susceptible.

Through international football engagements and on club tours Dean was privileged to dine and wine in the best hotels in Europe. Many distinguished people sought the honour of sitting at his table. But whilst they were ordering various wines Dean persisted on the waiter providing him with a large jug of beer from which he liked to help himself during the meal. His upper crust company, he recalls, were influenced and abandoned their exotic wines when he granted their polite but urgent requests to share his jug of beer! He refutes any charges of inverted snobbery. Beer is best!

On one occasion when he was dining with the Earl of Derby, Dean observed his Lordship dispense with the aid of cutlery, to handle a chicken leg and consume it in the traditional aristocratic style of Henry the Eighth. Dean was highly delighted with the Earl's table manners and recalls his own reaction with this characteristic comment. 'I thought if that was good enough for Lord Derby it was good enough for me!' So he proceeded to follow suit. And on reflection he regretted the numerous occasions when he had previously pandered to what he thought was etiquette which involved him engaging in unsuccessful battle with certain items of meat and game by employing the conventional armoury of knife and fork!

Dean retained his home-spun attitude and deliberately set out to avoid any form of pretentiousness of behaviour with the upper social set in which he often found himself. No doubt that is why he never became swollen headed about his achievements. There was an in-built trait in his character to reject anything that smacked of what he called 'toffee-nosed' attitudes. A sign of the times perhaps. Most working people were more conscious of their class origins and resented (sometimes quite wrongly) anything they thought emphasised the superiority of the behaviour of their so-called betters – 'manners' which appeared false to them.

Another example of this is illustrated by Dean's story of being invited to a studio in London's Wardour Street to be filmed and interviewed for Pathe News, then a popular feature in the cinema. Dean describes the visit as follows. 'I was greeted by a right cissy of a bloke who was talking in a high pitched voice with a bloody great plum in his mouth. 'Oh Mr Dean,' he said, 'would you mind sitting here while I make up your face – only some powder and rouge – just to take the shine off your face for the film.' I told him that if he attempted to powder me up to take the shine off my face I'd put a bloody shine on his!' The film producer's proposals were interpreted as almost an exercise in emasculation and Dean's spontaneous reaction seemed a natural enough one for him to make in those times. Eventually the situation was resolved, the film made, and Dean submitted to what was for him an experience not to be revealed to his friends.

Dean never could tolerate people who failed to use simple words to address others. He deplored those speeches made at social functions by people who indulge in a vocabulary beyond the scope of their audience to understand. Such utterances are false, he asserts, and only designed to impress, particularly when they emanate from people of his own background. Although he has the greatest respect for one famous football manager who is now retired, Dean (now in his early 70s) jocularly perhaps, says, 'Take Bill. Some of the words he uses in his speeches, my goodness, if you asked him what they meant, he wouldn't be able to tell you!'

Dean clearly delights in telling the story of a famous amateur international goalkeeper (who was also an Olympic high-jumper and all-round sportsman) and an appearance he once made for Everton. This chap, whom we shall call 'Mr X', was born in Liverpool, with a comfortable family background, certainly not one of the period's many 'hungry' footballers. On the occasion he played for Everton, which Dean refers to, Mr 'X' must have been in his late 30s. No doubt Dean's highlighting of the story is because of Mr X's middle-class background. In the late twenties there was an occasion when Everton had no regular goalkeeper available and the club was desperately trying to find a temporary substitute. It was decided to seek the help of the famous amateur goalkeeper Mr X, who had played a number of times in Division One and also (although an amateur) appeared twice for England in professional internationals. Mr X accepted the invitation and duly turned out for Everton in a match against Leicester City.

Dean alleges that before the match Mr X arranged for a private photographer to attend the ground and take action pictures of him keeping goal during the game. At one stage of the match Everton were winning 4-0 and their 'keeper had little to do, nor apparently had his photographer! Then out of the blue Leicester staged a revival, mainly due to the skill of Ernie Hine, their famous inside-forward. And, Dean alleges, the revival was also due to the mistakes made by Mr X. The final result was that Leicester won 5-4. Mr X had not anticipated he would have to pick the ball out of the net five times! Each time this occurred the photographer took a picture of the event. These pictures formed the only pictorial record of the game for the goalkeeper. 'And not one he had anticipated,' muses Dean, adding, 'that served him right, the big-headed so and so!' Dean obviously concluded that as an amateur, Mr X was a member of the upper crust. And this brought out Dean's prejudices, which incidentally were not lessened by the fact that Mr X received, according to Dean, £26 expenses from the Everton club for appearing in the match. No doubt Dean was embittered by the comparative wages of a professional which in those days, were only £8 per week.

Dean has other memories of circumstances he interprets as injustices caused by the power of the establishment (which for him means a non-political upper crust) and its influence in the realm of football. He was never impressed much with the administrators of the game in the twenties and thirties. Very few of any of the top men in the football business, he argues, were drawn from the ranks, and the names of many who held high positions in the FA and Football League were often the subject of Dean's criticism. Dean alleges, for example, that a relative of a top administrator became a football referee and after only a few years was chosen to handle the Cup Final at Wembley. He asserts this was blatant queue-jumping arranged through the old boy network. To top the incident Dean points out that the occasion was one in which for the first time a special Cup Final medal was struck for the referee. Dean alleges that such nepotism was commonplace in those days.

Dean is certainly not anti-establishment in the political sense, but he carries much resentment about the general administration of football in his day. He never complains about the Everton Club, referring to it as his beloved Everton, but his views today are no doubt coloured by the great disparity which exists between the benefits modern footballers receive and those of 50 years ago. One of Dean's great virtues is his modesty and this is no doubt founded on his high regard for ordinary folk and his rejection of any form of hypocrisy in social behaviour. If you live through hard times and survive to witness progress in your profession it's difficult not to develop some prejudices from the inevitable comparisons of past and present. In some areas these were more justifiable than in others. Football appears to be one of them. But Dean had not turned sour over this. He still loves football and will defend it to the last ditch, only ever desiring that it should retain the full sporting elements free from snobbery, hypocrisy, and commercial intrusions, the latter often producing more adverse affects than the former.

An experience which Dean recalls serves to highlight an aspect of his character which was also revealed by an incident in Cologne, referred to later. During his last season with Everton, at the time when he had been relegated to the reserve team, he was called on to travel to London ready to deputise for Tommy Lawton, his successor at centre-forward, who had been declared a doubtful starter for the match with Tottenham Hotspur. A few hours before the game Dean was informed he would not be required as Lawton would in fact be fit to play.

Dean felt free to accept an invitation from some dear friends of his, Alec Jackson, Alec James, and Joe Hulme, all famous internationals of the period who happened to be at the ground before the Tottenham match, to join them in a few drinks. It was an enjoyable reunion for Dean and just when he was completely relaxed and having consumed two pints of beer he received an urgent message from the Secretary informing him that he would after all be required to fill the centre-forward spot, Lawton finally being declared unfit. He immediately rose to fly off to the dressing room.

Normally Dean ate very little before a match but he had consumed a lunch and worse still was a little heavy with the beer. Had he been certain of playing, his usual glass of sherry mixed with two raw eggs would have been his only pre-match intake. Nevertheless he went on to play a reasonable game, and despite the close marking he received, it was a clean and sporting encounter with Dean's performance his usual exemplary one. At the end of the match he followed the other players to the dressing room along the path overlooked by spectators, some of whom indulged in the usual back slapping of the teams as they passed by.

Dean was one of the last players to leave the field and as he passed the overhanging body of spectators one suddenly shouted into his ear, 'We'll get you yet, you black bastard!' Dean was extremely sensitive to such insults and reacted immediately. To an approaching policeman who had over-heard the remark Dean said 'It's alright officer, I'll look after this,' and he thereupon promptly punched the offender, knocking him flying into the crowd. Cheers followed from some onlookers, but the policeman rushed towards Dean, only to shake him by the hand and comment rather enthusiastically, 'That was a beauty, but I never saw it, I mean officially or otherwise!' The twinkle in the eyes of the policeman was a delight to Dean. He says he always has, since that incident, taken the view that London 'bobbies' really are wonderful. Dean says the event is an example of the prejudice that exists with some football spectators. It is also perhaps, an example of how a man like Dean, who on the football field was a model of control, can react outside of it. He loved football so much he respected its rules on the field of play more sometimes than those which operated in other areas of life.

There are many stories in circulation which serve to emphasise the remarkable character of this great sportsman. His sense of humour and all-round athleticism were frequently demonstrated, sometimes other than on the football field. One story, told by Dean's friends, some of whom were witnesses to the event, not only provides evidence of the man's athletic prowess but also to his tremendous spirit of sportsmanship.

In the summer of 1930 Dean joined a party of friends on an excursion to Scotland to spend a few days at the Ayr races. Freddie Tarbuck, a Liverpool turf accountant, a man who has already been mentioned as a friend and admirer of Dean, was in the party. Freddie was a great character, and no doubt his son Jimmy, the famous comedian, owes something to such heritage.

Freddie was particularly interested in one feature of the programme at Ayr. When the first day's racing had been completed, Freddie's attention was drawn to an additional event which, it had been announced, would take place on the racecourse that evening. J. Smith, the Ayr United footballer who was also a Powderhall sprinter, had been entered to compete with other athletes in a special 100-yard handicap race. Racegoers and bookmakers stayed to witness this men's running event, and also to take advantage of the further opportunity to indulge in a flutter which the race presented.

When Tarbuck learned that the race was open to all-comers, he immediately took the step of entering Dean's name and at the same time enquiring about the odds his entry would attract. Dean was regarded as an outsider, and as such his chances were quoted at 100/1. Freddie, highly delighted, went off in anxious search of his protégé. He found Dean sipping sherry in a bar-tent situated on the course. 'Bill', said Freddie enthusiastically, 'I've entered you for the 100-yard handicap race which takes place in about half an hour. I'm afraid there's no handicap allowed for late entries so you'll have to start from scratch.' Initially, Dean's reaction was not entirely encouraging for Freddie. Having consumed several sherries Dean was not at all sure he should accept the challenge. Normally he would have been drinking a few pints of bitter, but as draught beer was not available on the racecourse and he disliked bottled beer or spirits, sherry was his alternative. However, sherry was his normal pre-match intake at football, so after a little persuasion he agreed to participate in the race.

Then the problem arose of providing Dean with running kit. Freddie managed to obtain some pumps, but failed to procure a pair of shorts. 'You'll have to run in your underpants, Bill,' Freddie said, reassuringly, 'I'm sure no one will notice and you'll be accepted.' Freddie was determined to have no impediment in the way of Dean competing in the race. He had placed a wager of £10 on Dean and stood to win a small fortune. Indeed, his enthusiasm grew with every minute that ticked by. His protégé received advice in profusion. Freddie gathered some discarded corks (from Guinness bottles) which he handed to Dean with the instruction, 'Grip one in each hand, Bill, you'll find they help you to run faster!' Dean responded with a typical witticism. 'I'm well aware of the purpose of the cork grips Freddie, but if you'd put a £5 note in each of my fists I'd run a bloody sight faster again!' However, Tarbuck's entry had to be content with the improvisations of borrowed pumps, the Guinness corks, and underpants!

The competitors finally lined up for the race. J. Smith was favourite at 6/4, and ran scratch with Dean, the latter at odds of 100/1. The race was over in about ten seconds. Dean won by two yards beating Smith into second place. Feverishly excited, Freddie Tarbuck rushed off to collect his winnings – a small fortune – from the bookmakers. In the meantime, Dean was being presented with a canteen of cutlery as his prize. Freddie returned to join a highly excited party of friends, rapturous about their football idol's success. No mean achievement to beat a winner of the Powderhall Handicap! Freddie, however, held out the cash he had won and is alleged to have said, 'This is a Godsend. It's just what I owe on the mortgage. As you know, I have no worldly possessions except a bed, a po, and a picture of William Ralph Dean on the wall. I must send the money home right away.' It was not confirmed whether he did or not.

There were scores of famous people with whom Dean became acquainted during his football career; not only those associated with sport but many who were engaged in politics and other areas of the public service. In addition, there were those he met from the world of entertainment for whom he had a special affection. As an entertainer himself, it was natural he should find more in common with show business people. One important difference was perhaps that the theatre depends on the illusion to entertain, whereas Dean's performances in his profession were no charade, but sporting realism! The common factor however, in this context, is 'live' entertainment, which Dean rightly argues was more prevalent in his day. Artistes – theatrical and sporting – were nearer the people as a result, sharing the sacrifices and sufferings of the times which yielded an abundance of kindred spirit – in shorter supply in the less fertile social and economic outlook of post-war society.

Dean enjoys the memories of the relationships he established with many professionals in other walks of life. He expresses the wish that his biography ought not to exclude mention of at least some of these people – people he liked, not because they were outstanding in their professions, but simply for the reason that they were nice, honest individuals, with whom he shared a stardom of a kind which was gloriously special to those pre-war days, reflecting perhaps a greater integrity than has been experienced in any other era. He makes no order of preference in referring to the names of such people. Indeed, he cannot remember all of them now, but those he mentions are, in his mind, symbols of a wonderful period.

During the twenties and thirties, when soccer teams visited the metropolis, it was a common practice for the players to attend a theatre show in the West End. The artistes made a point of introducing the team to other members of the audience, more particularly of course if the team was currently successful. Everton were always a popular attraction in London and inevitably its players, especially Dean, made many friends among the theatrical stars.

The inimitable Tessie O'Shea, Noel Purcell, George Robey, Flanagan and Allen, Dickie Henderson (Senior) and many others were stars with whom Dean found warm relationships. The latter was a particularly close friend. The Henderson family established a great tradition in the theatre, and Dickie Henderson junior was a small boy when his father introduced him to Dean at the Argyle Theatre in Birkenhead in the early thirties. When Dean suffered the loss of his leg in 1976, Dickie Henderson, on television shortly afterwards, made public his personal concern for the former Everton footballer, reminiscing with some warmth of his family's friendship with Dean. The sporting interests of artistes in the entertainment world were mainly racing and soccer, and artistes in the football world pursued racing and the theatre. Hence the bonds between the professions.

Merseyside produced a number of great footballing stars in the pre-war period but at the same time many of its sons became famous in the boxing ring – all contemporaries of Dean. There was a kinship between them all and Dean, who often visited the gymnasiums where the boxers trained, indulging in sparring himself, formed strong friendships with Nel Tarleton (contender for the World Featherweight crown), Ernie Roderick, Dom Volante, Jimmy Walsh, and many others who were outstanding in the fight game.

Two local politicians of the time, whom Dean had a great affection for, were devotees of sport and the memory of his association with them gives Dean particular pleasure. One was Mrs Bessie Braddock, who subsequently became M.P. for a Liverpool constituency and in the post-war years became a national figure. Bessie was extremely popular with the sporting fraternity because of her great work in support of local boxing clubs. Dean recalls that he and Bessie sat together as judges of beauty competitions, a panel, he asserts, which was a guarantee of incorruptibility. According to Dean, his experience of such events was of devious attempts by supporters of some competitors to influence or even bribe the judges. He says Bessie's integrity was her great virtue. He respected her not because she was a Labour politician but for her personal charm, sincerity, and honesty. Dean's words are 'I thought the world of Bessie.'

Luke Hogan, a former Lord Mayor of Liverpool, was a local personality who commanded Dean's respect. Dean says Luke was self-educated and although rising to high civic office, the man never lost the common touch. As Chairman of the Watch Committee Luke Hogan naturally held an official interest in the way local private social clubs were controlled and operated. He was always reasonable and understanding when such clubs fell foul of the law, particularly those places which were frequently visited by the local sporting personalities including Dean. When Luke ruled the working man got a fair deal, and it was this influence that drew Dean's admiration. Indeed the only people Dean respected had to be blessed with the simple qualities of humour, humanity, and honesty, characteristics which he himself reflected in no small measure.

11 International Experiences

IT IS NOT UNCOMMON in present day football for certain players to represent their country more consistently than their predecessors did. There are a number who can boast of over fifty international appearances, but all belong to the post-war period. In the pre-war years, it was rare for any footballer to gain more than twenty or so caps. The difference is no doubt due to the fact that with the increasing challenge of post-war continental football England teams are now managed to provide for a planned stability and continuity in playing strength, a policy scarcely envisaged in international pre-war soccer. At international level today outstanding players are developed and retained in a similar way to that followed by League clubs. Individuals of a high standard are provided with opportunities to gain as many international caps in one season as their counterparts of 40 years ago could expect to achieve in a whole career in football.

Dean, the outstanding centre-forward of his day, and possibly of any period in soccer history, was capped for England on sixteen occasions. It is a sad reflection on pre-war football administration that such an outstanding player as Dean was six years gaining his relatively meagre total of international caps. His form throughout his first three seasons in the higher sphere of soccer was truly phenomenal. In Division I from 1925 to 1928 he scored 113 goals in 104 matches. Such consistently good form brought him only nine caps. Between 1925 and 1933 he played in 272 league games and scored 270 goals. Admittedly the international fixture list during that period was extremely limited. Home internationals predominated and continental fixtures were less numerous than today. So when comparisons are made with modern players (who may boast a host of international appearances) such factors have to be taken into account. Dean's collection of sixteen international caps could be judged to equate in achievement with some players who have gained fifty caps in post-war football.

Dean's first international appearance was against Wales at Wrexham on February 12 1927, just five months after his return to football following the serious injuries he suffered in the road accident in June 1926. In the previous season, 1925-26, Dean was a leading scorer in the First Division, having scored 32 goals, but he had failed to. gain a single cap! Apparently such form was just not good enough to impress the selectors! In that first international against Wales he netted two goals. No doubt the selectors were then convinced that Dean was of international standard.

The match against Wales produced a story which Dean relates with great amusement. It is well known that there are some footballers today who are recognised 'cloggers'. It would be kinder, but an understatement, to say they indulge in hard tackling and are generally robust. Between the wars first-class soccer also had its share of such players. Dean names some of the established villains of this kind of play who plagued the football grounds during his career. He cynically describes them as 'men who would kick their own mother for a shilling'. Dean ought to know, because he was a main target for many of the big booters of his day. And what boots! Such primitive football accessories if worn today would be regarded as offensive weapons. Of course 'cloggers' so well equipped were the hazards of any run-of-the-mill centre-forward. But with Dean, who was a consistent goal-scoring threat, such tactics were employed more frequently against him than most. He suffered fifteen major injuries, not all the result of 'cloggers', but he received more stick than most. Some of this unscrupulous play contributed to his injuries and to many other physical discomforts. However, Dean possessed exceptional courage and good humour, without which he could scarcely have overcome such tribulations.

To continue with Dean's story of his debut in the England v Wales match, the Welsh full-back was Alfie Jones, who played for Wrexham in the Third Division, a section of the Football League not exactly renowned for soccer finesse. Jones could not be accused of being one of the worst type of 'cloggers', but he was a hard tackler and adopted a style of play consistent with that normally produced in the lower sphere of Division Three. At half-time Dean was getting a bit fed up with Jones' methods. They walked off the pitch together, Dean lodging a complaint with Jones about some of his strong arm tactics. Jones responded by making a puzzling remark.

'If I have any more of your complaints I'll tell my auntie of you!' Dean, rather astonished, came back with 'I don't give a damn about your auntie—I'm warning you, lay off the dirt, mate!'

'I'll bet you do care about her,' retorted Jones, 'she happens to be your mother!' Dean found this statement incredulous, but Jones' auntie was indeed Dean's mother. The England centre-forward had not met his cousin for some time and failed to recognise him. Now Wales has something to boast about in Dean's ancestry! He emphasises that Jones' style of play was much improved in the second half. Perhaps Jones feared his cousin would complain to *his* auntie about *him!*

The match with Wales was drawn 3-3 and Dean had made a highly successful international debut with two fine goals. Following this performance he was selected for a spring tour of the continent in which England played Belgium, France, and Luxembourg. And what a successful tour for the English team, particularly Dean! Against France, England won 6-0 with Dean scoring two goals. Belgium were then thrashed 9-1 – Dean getting a magnificent hat-trick. A further hat-trick was achieved by him in the match against Luxembourg, with England winning 5-2. In four internationals he had bagged ten goals. Shortly afterwards a most important international was to be played against Scotland on April 2 1927, and Dean had established himself as certain to lead the England forward line for some time to come. He was duly selected to play against the Scots.

The match against Scotland played at Hampden Park turned out to be memorable one. England had not won in Scotland for 23 years. Dean had just turned 20 years of age and for the first time in his life walked out on to a pitch surrounded by 140,000 spectators. And he did this without tension or nerves of any kind. This greatly partisan Scottish crowd had a reputation for producing a sound – they call it the 'Hampden roar' – thunderous in the extreme, and which could test the courage and nerves of the bravest of men. Dean, however, was oblivious to it all and only wanted to get on with the game. Such maturity has rarely been witnessed in a player of his youthfulness!

Dean had travelled up to Glasgow on the previous day. He collected his expenses, calculated by the football administrators to the last half-penny! They even questioned the penny fare on the tram car from his home to the ferry boat, by which he crossed the Mersey to the Liverpool station. There he entrained for his journey to Scotland. On the way he was faced with making a decision whether to take a medal or the £6 fee, the optional rewards for playing in international matches in those days. Dean says he decided to have the £6 cash but as things turned out he might as well have opted to take the medal. Due to the favourable result of the match he was to receive a surprising monetary award from a private donor.

Gate receipts for the England v Scotland match on that day are difficult to confirm but Dean asserts they were in the region of £38,000 which, having regard to pre-war charges, seems a feasible assessment. At £6 per man the 22 players who provided the entertainment received less than half a per cent of the takings. Really an appallingly unjust share, and compared with today, appears to have been an unforgivable exploitation of the professionals who took part. However, there was a patriotic Englishman named Payton, a Bradford mill-owner, who offered the English team £10 per man if they won and an added bonus of £10 per goal to each player who scored. There was no better incentive so far as Dean was concerned! He went on to play a magnificent game, which it may be said was not achieved solely on the basis of the monetary attractions.

Before the game the team indulged in no ball practice nor any discussion about team tactics. On the morning of the game the players went sight-seeing in Glasgow. They returned to their hotel and after a light lunch were taken to the ground at Hampden. The game was a ding-dong affair with the English having the better of the first half. However, the score sheet was blank at the interval. In the second half the Scots, perhaps more frustrated than the English, pulled themselves together and went ahead with a goal by Morton. Hill, the England captain and centre-half, was injured and nursing a deep cut on the head was on his way to the dressing room when Scotland scored. It was ten minutes before he returned and then to be more or less a passenger for the rest of the game. No substitutes were permitted in those days and England struggled for a time, but then revived and, through the opportunism of Dean, equalised. Despite being tackled by both full-backs, his speed and evasion beat them and he was able to hit a grass-cutter of a shot to leave the Scottish goalkeeper helpless. Just before the end Dean got the winner for England to register the first victory in Scotland for 23 years. In five consecutive appearances for his country Dean had scored 12 goals!

When the victorious team returned to the hotel they were welcomed by their benefactor Mr Payton, the Bradford businessman, who directed them to the mantelpiece in the lounge. Eleven separate piles of £1 notes were set out across the top. One stack of notes was taller than the others. 'That's yours Dean!' he said, enthusiastically. With equal enthusiasm Dean picked it up. Thirty whole pounds! Dean had an extra

£20 for his two goals and felt he had won a fortune. The sum represented almost four weeks' wages. And Dean, no doubt in concert with all the others players who received the miserable £6 fee, wondered where the balance of the £38,000 gate receipts for the match went after the players' fees had been met. No congratulatory gestures were made to him by the English football administrators who attended the game. Not even a handshake!

Dean played in three more internationals against continental teams, all of which ended in clear wins for England. In 1928 (the 60-goal season) he was in the team that beat France 5-1 and Belgium 3-1. His only other appearance against a foreign team was when England played Spain at Highbury in 1932. Dean gives an interesting account of that match which mainly concerns the Spanish goalkeeper. Zamora was his name and he was acclaimed as the greatest 'keeper in the world. And so proud were the Spaniards of him that they paid him £40 per week (a fortune in those days), and made him captain of his country's team. In fact Zamora was reputed to be the highest-paid footballer in the world.

Prior to the kick-off the band played several well-known pieces and was still performing when the teams came out. Dean quickly noticed the Spanish team was not led by their Captain. Then Zamora suddenly appeared carrying a football. The band were about to march off when Dean dashed up to the bandmaster and asked him to play something with a Spanish flavour. Without further prompting the conductor caught on and immediately the band struck up a march from *Carmen*. Zamora was delighted and marched along the touch-lines towards his goal executing a kind of goose step and at the same time bowing to the crowds. All the England players were highly amused. Dean turned to Charlie Gee, his Everton clubmate who was also in the England team and said, 'Charlie, I'll bet you your £6 fee we get more than five goals against him!'

Dean was nodding towards Zamora. Charlie, who had some pre-match nerves, responded 'We may win, but five goals? No!'

'Are you on then, Charlie?' Dean asked.

'Yes, sure Bill, I'm on.' Charlie lost his £6 fee for his first international because England won 7-1 with Dean scoring only one of the goals, but he nevertheless provided passes which produced some of the others.

At the end of the game a sad Zamora sportingly went over to Dean and said through an interpreter 'I shall be no good in Madrid tonight.' Dean came back with a broad smile, 'And it seems you will be no bloody good in London tonight, either!' A satisfactory game for Dean – receiving altogether £12 for his appearance, including Charles Gee's £6. It was a memorable event for Dean because Ellis Rimmer, the Sheffield Wednesday outside-left, was also in the England team. Ellis played with Dean in the Birkenhead schoolboys side of 1919-21, and had also been a team mate when playing for his former club Tranmere Rovers.

Dean acquired a wide experience of continental football because in addition to playing in internationals he went on many tours with Everton, a club that regularly arranged end-of-season fixtures in a variety of countries including Switzerland, Denmark, Germany, Spain, and France. Looking back on those tours in the early thirties, Dean has some interesting memories. Although the world still has great problems to solve in the 1970s the troubles afflicting Europe when Dean was a young man were probably more serious than today, and English footballers on tour were frequently confronted with the harsh realities of the political situation which then existed.

Sport is one of those areas of human activity which is assumed to be non-political. The Nazis destroyed that illusion at the 1936 Olympics and many other systems of government have since given further evidence of how sport can be exploited for political ends. But whatever may be done to sport by politicians, footballers as individuals also cannot avoid holding personal views on matters other than soccer. When Everton toured Germany in the mid-thirties. Hitler and the Nazis were assuming greater power, a fact made abundantly clear to the players. Dean, who was at that time captain of the team, felt he had to make sure that no Nazi salutes were given by his players at the pre-match ceremonies.

Everton played four matches in the 1932 tour against German clubs and Dean alleges that some of the German teams were augmented by national players. The fixtures included one game against Dresden which was attended by Herman Göring and some of the other leading Nazis who held important positions in the government. Dean as captain, and holding a personal abhorrence of the Nazi system, was anxious to achieve a convincing victory. No doubt he considered it one way of demonstrating to the Germans that they were no master race. The teams lined up on the pitch whilst the national anthems were played and Dean says he had to pull the arm down of one player who, obviously trying to be diplomatic, had made matic, had made a move to give the Nazi salute. Dean's action brought screams of disapproval from the crowd but nevertheless this did not persuade the team to alter its boycott of the sign.

After the ceremony both captains walked to the centre of the pitch to call the usual toss of the coin. Both held a football. Dean noticed the German captain gripped a size 4 football and was attempting to put this on the centre spot. Pushing it aside, Dean placed his own size 5 football on the spot. (Size 5 was the ball normally used in League football). An argument ensued about which ball should be used but as neither captain nor the referee could speak the other's language Dean quickly pointed to the centre stand picking up the size 4 ball as he walked over. The German captain and referee followed in the belief that some of the important spectators seated there would decide which ball should be used. Arriving in front of the stand Dean held up the size 4 ball displaying it before the VIPs. He then bounced it and promptly kicked it high over the stand and out of sight. 'Right', Dean gestured, 'the other ball is the one we'll use.' And so it was accepted to the astonishment of the German captain, the referee, and to all those watching. Everton duly won the game, and Dean scored a hat-trick – much to the annoyance of the Germans.

A further incident occurred on the German tour which involved Dean with the authorities in Cologne. Jimmy Dunn, Dean and a few other players were in a Cologne pub one evening and Dean absented himself to do some shopping before the stores closed. When Dean returned about half-an-hour later the party had broken up, the German waiter explaining that Dunn had been robbed and had given chase to the thief. The police had been informed and were also involved in the chase. Dean rushed off to try and find out more about the incident. Eventually he found himself at the police station only to discover Jimmy Dunn under arrest and in the process of being charged. Dean remonstrated with the police and demanded Dunn's release. The thief had got away and Dunn was being held for causing a commotion. Two of the German policemen then produced rubber truncheons and waved them menacingly towards Dean. But Dean, although the prince of non-retaliation on the football field, became the opposite kind of character in a foreign police station when his friend and colleague little Jimmy Dunn was falsely under arrest. So Dean went for the nearest policeman who was holding Dunn and at the same time shouted 'Run for it Jimmy'. Dunn ran for his life, but Dean having knocked out one German, was attacked by the other. Dean remembers punching his way around for several minutes and then all went blank.

Dean woke up the next morning in a cell, his head covered, he says, with a dozen little 'eggs' and unable to open his right hand, later discovered to have two fingers broken, due to the punches he had delivered on those German noses. The 'eggs' were the result of the beating he was given by the policemen using their rubber truncheons to some effect. The police, discovering Dean's identity, had sent for Mr Cuff, the Chairman of the Everton Club who was travelling with the tour party. Dean was then treated with more respect, provided with breakfast and brought before the court. The Everton club paid the fine, which Deans says was the equivalent of £13.50. This was regarded by him as a small fortune and he appealed to Cuff not to pay it! He was happy in the fact however that Jimmy Dunn was not charged (he had got away) and pleased also that the policemen still bore the bruises he had inflicted on them the night before! What upset him more however was the injured hand which prevented him from playing cards for some weeks afterwards!

Another tour of Denmark in the summer of 1933 led to an interesting event. The Everton club at that time having achieved so much success in English football were welcome visitors to most parts of the continent. It is fair to say, with due respect to all the other first-class players Everton included in the club team, that none were so famous as the great Dixie Dean. His record-scoring feats were widely appreciated, no less on the continent than in Britain. And Denmark was no exception.

The Everton team was accommodated in a top class hotel in Copenhagen. It was one of those hotels patronised by the wealthy. In June 1933, on the day the famous racing classic, the English Derby, was run, the Everton players were enjoying dinner in the Danish hotel's well-appointed restaurant. Dean was conversing normally with his friends but at the same time kept up an anxious enquiry about the result of the racing classic. The information was apparently not easy to come by. However, one of the hotel waiters made it known that an electronic sign flashed news from a position above some adjacent buildings which could be seen from the windows of the hotel restaurant. The waiter advised Dean to watch the sign predicting that the result of the race could well be given some time during the evening. Dean left the table almost immediately to take up observation of the news sign.

The reason for Dean's anxiety was that he had gambled a substantial sum of money on a horse owned and entered for the race by Lord Derby. His Lordship (a leading owner of race horses and whose forbears were instrumental in establishing the English Derby in the racing calendar) had personally given Dean an assurance that the horse he had entered was almost a certainty to win the race. Hence Dean's confidence in the horse and his heavy investment. Of course, everybody knows there is nothing completely certain in racing, but whatever confidence one has when the race is over can be undermined whilst anxiously waiting for the result. So it was with Dean. The horse was called Hyperion and Dean waited to identify the letters of the name which he hoped would be flashed across the sign if and when they appeared.

It was some time before his patience was rewarded. Suddenly the letters were spelled out in the flashing bulbs of the sign .....DERBY.....HY..... he waited no longer. He knew no other horse in the race had those initial letters in its name. Hyperion had won, and wild with excitement he informed his colleagues who joined him in the cheering and general high spirits which were the cause of upsetting their table and its contents over a gentleman sitting at an adjacent table. Apologetically they helped to remove the debris from his lap and made further pacifying utterances. To their astonishment the injured guest dismissed their apologies explaining that he fully appreciated the reasons for their exuberance. The gentleman had overheard the conversation during dinner and understood. Apart from that he asserted he was a football fan and had already watched the team play. He then asked if he might join the party. The Everton group naturally welcomed him and following introductions were surprised to discover that the gentleman was in fact Jean Hersholt, the famous Hollywood actor who was on holiday in his native Denmark. Mr Hersholt accompanied the team for the remainder of the tour, becoming a firm friend of Dean and the other players.

In the June of 1934 the Everton team made a summer tour of the Canary Islands to play a series of matches with the local Spanish clubs. Dean describes some hair-raising situations that he and his team mates experienced. The Civil War in Spain had not begun, but trouble between rival factions was evident in 1934. Rival forces were involved in armed conflict in all parts of Spanish territory and quite a bit of shooting went on in Tenerife where the Everton team were accommodated. And not only was there civil unrest but Dean says leprosy and other diseases were at that time prevalent in the islands.

The hotels then were nothing like as luxurious as they are

today. Jimmy Dunn and Dean were billeted together as usual. One evening in Tenerife they were returning from a visit to a place of entertainment when they heard the whistle of bullets being fired much too close for their comfort and they had to react quickly to find a means of escape. Not being well-acquainted with the back street geography of the place they scaled the nearest wall, only to find they were compelled to follow the desperate course of jumping garden walls, crossing roof tops and taking many diverse routes before they finally reached their hotel in the early hours.

Dean recalls that the inconveniences of the hotel, especially the variety of irritating insect life which was harboured in that locality were more than enough burdens to be tolerated without the additional hazards of civil conflict. So Jimmy Dunn and he decided that come what may they were leaving the place at the earliest opportunity. The *Dunbar Castle,* a banana boat, was leaving for England the following day. They were on it, travelling without the rest of the team and in the circumstances felt it was a justifiable course. Dean says that as a result of their decision there were no repercussions from the club, the team having completed its itinerary before they left.

Another experience of a summer tour which Dean recalls occurred in Switzerland in the early thirties. A fixture was arranged against a club which was experimenting with the new idea of floodlighting. The directors of Everton, including Chairman W. C. Cuff, were somewhat apprehensive about the proposal of the Swiss club to play the match under lights. Mr Cuff thought his players might suffer injury performing under such conditions. The Everton team were consulted and the players agreed to give their approval. Dean, always ready to exploit a situation to gain a monetary incentive, went to see Mr Cuff privately before the game commenced and proposed that each man be offered ten shillings for every goal the team scored. After some deliberation this was agreed.

Everton won the match 10-1, and the players obtained a useful supplement to their spending money. Dean claims this was the first time in history that an English First Division club had played a match under floodlights. However, it is a fact that experiments of this kind had taken place in English football some years before, so Dean may not be strictly accurate in his claims. Nevertheless, the Swiss event he refers to may well have been the first occasion an English team played under flood-lights on the continent.

Today, with vastly improved travel facilities, the modern

footballer gains a more rapid and extensive experience of the game around the world than that achieved by Dean and his contemporaries. But in the context of the period of his playing career Dean gained a knowledge and understanding of soccer and indeed a personal popularity to bear comparison with most players both then and now. He still receives acknowledgements of the renown he achieved. Post cards and letters arrive vaguely addressed to 'Dixie Dean, England', or Liverpool, or Everton, or Merseyside, which ultimately find him. They come from a variety of sources both home and abroad. Young people still want his autograph and older people are continually accosting him to express the appreciation of the pleasure he gave them in their youth, always recalling and confirming his spectacular skill on the football field.

12 Decline at Goodison

THE 1928-29 FIXTURES opened with Dean continuing his goal-scoring spree just as dynamically as he had left off in the previous record-breaking season. Everton, as defending champions of Division One, visited Bolton for the first match and before a large crowd, much augmented by supporters from Merseyside, won 3-1, with Dean scoring all three of his side's goals. Within a week of this victory Dean achieved another hat-trick in a convincing home win when Everton beat Portsmouth 4-0.

Everton, and Dean in particular, were riding on the crest of the wave of the previous season's successes and naturally became an extremely popular attraction. Soccer fans everywhere wanted to see the goal-scoring wonder of the age. Football crowds can be fickle, but at least tend to maintain a consistent admiration for any kind of outstanding achievement. An example of this in the modern age is that of Manchester United, a club which is still a crowd-puller whether or not the team happens to be currently successful. Such interest is based on the outstanding record of the club.

In 1928-29 Dean's records were an attraction in themselves, but as he continued to display the form which produced them, this created additional appeal, and crowds flocked to see him. Although the pattern of football was played on the basis of individual skills, and crowds thus provided with a variety of entertainment in positional play, Dean's particular role and flamboyant style combined to overshadow all others. However, due to the injuries he sustained, Dean played in only 29 League matches during that season, but nevertheless scored 26 goals, maintaining his consistency of averaging nearly one goal per match.

At the end of the 1928-29 season Dean's career record was 169 games – 168 goals! It transpired that at the end of the season Everton's fortunes reflected those of Dean. The club finished in eighteenth position in Division One and it seemed that their day of glory had disappeared and perhaps so had that of Dean. Not so, however. He and Everton were to revive and the centre-forward was to establish history of a kind normally created by those figments of the imagination inspired for the purpose of filling *Boys Own Paper* or other story books designed for youthful consumption.

It is interesting to note that during that period of development in soccer many of the stars of top-class football were syndicating articles, which appeared in the pages of the Press and sporting periodicals published in some profusion in the twenties and thirties. Most present-day followers of soccer believe it is a far cry to those early days and are often deluded into thinking that the philosophy of intuitive play then applied to the game meant the absence of any profound study of the broader techniques.

It is evident, from a perusal of the articles produced, that many aspects of the game were indeed studies in some depth. Superstars like Alec James, George Camsell, Hughie Gallagher, Charlie Buchan, Alec Jackson and many more (even Dean himself) who were the authors of such analysis and comment on the soccer scene showed the keen understanding of the game, and its potential, which then existed among the players. Indeed, some modern soccer administrators might be surprised to learn how relevant those articles could be today and possibly provide them with some pertinent lessons on the game.

The contributions made in most of the writings concerned tactics, but were mainly projected in the context of the blending of individual skill in the team sense, and the recognition of each player's positional talents without the need for overall directions. In one article, Jack Hill of Burnley, the England captain and centre-half, refers to some players as 'master tacticians', meaning no doubt that they successfully exploited their individual skills to suit team potential.

Dean recalls that some time in the early thirties Everton decided to call players together to discuss team tactics for the first time. A large table was marked out as a football pitch with eleven figures representing the Everton team. The secretary of the club, whom Dean says hadn't a clue, even about the shape of the ball to be used, talked endlessly about projected moves by the team, and overcome by boredom, Dean fell asleep. Then suddenly, Dean was awakened, and looked up. He saw the reality of the tactics being described, grabbed his hat which had reposed on his knee, and threw it across the table scattering the carefully placed figures. 'What on earth was that for?' was the chorus in response to his action. 'That', retorted Dean, 'is the opposition!'

Another story, not confirmed as being strictly true, which

Dean says occurred during the season of decline, concerns an idea conceived for using musical accompaniment during training sessions. The trainer, proudly disgorging news of the experiment to his friends, reported, 'I've just obtained a radiogram for the team.' A depressed Everton supporter responded, 'I reckon that's a bloody good bargain!'

George Camsell, a centre-forward of great repute, writing on the subject of goal scoring, mentioned that Dixie Dean 'provided as pretty a pass as anybody in the game', although Dean was the greatest goal-scorer of all time. Camsell knew, as an ace goal-scorer himself, that it was the kind of passes he received from his colleagues that mattered as much as anything in analysing goal-scoring methods. So it was that Dean, because he knew how the ball should be received, developed masterly techniques in the way he presented the ball to his colleagues. Camsell described Hughie Gallagher, another of the super centre-forwards of the time, as being the 'wiliest tactician in the game'.

Most of the articles of the time seemed to point to the general acceptance that a professional player was expected to be capable of blending his skills into a team without the necessity of being subject to direction by managers or other administrators. Is this something that the modern game needs, perhaps to halt the decline into mediocrity which many observers predict is likely to happen under the present over-organised approach to professional football?

The 'freedom for skill' philosophy of the pre-war days provided for a more natural development and gave the game of football more character, at least at the professional level, which it can be argued produced greater variety and flowing football. Alec Stevenson, former Everton inside-left and contemporary of Dean, who was a talented ball player and in modern parlance might be called a link man, is emphatic that individual skill is confounded by current methods, asserting that managerial directions generally operate to the detriment of the game.

The fluidity of any soccer match embraces such a wide variety of situations that players need to have more freedom to exercise their individual talents, in order to snap up those advantages which the natural ebb and flow of every game invariably provides. During the period between the wars it was evident that players were of a very high standard and in the final analysis no less knowledgeable or sophisticated about the game of soccer than the professionals of today.

Dean continued to collect goals with great consistency during the first half of the 1928-29 season, but increasingly, opposing teams were adopting 'stopper' tactics which to a large extent contributed to Dean suffering from a variety of injuries and caused his absence from many of Everton's fixtures. The club was not only concerned about the lack of success when Dean was absent, but also the fininical losses. The presence of the superstar added thousands to the attendance of any match. On New Year's Day 1929, the day when most people had inspired hopes for the future, Dean scored a hat-trick against Derby County, a match which Everton won 4-0, thus uplifting Goodison hearts and providing the best possible compliments of the season. Alas, due to more injuries, the year did not turn out as anticipated.

One week later Madame Tussauds, the wax museum of world-wide fame, honoured Dean by producing a life size model of him which was put on view in the 'Famous Sportsmen' section. Appropriately enough, Dean's wax figure stood next to that of Jack Hobbs, a great sportsman who was subsequently knighted for his services to cricket. One question which immediately springs to mind is 'had not Dean done as much for football?' Perhaps in those days professional football was not the kind of pursuit to impress the Establishment as much as some other sports did.

It was about this time that Herbert Chapman was in the process of building a football team for the Arsenal club, a team which was to attain such outstanding successes during the thirties. Naturally, Chapman had his eye on all the outstanding players in English football and could scarcely exclude interest in Dean, who was, after all, the most brilliant centre-forward in the League. So Chapman made a private visit to Goodison Park with the object of persuading Dean to sign for the London club. Dean says Chapman offered a blank cheque to the Everton board, demonstrating his determination to obtain the services of Dean at any price. However, William Ralph was equally determined not to leave Everton.

Whether Everton would have allowed Dean to go even if he had expressed a desire to do so will never be known. The facts are that Dean did not want to leave and a disappointed Chapman returned to London with the knowledge that perhaps there were exceptions to the rule that money could buy everything in life. In many cases it is supposed that money in football can purchase anything at all. Chapman did more than anyone else to prove such a point by indulging in a spending spree which allowed him to construct one of the most amazingly successful teams that has ever been seen in the history of soccer. Chapman's purchases included David Jack and Alec James at £9000 and £10,000 respectively. That was a fortune beyond the dreams of most people who lived in those times. Of course, inflation was not a new phenomenon. In 1925 Everton paid £3000 for Dean. In 1929 Arsenal paid £9000 for James. Whatever James achieved he never proved to be a better bargain than Dean!

Herbert Chapman was undoubtedly one of the outstanding manager/coaches in the history of football and will remain so whatever happens in the future. He was the first to be acknowledged as a 'manager' in the modern sense of the term and in fact can justifiably be described as the father of the role, and perhaps the wisest of them all. Few clubs appointed managers in those days and fewer still allowed any individual the freedom to dictate and follow a personal philosophy in the way that Chapman did. Prior to joining Arsenal, Chapman had led Huddersfield Town to two successive Division One championships. Then, having established such a wonderful set up, he left Huddersfield and the team completed a hat-trick of Division One titles in 1925.

When Chapman arrived at the London Club it was rumoured that he had already established a liaison with the Bank of England, which was quite feasible in the context of the Bank in the twenties, and he certainly spent record sums on the purchase of the best players in the land. All, that is, except the great Dixie Dean! Chapman did not just buy players. He was astute enough to adopt new tactics and he is credited with transforming the game at that time by his methods in this respect. He became as famous as a 'manager' for changing the face of the game as he did over his expense account. His success has scarcely been matched since then, except perhaps by Matt Busby and Bill Shankly, the well known post-war managers.

Chapman introduced what became known as the 'third back' or 'stopper' centre-half into the game. This has always been regarded as part of his genius, and the idea solely attributed to him. Dean had some experience of meeting the 'new' tactic. He tells a story of the effect of this 'stopper' type of play on himself. Herbie Roberts, the Arsenal number five, had been groomed by Chapman to adopt this course of play, the main purpose of which was to tighten the defence, as its title implies. Dean, who eventually played against Roberts on a number of occasions, recalls the first encounter he had with the Arsenal centre-half in this role. Roberts, following strict instructions, followed Dean throughout the game almost as his shadow. Dean was an experienced and astute soccer player, much more than Herbie Roberts, so he decided to do something about it, though not by indulging in any retaliatory fouls, which might well have been the course adopted by some players. Typical of Dean, he waited an opportune moment.

During the second half of the match Dean asked the referee for permission to leave the field, a situation contrived to test Roberts' reaction. Herbie fell for it, and ran to Dean to enquire where he was going.

'You don't seem to be injured, why are you leaving the field, Bill?' Roberts asked.

'I'm going for a pee, Herbie,' retorted Dean. 'Hasn't your manager instructed you to come with me? Come on, you'll get into a row if you don't!' The embarrassed Herbie quickly ran to a position where he could observe Dean's return, in order that he would not neglect his instructions!

Such close marking was not the total intent of the 'stopper' play, but against someone like Dean, who was as dangerous as a combination of three men, Roberts' 'stopper' role was restricted to the close marking method of blotting out the single player, wherever this happened to be appropriate, proving perhaps that whatever tactics might be employed in football, an individual with exceptional talent can cut through them all.

There are some football historians who claim that the 'stopper' or 'third back' game was not entirely an original idea when Chapman sought to apply it in 1929, when the tactic peculiar to Arsenal became so famous. As with many of the tactics which have been developed in the game over the years most of them can often be traced way back in one form or another. The really successful things in life are basically simple. And so it is with football. Even in the twenties and thirties a variety of old tricks and tactics were receiving fresh dressings and put forward as original ideas.

No doubt there is always room for original thought to be applied, even in a basic game like football. However, for modern exponents of the game to assume that their predecessors over the past 90 years had so little imagination that they did not cover most of the possibilities in the range of tactics is sheer arrogance and tantamount to insulting a host of intelligent men. In 1929 professional and highly competitive League football had been played for over 40 years, long enough for those engaged to have explored most of the angles, and ensure that there was nothing that was fundamentally new to add to the dimension of the game.

Dean and his contemporaries inherited a great measure of experience, and contrary to what some of the modern soccer experts seem to think, it would be quite wrong to hold the view that football in the past was performed entirely in a simple-minded and crude fashion, concluding that comparisons of achievement with today's standards are somehow incompatible. For example, a 'banana' kick, the art of bending a shot to deceive goalkeepers, is referred to in the 1970s as though it was some modern phenomenon. Dean was an exponent of this method of kicking a ball, scoring a number of goals that way. Other imaginative individual performances reveal they could not have been the product of stereotyped play which many believe to have been the football pattern of that era. For example Cliff Bastin, the famous England and Arsenal forward, scored 33 goals in one season playing as a wing forward!

Jimmy Dunn, the Everton forward, was just as enterprising and tricky as any of the modern players. Once or twice he tried to get away with backheeling a free kick! Professionals today more often try to get away with the less imaginative shirt pulling and other crudities which are, of course, not entirely new. In one match Dean lost two pairs of shorts! When Dean jumped to head a ball his opponents had no answer except the ruse of placing their fingers in the waist of his shorts to rip them off by the momentum of his powerful leap skywards!

In one period of the 1928-29 season Dean suffered a variety of injuries which kept him out of the team and needless to say Everton's fortunes declined. There were many changes effected in the team and a variety of tactics developed and adopted by players. In the local press the correspondence columns expressed concern about the club's poor performances. One letter contained a comment of some significance. On February 26 1929 a supporter wrote expressing his relief that in a recent match Everton had resumed the formation of playing five forwards instead of three! The implication is clear. How original are the modern tactics of 4-3-3 etc? The writer of the letter also joined with many other correspondents who urged the Everton selectors not to exclude Dean from the team if and when he was declared fit. There was a hint that supporters' confidence in the Everton administration was on the wane. The club already had two centre-forwards (besides Dean) and at the same time had just secured the transfer of another chap named Attwood from Walsall, at a fee of £2000. Dean was an England centre-forward, but the club at that time was always ready to change players if success was not constant – and the 1928-29 season was clearly failing for Everton. Panic had set in!

The winter of 1928-29 was particularly severe, and a number of football matches inevitably had to be postponed. A news item reporting a meeting of the Football League management revealed some of the sanctions which were imposed on clubs for not complying with the rules governing postponement of matches. It was announced that Newcastle, Leicester, Gillingham, Watford, Oldham, and Hull football clubs had each been fined 10 shillings for failing to notify the Secretary of the League of the postponements which had occurred! Looked upon even in the light of today's values, the fines imposed seem ludicrous.

Although Dean missed a number of matches during the first three months of 1929, it is not clear whether he was actually dropped or whether the injuries he suffered were the genuine reason for his omission from the first eleven. Doubts arose because he did play in one or two games for the reserve team during this period. The local papers made references to the rumours circulating about Dean, and supporters appeared to have some fears on the subject. Dean insists that his absence from the team was due to what the doctors described as rheumatism developing from leg injuries. Some sports writers inevitably summed up – Dean was suffering from 'Rumour-tism'!

However, Dean returned to the first team on April 11, in a match against Bury which Everton won 2-1, Dean scoring both goals. FA selectors were at the game and two days later announced the England team to play Scotland on April 18. Dean's name was included and his selection was the subject of some criticism by sports writers. It would appear that in the trial game the English selectors had played David Jack at centre-forward and his performance had impressed reporters. The FA selectors said that England wanted a team player, not one who played solo. Jack was accused of being 'too individualistic' in the role, so Dean was their man, as one more adaptable to team play.

Few footballers found themselves to be regular players for their country in those days. But although Dean had only 13 caps, he was in 1929 regarded as a regular. Critics were afflicted with a philosophy of change – often it was change just for the sake of it. In League football it was not uncommon for clubs to call on as many as 40 players during a season. This outlook was also reflected at international level. Nevertheless, England lost the game with Scotland 0-1 and the reports from Hampden Park were that Dean never saw the ball and the Englishmen gave a poor show. Dean was certainly not the player he had been in the previous season's match with Scotland. It was said, however, that he got no support whatever in the Hampden game. His own club continued to have doubts about his future, although he was still only 22 years of age. Only time would prove that whatever the misfortunes of the Everton club, he would never stop scoring goals for the team!

The season ended with Everton suffering one defeat after another – at home. A most unfortunate position to be in at the time, because the club was celebrating its 50th anniversary! On April 24 the Everton team, club officials, and many well known figures in the soccer world attended a gathering held in the Philharmonic Hall in Liverpool to mark the occasion and hear speeches reminiscing about Everton's contributions to football. The current season's performances were no doubt an embarrassment to such an event! Three days after the ceremony Everton were beaten at home once again, this time 2-4 by Manchester United. So the Jubilee year was somewhat marred, and a source of no inspiration. Everton finished eighteenth in the table but optimistically looked forward to redeeming themselves in the next season, at least before the anniversary year ran out in 1929! Little did they realise what a disastrous season the next one would turn out to be! It did, however, give credence to the theory that things have to get worse before they get better.

Despite the misfortunes suffered by his club, Dean never ceased to be a star attraction. Stories connected with him continued to appear in the Press. Some people suspected that when Dean was injured and could not play, announcements were often made to include his name in the side in order to deliberately induce more spectators to attend the match. It was reasonable to assume that many fans only made the effort to go to a game when they knew Dean would be playing, because attendances most certainly fell whenever he was absent. Conversely, members of the public often made contrary statements in leg-pulling exercises about Dean's inclusion in the team for certain fixtures. An example of one such story highlighted in bold type appeared in the *Liverpool Echo* during that time.

A big queue of football fans lined up for the tram from Victoria Street to Goodison Park one Saturday lunchtime. A policeman controlling the crowd espied a man in working clothes and shouted to him – 'Go home mate, and get your dinner and change your clothes. Dixie's not playing today – he's got indigestion!' The man he was addressing turned out to be Dean's father!'

Although Dean's football career was crowned with success, there was also a period which might be regarded as failure. This had to be a relative assessment, because at no time did he ever stop scoring goals. However, there proved to be a most trying time for two seasons between 1928 and 1930, both for Everton and himself. Following the championship win in 1928, the 1928-29 season was rather dismal but 1929-30 was a calamity, and in retrospect the worst season ever experienced by the club up to that point in time. Everton finished bottom of the First Division and were relegated for the first time in their history. As one of the founder members of the League, the club's pride was severely injured and there was no knowing when it would be restored, which only a return to the top sphere would achieve.

Many rich and famous clubs like Tottenham, Chelsea, Preston, and Wolves had experienced the drop and had discovered the difficulties of winning promotion from the Second Division, returning to what they regarded as their rightful place in football. Everton would be joining those clubs in the next season and knew the competition would be very keen for the two top places which would ensure a return to Division One.

To some extent the Everton club had panicked in the previous season when finishing 18th in the Division One table. But during 1929-30 the club spent large sums buying players in a desperate attempt to stave off what they eventually succeeded in achieving – the drop to Division Two. Many supporters made the point. 'It cost £100,000 to get into the Second Division – how much will it cost to get out?'

Dean played in only 25 games (but nevertheless scored 23 goals) during a season which ended in relegation for the club. He had a couple of major operations on chipped ankle bones, and developed what was described as a 'cold muscle' as a result. He was absent from the team on some occasions for periods up to five weeks. At that time the local sports pages published a weekly goal-scoring table (on the lines of cricket batting averages) showing leading individual scorers with games played, goals credited, and percentage goals per game, but despite his absences Dean's name was always in the leading three with an average of .9 or thereabouts per game.

Everton put up a great fight at the end of the season and gave signs that they might return to the First Division sooner than some of their cynical critics or lukewarm supporters predicted. The club had used 29 players during the season, with only two appearing in 40 games and three others in more than 30 games. Only 5 had therefore made 30 or more appearances. New players were tried and changed, but without success. It followed that if Dean was injured or even just out of form the Everton team would lack consistency and its fortunes therefore seemed to depend entirely on the great man. Nonetheless, it has to be said that the club did stage a revival at the end of that ill-fated season during a period when Dean made no appearances for the team in the concluding half-dozen games.

The last match of the season was played at Goodison Park against Sunderland, and Everton had to win it to have any hope of avoiding the drop. But of course the situation was worsened by the fact that the other teams in the danger zone had also to fail to obtain points in their final matches. There were sensational reports in the papers of anonymous allegations being made that the Everton v Sunderland game was to be 'squared' (an unusual phrase meaning to fix the result). Strong denials were made by the Everton club, the Chairman saying they would rather go down to the Fourth Division than 'sell it'.

Everton won the game against Sunderland 4-1, but unfortunately for Everton their rivals in distress also won, and this meant that the club occupied the bottom position. Everton had 35 points, and Burnley 36. Both went down. No doubt Burnley supporters were disappointed, but accepted the position. Everton fans, however, raised a great rumpus and at the annual meeting of the club strongly criticised the Everton Board and its administration. Letters poured in to the local press moaning about the club's misfortunes. Emotions were very much aroused. W. C. Cuff pointed out that of all the criticism received none had been directed at the players who were, after all, responsible for losing the games which caused the drop to Division Two.

The Everton club's balance sheet for that disastrous season was published in detail in the local press and showed a deficit (apparently the first in many years) of over £12,000. Receipts for gates were £51,456. Expenses amounted to £65,000, which included a combined total for wages and transfer fees of £35,000. Estimates were made of actual transfer fees being £25,000. Demands followed for the club to appoint a manager, but this Everton steadfastly refused to do. At the General Meeting of the club a vote of confidence in the Everton Board was carried by 82 votes to 61. Then the anger died down and the realities of the future were accepted.

So the season ended. The Second Division was an insult which had to be faced and the Everton team, board, and supporters had the summer to lick their wounds. The Open Golf Championship was held at Hoylake on Merseyside and no doubt helped to distract some attention. One of the entries supplied the name W. Dean. The local reporters were anxious to know if this was the footballer. It wasn't, but it would not have been out of place because Dean was about to develop into a scratch player. During that summer other events were taking place, like Sir Henry Seagrave breaking the water speed record on Lake Windermere by achieving 96.41mph. Clara Bow, the film star, was appearing at local cinemas and being advertised as 'See and hear the "It" girl flashing "It" as she never flashed "It" before!' Economic and soccer depression could be countered by such light relief, or so it appeared.

13 A Unique Heading Ability

DEAN'S REMARKABLE ABILITY for heading a football contributed as much to his fame as any of the other no less exceptional skills he brought to the game of soccer. He scored goals with unrivalled consistency throughout his career and although there is no accurate record available it is reasonably estimated that he scored two-thirds of the total with his feet (both right and left) and one-third with his head – about 130 goals. Just precisely how many goals he made for his team-mates by passes provided from his heading is impossible to say, but according to all reports they were quite numerous.

Football, by its title, implies that the emphasis is on controlling the ball with the feet. Handling is not allowed but heading the ball is not only permitted but encouraged, and the exploitation of the use of the head is something that fascinates not only players but spectators as well. Naturally players find it much easier to control the ball with their feet, albeit that in many cases some individuals have a limited dexterity in that respect and use only one foot, either right or left, yet are accepted as reasonably skilled professional footballers.

Most players appreciate the value of developing the art of heading the ball, but the risks involved often deter them from becoming really efficient. There is a predominant school of thought which says that good football is played only on the ground, and keeping the ball in the air is regarded as low-rate stuff. That is, of course, valid judgment in some respects because it is fairly obvious that the ball cannot be controlled as skilfully in the air as on the ground. But the advantages to be gained from projecting the ball over the heads of opponents are many and matches can be won by the intelligent exploitation of such tactics. However, the numbers of players who have acquired the art of heading a ball to any great advantage are few. No doubt that is why matches in which high kicking predominates become ragged and present poor entertainment. The lack of skill in the air shown by the majority of players makes any individual who masters the art a rare bird indeed.

Not only are there risks attached to the heading of a football, but many hazards exist in players rising or diving to use the head which can often involve serious collisions with other players. Some achieve great success on the basis of a singular capacity to dribble and control the ball with their feet; others in their ability to read the game and provide accurate passes; some with tackling and defensive skills with feet and head; some in their shooting power. Very few players acquire the art of combining and perfecting all the skills demanded by the game. Pelé, the Brazilian wizard, is one of the few modern examples of a player who is able to co-ordinate in his performance a mastery of all the skills to be exploited in soccer. It is perhaps his ability to head the ball so skilfully that gives him the edge over others who may be his equal in other departments of the game.

Dean possessed all the attributes of the complete player. His shooting was equally powerful with either foot. His dribbling and control was equal to the stars who shone on that particular skill alone. His speed was phenomenal, and his reading of a game second to none. His gift for heading the ball, however, was unique. To be unique in such an art in those days meant something different from the application it may receive today. In Dean's day it required a courage and confidence beyond anything demanded by the modern game. The ball consisted of an all-leather casing which was subject to soaking, often making it increase and vary in weight during the course of the match. It was laced on one side, causing protusions which presented greater hazards when coming into contact with the head.

Dean's capacity to out-leap most, if not all his opponents, was obviously a major factor in his success in heading so many goals. His athletic power was a source of wonderment in everything he did. Wherever he went, visiting clubs, garden fêtes, or other areas of social contact, admirers would exhort him to demonstrate his skills even in situations where facilities for so doing were extremely limited. He was a hero of all small boys who often persuaded him to kick or head a ball with them. If he visited a travelling fair, a popular source of entertainment in those days, he was recognised and earnestly requested to participate in 'Beat the Goalkeeper', a game which no respectable fairground would be without in the twenties and thirties.

Older fans who received Dean in their clubs on social visits were similar in their enthusiasm to the small boys who demanded that he demonstrate his prowess, adoring him as some travelling entertainer. Unselfishly and without arrogance Dean was prepared to please anybody. Kids thought the world of him and when he was around even adults became overgrown schoolboys. And so it was that whenever he visited a club where a billiard table was installed members would request him to demonstrate his power to jump. After removing his shoes he stood with both feet together and would leap straight on to the table clearing the edge by a goodly margin and land, still with both feet together, without disturbing the baize!

A professional man, an Everton supporter since the twenties, was asked if there was any modern player who could be described as reminiscent of Dean where heading was concerned. He replied, 'Yes, occasionally I have seen one or two goals scored with the head which have reminded me of Dean. But the difference has been that Dixie could still outleap the defence and score with two or three players hanging on to him!' Then he added, 'I have known Ron Pickering (famous in athletics) for a long time and he once told me that Dean would have made an Olympic high jumper had he entered the sport. Tommy Lawton was no slouch with his head, but he regards Dean as the greatest in the history of world football to date. And so do I!'

Dean's skill in heading a football of the type manufactured in those days was undoubtedly uncanny. He never suffered from the kind of concussion or other injuries experienced by many players heading that type of all-leather ball – except on one occasion in November 1928 when playing for England against Wales at Swansea. In the first minute Dean headed the ball and for no apparent reason went down holding his hand over his eye. Little notice was taken. The game went on and then Dean walked to the touchline to seek aid from the trainer. He told him his eyeball was affected and he could not see. The referee stopped the game and was requested to examine the football. It was discovered that the leather lace which bound the opening to the rubber bladder was loose and an inch and half of this was hanging out and had obviously caught Dean, lashing his eyeball to cause temporary blindness. The ball was replaced forthwith but although Dean carried on for the remainder of the game he was in great pain and his vision impaired. This is one hazard which modern footballers do not face.

The type of ball in use and the injuries it caused to so many players when heading made Dean's skills look all the more remarkable, indeed they were unique and were a continuous source of fascination to both players and spectators alike. Quite rightly more attention is given today to making sport safer and investigations are being made into what protection can be afforded to players in heading a football. The modern football by its design and weight presents much less risk than the one used by Dean and his contemporaries. No doubt if Association Football had become popular in the USA some form of protective cap would have been developed for the use of players. In Britain, however, such appliances would be regarded as 'cissifying' the game and therefore not to be tolerated!

Dean considers heading to be an art which can only be developed if you have the gift. His successor at Everton, Tommy Lawton, another outstanding centre-forward whose heading skills were greatly admired, did benefit from being groomed in this field by Dean himself. And although Tommy could score goals with his head, which did credit to the master, he did not have the superb all-round capacity in laying off the ball or passing which Dean possessed. Perhaps the administrators of the modern game will enlist the experience and advice of the greatest exponent of the art, if and when they decide to examine the dangers involved to professionals in heading a football? Dean's description of the design of the modern football sums up his attitude. 'It's more like one of Lewis's balloons!' he says. And he nearly always adds wryly 'Today they also play in bloody carpet slippers instead of boots.' Despite his opinion, it is reported that a number of players using the modern design of football have died as a result of injuries sustained through heading the ball. Of course if higher skills are developed, accidents to players might be reduced. Very few will ever acquire the skill or the techniques employed by Dean. Why, he could even head the ball down to the ground in such a way as to bounce it over the arms of an advancing goalkeeper and into the net! Nearing the end of his career, Dean became one of the few players who scored by heading a goal from a penalty kick. The ball was punched out by the goalkeeper following a penalty and Dean met it with his head and scored. That was during a game between Everton and West Bromwich on November 7 1936.

Dean was acclaimed more for his heading of goals than his ability to head in any other direction. But the fact is he gave his colleagues the opportunity to score many of their goals as a result of passes made by gliding the ball to them with his head. That effortless flick of the head which Dean possessed (in fact even now he demonstrates it when telling a football story and you realise just how exceptional it is) could send a ball to any part of the field with remarkable accuracy, in a way that will probably never be emulated. Many professionals in the game gained reputations on their skill of producing defence-splitting passes projecting the ball with their feet. Dean could achieve all that they did by directing the ball with his head.

Backheading the ball is a profitable skill developed by one or two players in the modern game. Dean's exploitation of this technique had to be seen to be believed. Not only could he deceive a goalkeeper by heading a ball into goal but he could also glide a ball to a colleague to send the 'keeper the wrong way, a skill which required all the exceptional reflexes of his great professionalism. Although training and experience sustained Dean in the art of heading a football his particular ability just had to be a gift which all the practice in the world could scarcely give to another human. There is no other way to explain it.

There have indeed been occasions when Dean, who incidentally made more intelligent use of his head in more ways than one on the soccer scene, exploited a situation commonplace in pre-war football but probably less so in today's game. In the thirties floodlights were not in use and matches played in the afternoon were often caught with a strong blinding sun, low in the sky, which on some grounds caused extreme problems for goalkeepers. Dean developed a tactic for those situations which frequently paid off. He would approach the opposing goalmouth facing the other way and anticipate a high ball intended to deceive the goalkeeper and without looking round he would watch the keeper's advancing shadow cast by the sun over the six yard box. Dean would then apply a superbly timed back-header directed away from the keeper into the goal. The variety of subtle touches Dean demonstrated in heading a football could only be sustained by magnificent reflexes scarcely emulated by any other player.

There is one story in the context of Dean's unique ability that possibly only he has the right to tell. And it is certain that no one else could illustrate the point of the story as well as he. He starts by saying that as a famous name and well-known figure in the pre-war days he was vulnerable to charges from any unmarried woman that he was the father of her illegitimate child. One such summons he recalls was served on him by a court in Bristol. He duly attended the Magistrates Court to face the threat of a paternity order. The magistrate addressed him, saying, 'Mr Dean you are charged with being the father of that woman's child over there – how do you plead?' 'Not guilty', Dean replied, 'I have never seen her before in my life.' 'Miss ————— you heard what Mr Dean has said – what evidence have you that he is the father?'

The woman, who was sitting with a 3-month-old baby boy on her knee, did not speak but proceeded to undo her frock and exposed her breasts. The baby immediately stood up on her knee and began heading each breast in the manner of a professional footballer heading a football (Only Dean can adequately perform the actions when telling this story). The magistrate looked on in amazement. 'That's sufficient evidence for me – you are *the* "Dixie" Dean aren't you?' 'Yes Sir,' acknowledged Dean. 'Then I'm going to grant this lady two pounds ten shillings a week', puffed the magistrate. 'That's very good of you, Sir,' Dean said approvingly, 'I think I am prepared to give her a few bob as well!'

Heading a football has its delights and its problems. Being unique makes it difficult to mask your identity, and the story above (fictitious, of course) is one which could only apply to him.

Argument among football fans perpetuates on the subject of Dean's unique ability in heading a football. On Merseyside, an area once blessed with having, in Dean and Tommy Lawton, two of the greatest exponents of the art of heading, discussion about the merits of these players persists to this day. An exchange of views overheard in a Liverpool pub in 1976 went something like this.

Liverpool supporter: 'Go on with yer, wack, I only just read in the paper last week that when Dean scored his 60 goals he scored 40 with his feet and only 20 with his head. He couldn't have been all that good with his head!'

Everton supporter's quick response: 'So what? He had *two* feet but only one bloody head!' A logical assessment. Dean's two powerful feet were something to contend with, but his head adequately competed, producing a balance others have rarely been able to match.

14 Record Scoring Spree

THE SEASON EVERTON would have to spend in the Second Division loomed depressingly ahead. Never before had the club faced such a prospect. The Everton players were ordered to report for training on August 1. The newspapers reported that Dean was the first Everton player to arrive, presenting himself one hour before the others. It was no doubt a sign that he couldn't wait to get on with the job of bringing the club back to the First Division, where it rightly belonged. Two practice matches were played prior to the opening fixture which was to be against Plymouth on August 31. The practice games each attracted over 10,000 spectators, an indication that the lower sphere of football Everton had in prospect might not deter support for the club.

Economic depression was getting increasingly worse at this time and with over 2 million unemployed there were no signs whatever of an improving situation. People were resigned to it all – even the President of the TUC was currently saying that the number of unemployed did not appal him! How different from today! The masses had their football and their heroes – a kind of safety valve releasing spiritual sustenance for their survival. Dean, as one of their heroes, had a major role to play. There were many outstanding sporting personalities at the time but the one who stood out in the most popular of sports had to be *the* hero. Without question this mantle was worn by Dean, and over the most bitter period of that depression he did not let those masses down.

When Everton visited Plymouth to open the season's fixtures, 34,000 spectators turned up and were treated to such a great game that many of them have never forgotten it. Everton won 3-2, but Dean did not score. However, his display was described as scintillating and it was from the passes he gave with his head that all three Everton goals were scored. The Plymouth crowd gave the Everton team a standing ovation and loudly proclaimed it as the finest they had ever seen. Dean's football skills were a thrilling experience for the West country fans. All of this was to be symbolic of Everton and Dean's contribution to Division Two for the whole of that season.

Everton went on in the first month to beat Preston, Cardiff, and Swansea, and crowds flocked to see their brilliant combination with Dean as the star attraction wherever the club played. If no misfortunes occurred, the signs were that Everton would sweep through and be back in the First Division in one season. Ben Williams, the full-back, had been appointed captain and as a player with previous experience in the Second Division he obviously took some credit for the team's early performances.

Before the end of the month of September, however, Dean was injured and in his absence Everton were surprisingly beaten at home by Port Vale, not regarded as very distinguished opposition. Dean soon returned and Everton went from one success to another, scoring goals in an unprecedented fashion with Dean providing for others and taking his share of the glut. By October 1930 one supporter at least (not the Press, or the club) was taking a tally of Dean's career total of goals. The fan wrote to the local paper and drew attention to the fact that Dean was rapidly approaching his 200th League goal and only required two more to reach the target, to add still another record to his already well-rated list.

Dean duly obliged on November 8 1930 against Wolves at Goodison Park. Everton won 4-0 and Dean, at 23 years of age, was the youngest player ever to score 200 League goals and the only player to achieve this in only 199 games of League football. There was no pre-match publicity on the significance of the record Dean might achieve in the course of the game. In fact Dean himself was not aware at that stage of the number of goals he had accumulated. Such statistics seemed of no importance to him. Afterwards, the Press and most sports reporters confirmed that this was characteristic self-effacement on the part of Dean. Sir Freddie Marquis, later Lord Woolton and a Government Minister, presented Dean with a gold medal to commemorate the event and Dean (who now has in his possession only a few of the many trophies he won during his remarkable career) proudly retains this memento.

It is interesting to note that following the record-breaking 200th goal the local sports writer in the *Daily Post* had this to say: 'Dean scored his 200th goal, a fine record considering his comparatively short career and but for a lapse last season his record would have been infinitely better.' What power of understatement! In the previous season Dean had scored 23 League goals in 25 matches! Lapse, indeed! No footballer in history had a record of such consistency in League soccer – or ever will, perhaps. One can imagine if any of today's players attained half the measure of Dean's goal-scoring feats how the media would latch on to any of the events and promote the maximum of publicity. Indeed, recently one centre-forward (with Everton) scored one goal in each of seven consecutive games –a total of seven and the reporters were conducting research as to whether or not it was a record. They were soon informed that Dean had exceeded this target on any number of occasions. Once he scored a total of eighteen goals in nine consecutive games! In fact there are few records in goal-scoring that he does not hold to this day.

Not only in reporting soccer were approaches different in 1930, but some administrative attitudes were somewhat peculiar. For example, in the 1930-31 season the FA issued bans in all directions. Many new ideas were frowned upon. In retrospect the bans look very stupid. They included no broadcasting of Cup or League matches; all public clocks on football grounds to be removed; no alien players (of course this still applies); no floodlights; Welsh teams must not include players engaged with English clubs; and the FA was seriously considering forbidding players from the same club being included on opposing sides in international matches!

In connection with broadcasting, the ban included the Cup Final and the BBC was compelled to devise a shrewd way of keeping listeners informed of the progress of the match. The BBC sent, as spectators, ten reporters to Wembley with instructions to each in turn to make an exit from the ground every 15 minutes. The first would then broadcast an account of the game up to the point where he left. By this method the whole of the game was covered. It seemed hard lines on the first reporter, but no doubt satisfying for the chap who was left to the last! There was also a classic case of a Celtic footballer who was deported to the USA and fined £80 for playing as an alien. The Home Office discovered that the poor chap had emigrated to America two years before and had returned (disillusioned with New York) to Scotland, his native country. Celtic signed him on but apparently by going to the USA he had made himself an alien. He went back, it is assumed, to a worse unemployment problem than existed in Britain.

An event occurred during the 1930-31 season which caused some upset to Dean. He had to appear in court to face a charge of careless driving. It was alleged that, driving without due care whilst attempting to pass a tramcar in the town of Birkenhead, he knocked down a pedestrian. Dean travelled about not in a racy type of sportscar, as might be imagined, but in a small Morris. Some people, ready to judge anyone in the public eye as being arrogant, particularly a dashing sportsman, assumed his guilt. The courtroom was packed for the hearing and many people waited outside. The case was dismissed, witnesses on all sides stating that Dean was not travelling more than ten miles an hour – some even said it was only five. Most people knew that Dean was not the type of person to flaunt his position or be inconsiderate. The pedestrian gave evidence in court and apparently was not seriously injured. Even when charges are dismissed against a man in the public eye, doubts often exist about him. In Dean's case his image was not tarnished in any way by the incident, nor indeed was his performance on the football field affected.

Everton continued to the end of the year, lapping up goals, points, and large crowds, in a record-breaking manner. When they played Millwall at the Den in London 20,000 turned out to see Dean and Everton. By December, Everton had scored 55 goals from 18 matches. The team led the Division by a margin of at least six points for the whole of the season. After 31 games they had scored 104 goals, gained 52 points and led their nearest rivals Tottenham, by 13 points. Dean had scored 36 League goals from 28 appearances.

During that memorable season Everton were within an ace of reaching Wembley and the Cup final. After beating Plymouth away 2-0 in the third round they were drawn against Crystal Palace in the fourth. The match provided the club with the opportunity to avenge the 6-0 defeat Palace had inflicted on Everton in a Cup-tie at Goodison Park in 1922. Dean tells a story about the goalkeeping aspect of the match. Tom Pope, an Everton reserve 'keeper of the time, nearly came to play in that 1922 game in place of Fern, who played throughout with a damaged hand. Tom Pope, who is now over 80 years of age and still living on Merseyside, told Dean he wished he had played in the match. Dean, with natural reaction, said 'surely you ought to be glad you didn't play – six goals! – you would always be remembered for it!' Pope, as droll as Dixie himself, replied, 'Exactly! That's why I wish I had played, no one remembers me now – for anything!'

The outcome of the match against Palace, played at Selhurst Park in January 1931, could not have been better for Everton. The old score was settled, just right, with Everton winning 6-0, and Dean bagged four goals. In the next round of the Cup Everton were at home to Grimsby Town and before 66,000 spectators the Merseysiders won 5-3. In the quarter-finals

Everton beat Southport 9-1 – Dean again hitting four goals. The semi-final tie was played at Old Trafford, Manchester, and Everton's opponents were West Bromwich Albion. The game was a disaster. Everton were clear favourites and before a 70,000 crowd should have had three or four goals in the first half. Spectators overspilled on to the pitch and the game was constantly interrupted with the problem. Over 300 spectators were injured. It was reported that a crowd of over 20,000 was outside the ground seeking to gain admission. And the match was between two Second Division sides! Dean wanted to forget the match afterwards. He himself had shot wide when in a position to score. He served a perfect pass to Wilkinson (a substitute for Critchley at outside-right) who also shot wide. The same player had had to move a police horse out of the way in order to take a corner kick! Everton lost by the only goal, scored by West Brom in the second half. Coggins, the Everton 'keeper, was blamed for an error which presented the goal to Glidden the West Brom captain. Everton were the superior side but it was not their day. The Albion went on to win the Cup.

By the middle of February 1931 Everton had on five occasions scored 5 goals; on two, 6 goals; on two, 7 goals; and on one, 9 goals. In two matches they had netted six goals before half-time. Dean was in superb form, and so too were the rest of the team. They played together with great confidence and skill. It was in the first half of the season that Dean had recorded his 200th league goal. In the latter half, on February 21, notice was given in the Press that he only required one more goal to establish another record – his 200th for Everton. On this occasion the local *Liverpool Echo*, no doubt having a desire to make up for their shortcomings on the previous 200th goal event, decided to publish an article about Dean's prodigious feats and made a premature announcement that he had in fact scored the goal to make the 200. Everton were playing Notts Forest that day and Dean failed to score! With his record, of course, you perhaps couldn't blame the paper for its prediction. Dean did, however, leave a black mark on the goalpost in that game where his shot had hit the upright. In those days the all leather ball made such marks and gave living proof of the hard luck that players often suffered from. That game was his 194th League appearance for Everton and he had scored a total of 199 goals.

The anticipation of the 200th goal in the *Echo* article seemed to place a spell on preventing the goal ever being scored. The goal did not come until April 4. Dean was selected for a trial game for England played on March 4 in which he recorded a hat-trick before half-time. But those goals did not count. In the next appearance for Everton he hit the bar and upright but failed to score. Then the Cup semi-final –'a blank'– but even if he had scored it would not have qualified for the 200 target. The saga continued with Dean being selected to play for England against Scotland, so he missed another League game for Everton. Then, in a League match against Millwall, he hit the bar. In the same match Everton were awarded a penalty which the captain had no hestitation in asking Dean to take. This was it, so everybody thought. But no, he hit the upright, the ball rebounded and he shot it into the net, but once again he was thwarted. The goal was not allowed – an opponent had not touched it from the taking of the penalty kick. A fortnight later in a game against Bradford City the goal came and another record was chalked up – at last!

The article which appeared in the *Liverpool Echo* anticipating the 200th goal still contained valid comment however, except for the amendment that he had attained the target in 198 games instead of 194. At that time a young Australian cricketer named Don Bradman was becoming well known by thrashing England's finest bowlers and making runs in Test Matches as had never been seen before. He might well have been described as the 'Dean of Cricket'. The article about Dean was aptly entitled: *Dixie Dean 200 not out – A Bradman of Football* and went on to say that William Ralph Dean today wanted but one goal to make his 200th goal in senior football. Here are some excerpts.

Dixie Dean, the Everton centre-forward, gets goals with a regularity that makes the register ring with features and facts.

But this milestone in his goal-getting life is almost as memorable as his 60 in a season – the championship season.

Yet through it all there is no selfish strain in his football character. He continues to be content to get or to give goals.

Think of it – 200 goals from this still young man in the space of five and a half seasons of football, some portion of which he spent in hospital with a motor injury that threatened he would never play again, and some spent nursing a damaged bone that was operated upon.

Dean's record up to the point of his expected goal (inclusive) today reads:

194 League appearances: total goals 200.

The season ended in great triumph and delight for the team, the club, the supporters and of course Dean himself. On the day Dean shot his 200th goal for Everton, a month before the end of the League fixture list, the club had been assured of the championship. At that point only 36 games had been played out of the maximum 42. None of the clubs chasing Everton in the Division were in the position to gain sufficient points to challenge the lead. This, perhaps, made Everton relax because the team lost a number of the remaining fixtures. Nevertheless when all the Second Division games had been played and the season was over Everton were seven points clear of their nearest rivals West Brom, the team that had knocked them out of the Cup.

Everton's record in Division Two was impressive. They had played 42 matches, won 28, drawn 5, lost 9, and goals for 121, against 66, points 61. In League and Cup they scored 143 goals. In the League Dean netted 39 goals, Dunn 14, Critchley 13, Johnson 12, Stein 11, White 9, Martin 7, Rigby 4, Griffiths 3, Gee 2, Wilkinson 2, McClure 1, McPherson 1, and Thomson 1. Both Coggins, the keeper, and Cresswell never missed a game. The team revolved round fewer players than in either of the two previous seasons and the sparkling forward line of Critchley, Dunn, Dean, Johnson and Stein played together like their predecessors of the Division One championship season of 1927-8, the surviving members of which were Dean, Martin, Critchley, and Cresswell, obviously a matter of some significance. Everton possessed a combination of youth and experience which could return to Division One with confidence and remain in the higher sphere for a long time to come.

At that time Dean was without doubt the inspiration behind the club's aspirations. It was argued that the team was even better than the one which had won the First Division Championship three years before. The forward line could combine to take advantage of their opponents' close marking of Dean. He was the recognised menace to all opposing teams and despite the strictures placed on him through the questionable methods adopted by some of his adversaries, and the benefit this often brought to his own colleagues, Dean went on scoring goals in a most remarkable manner. There could be no suggestion of a one-man team, but Everton's prospects would have looked less bright if the inspiring Dean had not been available to enter Division One as a member of the team. The season just completed had seen him score over 50 goals in League, Cup, and some representative games. And he was still only 24 years of age!

The Second Division table at the end of the 1930-31 season,

with Everton as champions, may be of interest and is reproduced below.

	P	W	D	L	F	A	Pts
Everton	42	28	5	9	121	66	61
West Bromwich A.	42	22	10	10	83	49	54
Tottenham H.	42	22	7	13	88	55	51
Wolverhampton W.	42	21	5	16	84	67	47
Port Vale	42	21	5	16	67	61	47
Bradford P.A.	42	18	10	14	97	66	46
Preston N.E.	42	17	11	14	83	64	45
Burnley	42	17	11	14	81	77	45
Southampton	42	19	6	17	74	62	44
Bradford C.	42	17	10	15	61	63	44
Stoke C.	42	17	10	15	64	71	44
Oldham Ath.	42	16	10	16	61	72	42
Bury	42	19	3	20	75	82	41
Millwall	42	16	7	19	71	80	39
Charlton Ath.	42	15	9	18	59	86	39
Bristol C.	42	15	8	19	54	82	38
Nottingham F.	42	14	9	19	80	85	37
Plymouth Arg.	42	14	8	20	76	84	36
Barnsley	42	13	9	20	59	79	35
Swansea T.	42	12	10	20	51	74	34
Reading	42	12	6	24	72	96	30
Cardiff C.	42	8	9	25	47	87	25

Before the next season began, summer intervened, and during that period Dean rejoiced in a double satisfaction apart from the vacation and the blessings of the warmer weather. A professional sportsman assured of dealing in a higher class of business when next the shop opened up at the end of the summer, he was also deriving pleasure of a personal nature, one which no business can possibly compete with. Dean had met a wonderful girl. Her name was Ethel Fossard, she was beautiful, and she was 20 years old. He intended to marry her. Although Dean was only 24 he had already lived what might be regarded as a full and exciting life which many of his contemporaries could scarcely aspire to if they lived to be 100. Dean was famous; he had been all over Europe and generally tasted the glories of the attendant adulation and good living denied to most working class people, particularly in those hard times. All this in spite of the relatively low monetary rewards he received for his unique talents.

There were, of course, many people who earned fame and fortune in a much easier way than Dean could possibly do. At his age no doubt one of the most enviable attractions of his position from the point of view of his particular generation was to be admired by the fair sex. He was a handsome young man and well sought after. Women did not enjoy the independence then that they have today. In their search for a husband, their considerations were to some extent different from the modern woman. Security perhaps was one. But this was one thing Dean could not offer. Just like today's pro footballers, there was no guarantee of long-term security. Nevertheless, having regard to all this he could command feminine admiration to his advantage. But he claims that even in these circumstances he was something of a loner. He did not exploit the position he enjoyed to gain the benefits of indulging in such delights. Sport, stag parties, drinking in male company, and, inevitably, gambling were pursuits which were perhaps the by-products of a professional footballer's existence, and Dean inexorably followed the path.

However, Dean did not entirely ignore female attraction. He had had one or two female friends, but with someone so famous and young it was not surprising that much gossip arose about his intentions on marriage, a normal consequence, particularly in those days, of any such flirtations. There had been one girl, the daughter of a publican, whose premises were not far from the Everton football ground in the Scotland Road area, and whom Dean visited fairly regularly. Dean, like most working class people who attain fame, was always generous to his less fortunates. Witnesses said that he would buy drinks for the old-timers who gathered in the entrances to the pub, and many of these were the elderly 'Mary Ellens' dressed in their traditional costume of huge black shawl and cloth cap. It was perhaps not the best way of helping them but in that terrible depression it afforded a relief to their miserable existence as much as football entertainment did for their husbands on a Saturday afternoon. The daughter of the publican, whom Dean will not name, was not in very good health and died young after a serious illness. Dean was very upset, and it was another year before he met his future wife.

Dean went to dances and the various social pursuits which were popular in those days, but he attended these functions rather infrequently and he invariably went on his own. He became acquainted with Ethel under very different circumstances. Ethel Fossard was employed at an establishment not far from Dean's home in Birkenhead. She was courting a young man whom Dean knew as a neighbour. Tragedy struck when the young man became seriously ill and died. Dean attended the funeral and it was whilst at the graveside that he met Ethel Fossard for the first time. Then he saw her again and a series of meetings followed, ultimately becoming a courtship. Dean then popped the question and the wedding was arranged to take place in the summer of 1931.

The actual date and time of the wedding was kept a closely-guarded secret for obvious reasons. Thousands of football fans and others who naturally love to see any event involving a public figure, particularly a wedding, would flock to the ceremony. Even the guests were not told of the name of the church. They were asked to call at the bride's house on the day of the wedding to be given the details. However, when Dean and the best man arrived at the church they had to wait outside because the previous wedding on the church's agenda was being conducted inside. The church was St James', situated not far from where Dean lived, and of course it wasn't long before his famous face and figure was recognised. The word spread like wildfire and before the wedding could be performed literally thousands had gathered outside the church. Special contingents of police were called out to control the throngs of people and provide an escort for Dean and his bride to get away.

Dean did not embark for some exotic destination for his honeymoon. He went on a tour of the race tracks of Britain with his bride. He says it wasn't that he wished to deny his young wife the normally accepted fortnight of bliss in a small hotel somewhere on the continent, but by mutual consent they went off in his car on a sporting spree, meeting all manner of people involved in the sport of kings, and whom he knew so well.

Ethel Fossard was a beautiful girl, tender, gentle, and cultured in her ambitions – perhaps the complete antithesis of her husband in the latter characteristic. She was to bear him three sons and a daughter. None of the boys ever took up professional soccer!

15 Champions Again

WHEN THE FOOTBALL SEASON opened in the autumn of 1931 the Everton club and its supporters rejoiced in the prospect of being involved in top class football for the next eight months and also of course the opportunity to prove that they deserved a place in the top sphere. But whilst they indulged in such euphoria the nation was facing the most severe financial crisis in its history. The number of unemployed had reached record levels and vast numbers faced what must have been a very hard winter. Protest marches, demonstrations, and even riots took place in some of the major cities. A General Election was ordered and a Coalition Government was formed with a 500 majority to steer the nation out of the economic mess. Severe measures were taken and wages were reduced in a number of industries, but seemingly footballers escaped the axe.

Dean was now married and rented a house from the Everton club not far from the ground at Goodison Park. It was certainly not the mansion that a modern superstar would be furnished with today. Indeed, Dean says it was plagued with cockroaches and he got out of it as soon as possible. The politics of the day did not arouse Dean's interest all that much, except for one issue which he will talk about. Dean himself had been a railwayman and indeed his father was still employed as an engine driver. Mr J. H. Thomas, General Secretary of the National Union of Railwaymen, had joined the Coalition Government in 1931 and had therefore acquiesced in the policy of that Government in reducing railwaymen's wages from 44 shillings per week to 38 shillings. Dean, echoing the sentiments of most railwaymen, expressed a strong detestation of that particular politician. Mr J. H. Thomas ceased to lead the NUR and as a punishment the Executive Council refused to award him the pension he should have received for his services to the union, a penalty which caused Thomas great bitterness and outrage towards the NUR. Dean says he was entitled to hate that man. In 1936 Thomas resigned from the Government after an unauthorised disclosure of Budget information. Dean, still affecting a loyalty to his railway background, condemns Thomas and cynically refers to these events as one of the causes of his disdain for politics in general. Football was Dean's business, and he stuck to it as something independent of the political scene.

During the first eight weeks of the season in which they returned to the First Division, Everton produced plenty of evidence that the club was going to be a force to be reckoned with in the championship race. At Anfield in September Everton beat Liverpool 3-1 with Dean scoring a hat-trick, all the goals coming in the first 21 minutes of the game. By the end of October Everton had beaten Sheffield United, away, 5-1; thrashed the other Sheffield team, the Wednesday, at Goodison 9-3; swamped Newcastle 8-1 and in all scored a total of 44 goals in 13 games! Dean had a couple of hat-tricks and in one game had netted 5 goals. Many goalkeepers were no doubt suffering from the strain of picking the ball out of the net!

Such prolific goal-scoring on the part of Dean perhaps prompted the press to interview him, a report of which appeared in the local *Football Echo* in 1931. It was paradoxically entitled 'Goalkeepers I Hate, by W. R. (Dixie) Dean.' By getting such a crop of goals one might have thought 'hate' inappropriate! The sub-title of editorial comment under the heading is indeed interesting. It said 'England is in need of a centre-forward . . . the belief is rife that there will be a recall of Dean of Everton'. Despite his consistently good form he was not called on to play for England in any home internationals that season. Before the 1931-32 season ended he was selected to play only once for his country, against Spain, and his final international appearance was to be against Ireland in 1932. Yet throughout he continued to maintain a regular rate of scoring at an average of almost one goal per match!

The report of Dean's views on goalkeepers reveals (in retrospect) some interesting points. Here are some excerpts.

When I am old and grey I hope to be allowed to go into goal and spend my declining years therein! That is how I feel about it. Have you ever studied the position of goal? The men who play there are allowed to warm themselves by walking up and down, and if you go near them the tear-falls can be heard miles away. Actually, goalkeepers are the best friends I have got – outside the field – but inside the field they are the people I have always hated.

For some strange reason the goalkeeper is given a special dispensation. He of all men must be cloaked. In the old days they used to haul them in the dressing room every week. Judging by the stories our secretary tells me. But all that is changed. To-day be assured that if you are a centre-forward and you try to connect a boot with the ball when the goalkeeper is in possession, the 'bird' is a certainty.

Enough on that line, however. The purport of my chat isn't so much the way goalkeepers are treated, but about the goalkeepers I have played against, found hard to beat, and why they are hard to beat. I want to talk about some of the best men of my time: their methods. You can pick where you like, but for sheer intuition and ability and agility rolled up into one little piece commend me to 'Leesh' Scott. He plays for a club that has been made famous by its string of goalkeepers – none of them cost more than a tanner or so, but they run along this line with rare success: Doig, Hardy, Campbell, Scott, and sometimes Riley. What a collection of stars.

I never played against Sam Hardy, but it is sufficient to know that he himself tells me there was never one quite so good as Scott. I ought to know something about what he can do. I had my first Derby day against him, and could not score. This may sound selfish criticism, but I certainly thought him uncanny. If I drew up a chart of goalkeepers in order of merit, as far as my judgment is concerned. I would place them this way:

(1) Elisha Scott, Liverpool FC
(2) Harry Hibbs, Birmingham
(3) John Thomson (the late), Celtic.

(with the belief that Thomson would have gone to the top in due course but for his wretched accident and death).

Hacking of Oldham, in his greatest mood, was a very able goalkeeper, and one of the few who doesn't display nerves. Oh, yes, we who often stand quite near the goalkeepers, can tell you readily the goalkeepers who are bundled by bustling forwards into a state of nervousness that shows itself on the face and particularly in the eye.

Hacking was strong and rousing, whereas a man like Hibbs adopts a very natural style, and a beautiful action. In fact, I reckon Hibbs should be taken slow-motion for the purpose of the future generation of goalkeepers. Hibbs has a dive method to take a cross-grained shot and is alone in reaching those going-away shots, but Scott seems to be best with a point blank charge. It can't be luck when a goalkeeper goes on saving penalty kicks. Scott saved one at Chelsea the other day that they reckon Odell drove in at a furious pace. Don't tell me it was a lucky save; Scott does these things uncannily, and I think one of his means towards saving is that he is never still. So soon as the attack against him crosses the half-way line watch Scott jump.

As showing how easy goalkeeping is – joke over! – one has only to remind you that when a team goes away they never think of sending a goalkeeper as reserve; it is always a half-back, forward, or full-back. Never a goalkeeper! Standing between the goal-posts you begin to wonder how some of them reach the point of the ball, but having seen the able Coggins and Sagar of our club pounding the balls out I have ceased to wonder how they do it and why goalkeepers are in the ascendency. I have come to the conclusion that it's a gift. Otherwise how could you explain the work and worth of the continental goalkeepers.

Everywhere the cry is for new styles – save in goalkeeping. This phase goes on growing better and better; yet we forwards keep getting a goal or two, and thus the game is saved from the stalemate that would arise if forwards were unable to score and goalkeepers stopped everything.

The first half of the 1931-32 season proved an astonishingly successful period in which Everton and Dean indulged in a goal-scoring spree that may never be emulated. By the end of the year, with only half the League fixtures completed, Everton had scored 78 goals. The fantastic rate of scoring led to speculation that Dean would be challenging his own 60-goal record by the end of the season. Comparisons were being drawn to the 1927-28 goal-making epoch. For example, after 18 games in 1927 Dean had 27 goals and in 1931 having played the same number of matches, he had 24 goals. Dean's form was described as surpassing anything he had previously achieved, and the predictions for this greater success seemed therefore to be justified.

So many high scores were being registered by Everton, particularly at home, and against teams well placed in the League, that the supporters and even sports commentators were describing the team as invincible. There was indeed wild speculation about the side's potential. No doubt recent successes were the cause of such intoxication. After all, it was heady stuff! Inside a few months the team had scored nine goals on three occasions. In four matches against some of the best sides in the First Division, Everton had scored 33 goals. Nine against Sheffield Wednesday and Leicester City, eight against Newcastle, and seven against Chelsea. There were three fives and a number of fours in other games. Supporters were inundating the local Press with letters suggesting that in order to make Everton's future matches a fair challenge, opposing teams ought to be given several goals start. Some even proposed a figure of six!

Dean had registered a number of hat-tricks, bagged four in another game and scored five against Chelsea, four of which came before half-time. Interesting to note that in that game, played on November 14, the players did not leave the field at the interval because the light was so bad! They turned round almost immediately in order to limit the possibility of the match being abandoned. No floodlights existed then to prevent such embarrassments. In this game Dean gave a masterly display of heading techniques which reporters say had probably never been seen on any football ground before. Four of Dean's goals were scored with his head, but he also presented his team-mates with opportunities to score many more, all from passes made with his head.

Another noteworthy aspect of the game against Chelsea was that although Everton won 7-2, whenever Chelsea attacked, Everton would have nine players in defence, a tactical feature which is often supposedly thought to have originated in modern football. Chelsea fielded Alec Jackson and Hughie Gallagher, the Scottish international forwards; and O'Dowd (an England player) a new signing with a great reputation at centre-half, made his debut for them. Although O'Dowd played well he was no match for Dean, who was in brilliant form.

Everton at that particular period were classed as the best football combination in the land, and with some justification. The club was leading the First Division and winning matches in the manner already described. Dean was the leading goal-scorer in the Division and in such outstanding sparkling form it might have been assumed he would be automatic choice to lead the England team in the home international played against Wales at Liverpool on November 11 1931. Dean was not selected, but Waring of Aston Villa was chosen as centre-forward. Of course Waring was an outstanding player and worthy of a place in any international eleven. Waring was a product of the Birkenhead nursery that produced Dean, and although Merseyside interest in the Wales match was sustained by his inclusion, Everton supporters were greatly disappointed that their own idol had been left out.

The selection process for international teams is understood to have followed a rather complex voting procedure among FA administrators which did not always produce a co-ordinated plan or indeed the selection of the best players. It is not suggested that any of those included in international teams were not deserving of their places but there seems little doubt this is one area of football administration that can be said to have improved through the institution of managers. Dean had no ill-feelings towards his fellow townsman – he and Waring were firm friends – and selection of the centre-forward berth for either of them caused no animosity in their relationship.

At that time a number of examples of club penury appeared and the rather unenlightened administrators of football seemed to not only ignore a club's difficulties but add to them by imposing stupid restrictions. In November 1931, Newport County, a struggling Third Division club from South Wales (an area hit severely by the economic depression) was removed from the FA Cup competition because it was alleged to have indulged in promoting lotteries to provide club funds. Admittedly the laws on gaming and lotteries were much more severe in those days, but the punishment imposed on the club by the FA did not help. Another example of the poverty of some clubs in 1931 was revealed by the news that Rochdale could not even find the travelling expenses for their players to visit Barrow-in-Furness in a Third Division fixture. The newspapers gave some prominence to the fact that Gracie Fields, then a current singing and variety star, announced she was prepared to defray the expenses in order that Rochdale (her own town football club) could fulfill its fixture with Barrow. Although smaller clubs in general had better gates than they do now, some of the Third Division clubs in badly depressed areas of South Wales, the North East of England, and parts of Lancashire, were in dire straits even though the two Divisions (North and South) of the Third Division which operated in those days had been specifically designed to facilitate economy in travelling.

Everton, regarded as one of the richest clubs in the land, had no financial worries however, nor indeed, it would appear, any problems about lack of playing success. Opposing teams were said to be frightened to death of the Everton forward line. Many people were inspired to write rapturous verse praising Everton's accomplishments and, of course, those of Dean in particular. The local Press published a number of such efforts. But in the midst of all their success Everton visited West Ham and came unstuck before a record crowd. West Ham had a goalkeeper named Dixon who put up a magnificent display, Everton lost their balance and at half time were 3-0 down. In the second half they pulled the score back to 3-2 but were finally beaten 4-2. The reports of the match said West Ham deserved to win but the result could be construed as a salutary lesson for Everton mainly for the sobering effects it would have on the team. Dean, however, was one player who emerged from the defeat with credit. Again his play was described as superb and he gave another masterly exhibition of heading power.

This defeat obviously taught Everton a lesson. They came bouncing back, and before the New Year had registered five goals against Middlesbrough and another five against Blackburn with Dean recording another couple of hat-tricks. However, he was receiving more than his fair share of injuries – the inevitable consequence of being a successful forward. But he had the amazing virtue of retaining his good humour and never complaining or retaliating to any of the questionable tactics which were being used by opposing defences in their desperation to stop his goal-scoring habits. Many witnesses to his exploits during the period speak of the times Dean went to the touchline with his leg bleeding profusely, but without complaint had cheerfully returned to the field to play and relied purely on his football skills to overcome the crudeness of his adversaries. This remarkable quality which Dean possessed is one to which testimony has been consistently given throughout his career, by players, spectators, and sports writers.

For Everton's first game in the New Year Dean was absent with a damaged ankle and the team were beaten 4-0 by Birmingham. Comment about Everton's performance included 'the mastermind was missing' and 'the team was like sheep without their shepherd'. The following week was the occasion of the third round of the FA Cup, and Everton had been drawn at home against their neighbours and old rivals, Liverpool. What an occasion! Everton were the clear favourites, Liverpool not enjoying anything like the success their rivals had attained in the League. But the question was, would Dean be playing? He was named to play the day before and the fans looked forward to an exciting match. There were 60,000 present and they paid over £6000 for the privilege. Everton supporters received full value in the first minute. A report says: 'In less than a minute Morrison and Tiny Bradshaw in the Liverpool defence confused each other in mid-field so that Dean – the Blue Devil of their dreams – got the ball. But he was forty yards out. No danger yet. Up came a back to tackle. Dean swerved, the back slipped, and the Blue Devil of Goodison Park was on his way. The route was clear to goal. He strode forward, shot with his left foot from twelve yards, and as Scott dived, the ball hit the near post and spun into the net.' A minute of Dean magic. Liverpool, however, came back, equalised before half time, and in the second half scored again to win the match 2-1 and put Everton out of the Cup.

Now Everton were able to concentrate on the League championship – a race which the club had very good prospects of winning. In 32 games the team had passed the 100 goals mark and with 10 games to play needed 28 goals to beat Aston Villa's record 128 in the 1930-31 season. In a game against Huddersfield, Dean registered another hat-trick in Everton's 4-1 win. Rapturous praise poured on Dean for his performance, particularly for his heading of one goal. A report said 'Dean showed his brilliance in beating a man who can use his hands. He backheaded the ball, bewildering the Huddersfield goalkeeper by the method of heading behind him with a sense of timing that was superb.' Perhaps there is only Pelé in the ranks of modern footballers who could compare with the sheer genius and professionalism which Dean consistently displayed in heading a football.

The Easter programme was an extremely tough one. Everton, however, gained four points from three games, two of which were against title challengers West Bromwich Albion. An aggregate 150,000 spectators attended the three matches. Everton, escaping injuries during the period, were fortunate in fielding an unchanged side for match after match, despite the fact that each game they played became successively harder as the race for the championship drew to a close. Indeed Everton's team was being announced in the press 'team as usual'. An unusual step for the local Press, normally providing as it did so much detail of this kind in a repetitive way, days before a match was to be played. But the forward line of Critchley, Dunn, Dean, Johnson, and Stein was so regular that team selectors could have invested in a rubber stamp to save writing the names! However, it had to be admitted that in the closing period of the season goals were becoming a much scarcer commodity than they had been early on.

Arsenal were challenging Everton for the title and also cherishing ambitions to win the Cup. Alas for them they were beaten by Newcastle in the final. Furthermore, the London club's challenge for the Division One championship petered out and Everton were assured of the title before the League programme was completed. So Everton's final fixture of the season against Portsmouth had no bearing on the outcome of top of the table placings. The game against Portsmouth was almost a case of history being repeated. Four years previously when Everton last won the championship of Division One their last match of the season was at home and the League President John McKenna was in attendance to present the trophy to the Everton captain Warney Cresswell. John McKenna was there to perform the ceremony once again but this time it was to hand the trophy over to the player who was the star of that memorable occasion in 1928, none other than William Ralph 'Dixie' Dean, who had since been elevated to the captaincy of the Everton club. In 1928 the final game contained all the drama of Dean reaching a record 60 goals. In 1932 the match against Portsmouth had nothing exciting to offer and indeed became something of an anti-climax.

Over 50,000 spectators attended the match against Portsmouth mainly, it was supposed, to reflect in the end of the season glory of the Everton championship success. In particular the crowd wanted to show their appreciation of their idol, Dixie Dean. He had scored 45 League goals and some might have expected perhaps five goals from him in this game to make his half century. Portsmouth were not exactly a pushover but at that time they were not the best of opposition. So anything was possible. Happy anticipation prevailed. Half-an-hour before the game commenced it was announced Dean would not be playing. Disappointment turned to astonishment when Dean led his team out on the field. What was going on? The crowd drew their own conclusions when Everton gave a most inept display and Portsmouth won the match 1-0.

The ceremony of presenting the championship trophy to Everton lost some of its expected glitter. Dean, who accepted the cup from the President, made a typically honest comment: 'After today's performance I'm ashamed to take it.' However, he thanked the team and supporters and as captain he cracked the flippance 'One word from me and the team did as it liked!' This was described as a daring comment by some newspapers reporting the event. But Dean never stood on ceremony. Some thought Everton had entered the game in a careless manner – perhaps the team was not fit for a number of reasons. Dean himself had an atrocious game and speculation abounded as to why it was announced that he would not play and then he was apparently restored to the team within half an hour of the kick-off. Had there been some unofficial celebrating before the start? Dean asserts that this was not the case.

But Everton had already been assured of the championship and despite the disappointment of the Portsmouth game the contrasting situation which faced Liverpool on that last day of the season made Everton's lapse seem very minor indeed! Liverpool, playing at Burnden Park, were trounced 8-1 by Bolton Wanderers. Everton and Dean could afford a gloating satisfaction that their neighbours would have to carry the ignomy of such a defeat throughout the summer, whereas Everton held the outstanding prize of Division One to parade during the break and proudly defend next season.

Mr Cuff, the Everton chairman, said it was all-round ability that had won two championships in successive seasons and the team's spectacular forward play had been good for the game as a whole. With such a measure of success no-one could detract from the efforts of the team as a whole or the forward line in particular, but the leadership and brilliant play of Dean was without doubt a major factor in the club's great achievements over the period.

Football League First Division – 1931-32

	P	W	D	L	F	A	Pts
Everton	42	26	4	12	116	64	56
Arsenal	42	22	10	10	90	48	54
Sheffield W.	42	22	6	14	96	82	50
Huddersfield T.	42	19	10	13	80	63	48
Aston Villa	42	19	8	15	104	72	46
West Bromwich A.	42	20	6	16	77	55	46
Portsmouth	42	19	7	16	62	62	45
Birmingham C.	42	18	8	16	78	67	44
Liverpool	42	19	6	17	81	93	44
Newcastle U.	42	18	6	18	80	87	42
Chelsea	42	16	8	18	69	73	40
Sunderland	42	15	10	17	67	73	40
Manchester C.	42	13	12	17	83	73	38
Derby Co.	42	14	10	18	71	75	38
Blackburn R.	42	16	6	20	89	95	38
Bolton W.	42	17	4	21	72	80	38
Middlesbrough	42	15	8	19	64	89	38
Leicester C.	42	15	7	20	74	94	37
Blackpool	42	12	9	21	65	102	33
Grimsby T.	42	13	6	23	67	98	32
West Ham U.	42	12	7	23	62	107	31

16   Hat-trick of Successes

DURING DEAN'S SERVICE with Everton between 1928 and 1932 the club won the championship of Division One twice and Division Two once. On each of these occasions Everton scored more than 100 goals. In all its 98 years' existence to the present day in no other season did the club exceed the century mark in goals scored. Dean's presence in the teams that achieved such remarkable scoring feats is of some significance. The sum total of those three seasons' goals was 339, with Dean contributing 144 from 114 appearances. By any standards, a phenomenal individual achievement which the English Football League has not witnessed from any player either before or since.

The 1932-33 season was the last occasion Everton gained a major honour whilst Dean was with the club. The ratio of success acheived by Everton during Dean's service was remarkably high. In 88 years of League membership Everton have won the Cup three times and taken seven Division One titles. A success rate of 1 in 28 and 1 in 12 years respectively. Indeed, the FA Cup success in 1933 was the link which kept Everton from complete obscurity in Cup history over 60 years, the club having won the tophy in 1906 and subsequently in 1966. The 1933 final was a shining light and even brighter in retrospect. For Dean, who captained the victorious Everton side in that Cup Final, it was the crowning point of his remarkable career.

The season which commenced in the autumn of 1932 provided the opportunity for Everton to complete a unique hat-trick of successes, if by following their two consecutive title wins of Second and First Divisions, they could win the FA Cup. Everton were in form and had a great captain in Dean. He was still young and at 25 years of age only required a Cup-Winners' medal to achieve every honour in the game at that time and so fulfil the dream of all professional footballers. He was the most prolific scorer of goals in the English League and when that season began he had played 269 League games and netted 275 goals.

Everton, no doubt like every other club, set out to win the Cup every year, but the 1932-33 season took on a special significance for them. Two seasons previously the club had reached the semi-final of the Cup and narrowly missed reaching Wembley, but their prime target then was gaining the Division Two title, and this they had done. Now, as defending champions of Division One, they faced the season with great confidence. A good Cup run was in prospect. Of course it would help if a secure position in the League was obtained during the first half of the season before the Cup-ties began in January of 1933. This was in fact achieved and Everton confidently awaited the draw for the third round of the Cup in which they and other First and Second Division clubs traditionally made their first appearance.

Everton's Third Round tie was against Leicester City away, a match which they won 3-2 with Dean scoring one of the goals. A home tie against Bury gave Everton no trouble in the fourth round, where they won 3-1 before facing another home tie in the fifth round against Leeds United, which finished with a convincing win for Everton by two goals to nil, Dean scoring once again. The luck that is an essential ingredient of all Cup success was retained when the club found itself drawn at home to Luton Town in the sixth round. Luton were a moderate Third Division side and faced a formidable task at Goodison. Nevertheless, Everton had suffered defeats at the hands of lowly opposition in Cup-ties before and therefore took this game very seriously. They were experienced enough to know the Cup could be a great leveller. As it turned out, Everton won handsomely by 6-0 and entered the semi-final to find that their opponents were to be West Ham United, a team with a poor record lying near the bottom of the Second Division.

The match against West Ham was arranged to be played at Wolverhampton and Everton were the clear favourites. Dean had scored in every round so far and his confidence as captain knew no bounds. His team was now set for Wembley and it appeared that nothing could stop them. But the game against West Ham proved to be no pushover. Critchley, the outside right who had been displaced earlier in the season, was brought back for this game in place of Geldard. In the opening period Everton gave a very nervous performance and with the score 1-1 at the interval the game was wide open for either team to win. It was Critchley who managed to scramble a goal in the second half to give Everton victory by two goals to one. It was a near thing, but Everton were in the final at last. And what a classic contest it would be, for their opponents were to be Manchester City, a First Division side of great talent. Moreover, it was an all-Lancashire final certain to attract an eager and passionate following of supporters for both teams.

Intense excitement developed in the six weeks before the final. Everton had one of the best forward lines in the League and Manchester City possessed a half-back line of great skills in Busby, Cowan, and Bray. Pre-match speculation went on in those days no less than that created by modern Cup finals. There was discussion on the colours to be worn by the respective teams. Both clubs normally wore blue and the FA had allocated red for one and white for the other. The clubs exchanged views about which colour their players should wear. City wanted red and Dean advised his directors to concede to their request without argument. First, he didn't want Everton to play in red (for obvious reasons) but he argued that to play in white would give his team a psychological advantage. And so it was that Everton wore white and City red.

Another item that had to be settled was the wearing of numbers on the players' shirts. For the first time in the history of the final players would be identified by numbers, but as they would be numbered from 1 to 22, which team would be allocated 1 to 11? Everton were chosen to wear the first sequence. Another matter of interest was that the referee, Mr Wood of Sheffield, was offered five guineas or a gold medal as his reward for taking charge of the game. Whatever he decided upon, it was obvious he could only be doing it all for the love and honour of football. It is said that our Judges are highly paid in order to prevent corruption. But a poor referee controlling the major sporting event of the year, and making vital decisions, was considered to be worth only five guineas!

Although the Cup final retains its importance as a national event, in the decade before the war it was regarded as an even greater attraction because arguably it had much less competition. Today many other glittering occasions appear in the world of sport to blur the focus which once concentrated so intensely on the Cup final. The run-up to the game in 1933 was perhaps not exploited in the utterly commercialised way it is in the present day. Dean says he and his men had to forego the drinking of alcohol three weeks prior to the match. It appears that they would endure any sacrifice, even the ban on beer, to achieve success! Dean recalls that on the eve of the game the team went to bed at midnight after a supper of tripe and onions.

Always the imperturbable character, Dean was able to inspire his team with his own calmness and project the relaxation so essential to alleviate a daunting situation. Comic relief was always welcome and Dean says footballers in those days revelled in light-hearted banter both on and off the field. Jimmy Dunn, with whom Dean was a very close friend, indulged in all manner of practical jokes. A commercial offer of supplying the Cup final team with a full rig-out of suits, shirts, shoes, hats, and topcoats was gladly accepted. When they were delivered Jimmy Dunn mixed the sizes up so that when the team tried them on they looked, as Dean recalls, like extras for a Mack Sennet comedy! The pattern of the attire was fashioned in the style immortalised by the Chicago gangsters of the time. A photograph was taken and is one of Dean's proud possessions.

Dean remembers that one of Dunn's favourite tricks when the team was staying in a particularly posh hotel was to pin a pair of kippers to the underside of the dining table and leave them. A few days later the management were at a loss to discover the source of the putrid odours which filled their restaurant, much to the sordid amusement of the Everton players who all knew Dunn had been at it again. Disgraceful conduct, perhaps, but they were never more violent than that, says Dean!

Footballers got very little bonus out of the entertainment they provided in those days and Dean, like many of his contemporaries, naturally thought soccer must nevertheless have been a profitable pursuit for the administrators of the game. He argues this point quite strongly. Even when a special bonus for players was more than justified, such as appearing in the Cup final, or even winning the trophy, individuals were not paid an award in cash. Instead they were presented with vouchers which could be used to purchase goods from nominated traders. Dean says he was presented with a bonus of £30 worth of vouchers for winning the Cup – and he was captain of the team!

The teams reaching the final in the thirties no doubt made a profit, and it is well known that the Cup has always been regarded as a good money-spinner for clubs. In 1933, excluding the final takings, Manchester City profited to the tune of £17,942. In the first round City played Gateshead and forced a replay, the game ending in a 1-1 draw. Their share of that gate was £479! Everton, who did not have any replays during the course of reaching Wembley, gained a sum just short of that made by Manchester City – £17,164, excluding the final takings. That would represent a considerable sum in those days.

The pre-final excitement reached fever pitch, and throughout Lancashire the population of that depressed county forgot all its economic troubles to concentrate on the Wembley contest. The teams were announced. Everton brought back Geldard, their flying winger, a move which caused some controversy among supporters because he was replacing Critchley, their hero who had scored the vital winning goal in the semi-final against West Ham. It was a difficult decision that had to be made, and Dean confesses he had a hand in it as captain. The full team was: Sagar, Cook, Cresswell, Britton, White, Thomson, Geldard, Dunn, Dean (captain), Johnson, and Stein. Manchester City's teamsheet read: Langford, Cann, Dale, Busby (now Sir Matt), Cowan, Bray, Toseland, Marshall, Herd, McMullan, and Brook. Two teams with many international players, some of whom will remain immortals in the game. A great exhibition of football was in prospect on that Wembley turf. Dean, wearing the Number 9 jersey, was the first centre-forward at Wembley, appropriately enough, to assume what has now become perhaps the most famous number in football.

The London Midland and Scottish railway – the famous L.M.S. – laid on 40 special trains to take supporters from Lancashire to London, providing a reserved seat for everyone, with 700 on each train. A delightful episode in the history of steam. From Merseyside, the crowds, armed with every conceivable makeshift musical instrument to entertain themselves during the journey, embarked in high spirits. They sang songs to the accompaniment of banjos, ukeleles, combs and paper, mouth organs, whistles, singing the praises of their heroes, particularly about the man who was the very symbol of their worshipful fervour, the great 'Dixie Dean'. The crowds were on a great day out and even the rhythm of the wheels (that we hear less of today) inspired additional syncopation. Supporters also went by charabanc and every other means of transport. At Euston Station their rivals from Manchester engaged in happy and carefree contests to make the loudest din imaginable without rancour or aggressive behaviour of any kind. Football supporters seemed to reflect a true sporting spirit which added such tremendous delight to the game of soccer in those days.

His Majesty King George V was unable to attend the Cup final through illness and the Duke and Duchess of York attended instead. The Lord Mayor of Liverpool sat with the Duchess (now the Queen Mother) and pointed out the Everton players to her. When the Lord Mayor attempted to identify the great man – 'That's Dixie Dean' – she rebuked him in a politely Royal manner. 'Even I know Dean,' she said. Of course, who didn't? At the beginning of that match he had the record of having scored 298 goals in 308 League games. With such a wealth of experience he was reassuring his men and trying to relax them to dispose of the inevitable pre-match nerves. Dean recalls that Warney Cresswell, Everton's famous full-back, was puffing his pipe and effusing a calmness which acted as a tranquiliser to settle all their nerves. 'And Warney', Dean declares, 'smoked the cheapest tobacco on the market!'

Nearly 100,000 people created a tension and an infectious atmosphere from which no player in either team could be totally immune. The Manchester City players knew that the greatest danger to them was Dean. Robin Bailey, a well-known critic of the time, had written an article about Dean published in September 1931 in the *Liverpool Echo*. Here is an excerpt:

Watch old Dixie! Keep your optic on that bloke Dean, were the warnings at the Den when Everton played Millwall last season. Once I saw him on a Northern ground in a Cup-tie, and the Liverpool regiment of fans were there in full blast: 'Give it to Dixie! Give it to Dixie!' was the avalanche of advice that drowned every other shout. Even the rattles and sirens had no chance against it.

An American reporter in a spirit of curiosity once accompanied me to a match in which this tall, curly-headed youth was in action. He watched and listened, as a well-trained newspaper man does whatever big town he comes from.

'Say, which are the Dixies?' he asked after five minutes. I handed him a programme.

'What's the big idea of this Dixie stuff?'

'That is the name of the Everton centre-forward. He's a great footballer, a sort of Babe Ruth (greatest of all baseball stars) of England.'

Thereafter, the field glasses of the American were trained on Dean, wherever he roamed — and he does roam. Our cousins from the other end of the Big Ferry are tremendously interested in successful and magnetic personalities.

So, as a matter of fact, are we all.

The most thorough and technical tribute I ever heard laid at the studded soles of the famous Dean, who is not gloomy, came from Alf Messer, the Tottenham Hotspur centre-half.

During his several campaigns at Reading (who did pretty well in the Cup) in representative games, and since he went to White Hart Lane this masterly pivot has faced all the leading centre-forwards of England.

'Dean is easily the most difficult of them all to deal with,' said Messer. 'He's big, tall, quick, clever, individualistic, yet no centre leads or combines better with his comrades. Barring Charlie

Buchan, I never saw any other forward so deft with his head, yet he is no mere football aviator; always in the air. A great footballer and a sportsman.'

This was a formidable antagonist's summing-up of Dixie Dean, and such a long speech was all the more surprising, because Messer, like another artist, Frank Woolley, speaks seldom, and then usually calls upon few words.

And yet the first time I met this irrepressible Dixie Dean, cherry optimist and happy warrior of the Cup and League trails, he was in tears. He wept bitterly over what he thought had been his hopeless failure. It was after his first game for Everton against Arsenal at Highbury that I sought an interview with the expensive new forward just transferred to Goodison Park from across the Mersey. He did not think he would be able to hold a place in First League football.

But the 'old soldiers' in the side gave me that footballer's wink which tells me more than half a column of close print — it signalled: 'The boy's good. He's down-hearted about missing a chance or two, but he's the right stuff.'

That is what the winks wirelessed, and they were right. Here's to one of those old-fashioned Everton seasons, and Dixie at the head of the football 'batting averages'!

If he and his pals should breeze up to a certain stadium some time in April, well, the final would not be devoid of good football — as it has been on some deadly drab occasions.'

The game at Wembley in 1933 proved Everton the better side. Manchester City were really outclassed. Everton's players exuded confidence throughout and were able to control every move attempted by their opponents. Britton, Everton's right half, was particularly outstanding and Cresswell was intelligent, cool, and efficient at full-back. All the team played well. Without any sign of pressure the Everton forward line, renowned for its individual and combined skills, excelled and gave a demonstration of intricate ball play of the kind which some people believe has its origins only in modern football. They interchanged with an amazingly intelligent understanding which in forward play can only stem from the highly individual skills ordained of each. The *Manchester Guardian* reported, 'They were romping about and playing their tricks as unconcernedly as though this were almost an exhibition match at familiar Goodison Park.' In addition the Everton forward line contained the unique, potentially explosive power of Dean, a menace which haunted their opponents throughout the game. Matt Busby has already been quoted on this score!

The first goal came five minutes before the interval. Langford, challenged by Dean, dropped the ball and Stein was able to score with ease. Early in the second half Britton sent over a high centre, Langford waited to gather the ball, a fatal error because Dean was there with his head, and the City goalkeeper and the ball were in the back of the net. Some thought that Dean had acted unfairly, but Langford afterwards confirmed that it was a good goal and there wasn't a fairer player than Dean. Ten minutes before the end Dunn sealed Manchester City's fate by heading in a centre from Geldard to make the score 3-0 for Everton – the clearest margin of victory recorded at Wembley in a Cup final to that date. Everton had also achieved what was a unique hat-trick of success. And for Dean his dream had come true. The great man duly received the Cup and his medal from the Duchess of York. Her Royal Highness did not hide her great pleasure at doing the honour, or her admiration for Dean and his colleagues. A truly entertaining spectacle, and for a Cup final at Wembley an unusually good measure of skilful football.

Followed by the Everton team, Dean then proudly displayed the trophy to their supporters who were delighting in Dean's antics of raising the Cup to his lips as if he were drinking from it. Everton had won not only by reason of a talented display, but because they were relaxed and confident, a condition which had eluded the City players. One good reason was the role played by their captain Dean, and emphasised by Sam Cowan the City captain. 'Dean,' he said, 'was an inspiration to his men.' Glowing reports of the Everton performance inlcuded particular reference to the part Dean had played. Dean says his heart went out to Jimmy McMullan, the City player who was playing his last game before retirement. McMullan was in tears and Dean was strongly tempted to say 'Here you are wack, take my medal and I'll take yours.'

Some newspaper reports drew attention to the fact that Dean had not scored at Goodison Park for two months prior to the match at Wembley. He had, however, played a full season of 39 League games scoring what was for him a poor total of only 24 goals, plus his 5 goals in the Cup-ties. Some critics with short memories had supported Dean's exclusion from the England team because they claimed he did not possess the big match temperament! They had forgotten that at only 20 years of age he had thrilled over 100,000 Scottish partisans at Hampden Park and scored England's two goals to defeat the mighty Blue Devils for the first time in Scotland for 23 years. In his first Cup final (an equally tense occasion) as captain of the Everton team his big match temperament was probably the major factor in the brilliant victory achieved by his club.

The celebrations of the Cup triumph continued over the weekend, but Dean had to interrupt these to do quite a bit of film work with Pathe News, most of which was carried out on the Sunday. The team finally left London by train for Liverpool on the Monday afternoon, and on arrival there was received by one of the most enthusiastic crowds ever seen in the history of football. In those days it was an event in which most people sought refuge as a relief to the drabness of their lives. The Cup was a symbol of victory for the local community and the conquering heroes who had achieved it just had to be worshipped, an indulgence that no-one on Merseyside was going to be denied. The excitement of the occasion reached a fever pitch.

The police, anticipating the massive crowds congregating in the centre of the city, erected barriers in the hope of exercising some control. These were brushed aside and the wide area of Lime Street was filled to absolute capacity with people, which from above appeared as an endless sea of humanity covered with a confetti of cloth caps, that popular headgear of the thirties.

When the victorious Everton team arrived at Lime Street station they immediately boarded a coach and four, the vehicle used by the returning 1906 Everton Cup-winning team, to emerge facing the feverishly applauding crowds. Dean and his men were quickly overcome by an emotion which reflected that effusing from the milling thousands struggling to provide a passageway for the horses drawing the carriage. Dean, standing precariously high on the coach, held up the sacred trophy for all to see. Around the station alone the crowd was estimated to be over 50,000, and many were being pushed, buffetted, and pressured, suffering great inconvenience seemingly without complaint.

The team's tour of the centre of the city made slow progress to the Town Hall. Every street was a mass of excited people and a passage was cleared only with great difficulty almost yard by yard for the coach and horses to proceed. When the convoy finally arrived at the Town Hall, Dean was observed to be sweating profusely but this did not hide the tears of joy or the mixture of emotion and depth of feeling expressed on his countenance. His arms felt as though they were ready to fall off after holding the trophy higher and higher as demanded by the appealing fervour of those Merseyside crowds. Dean, the man who was rarely moved by the pressures of any kind of situation, had met his Waterloo. This was, he claims, the most moving experience he had ever known, or was likely to, even if he lived to be a 100 years old.

Goodison Park, Everton's home ground, was thrown open for fans to enter and view the trophy, a prize not seen on Merseyside for 27 years. A war had intervened and many thousands of those who had last witnessed such an event would not be there. Liverpool FC, Everton's close neighbours, had never won the Cup, so this was indeed a rare occasion for the local community. The Everton team, and the Cup, left the Town Hall to proceed along Scotland Road, Kirkdale Road, Walton Road, and County Road to Goodison Park. Half-a-million people lined the route to watch the coach pass by. Some sat on the roof-tops of houses, up lamp posts, and on any convenient or even hazardous vantage point. When the coach turned into Goodison Park there were more than 50,000 ecstatic supporters to welcome it, all the fans saturated by a glorious feeling that overwhelmed their senses. The Everton team was given due homage, the scene reminiscent of some tribal ritual with Dean as the omnipotent God.

The next time the Cup came to Merseyside was to be 30 years later when the style of life had changed, when new distractions had been developed, like television for example, taking some of the edge off the live importance people attach to events of this kind. Of course large crowds will still turn out for such occasions but it's likely that never again will there ever be such a massive, emotional response as witnessed in 1933. By comparison Dean considers that modern football spectators reflect only a superficial image of the enthusiasm of their 1930s counterparts.

The Cup final celebrations were followed by the normal aftermath. A decision was made that the ball used in the final would be presented to the club. Madame Tussauds, the famous London waxworks museum, honoured Dean by creating a new model of him to replace the one produced five years before.

There were a number of court cases involving charges against some Everton supporters of 'stowing away' on the special trains carrying fans to Wembley. Local magistrates, no doubt carried away by their own pride and satisfaction in the Everton triumph, showed an unusually lenient attitude to those charged. Most of the people appearing in court were let off with nothing more than a warning not to do it again. Rather surprisingly it was revealed that the number of cases of drunkenness which had occurred over that eventful weekend were no more than usual. Many who were charged with such offences inevitably proffered the excuse that they were celebrating the Cup victory!

Another consequence of the local Cup fever was one that befell Dean's brother-in-law. He worked for a Merseyside firm and like most people employed in those days was conditioned to a six-day week, having to turn in on Saturday mornings. He had obtained a ticket for the Cup final and was naturally eager to attend the game. A once-in-a-lifetime opportunity for him. He requested his employer to release him on the Saturday morning – a request which could have easily been granted without seriously affecting the business. His employer refused. However, Dean's enthusiastic relative could not resist the temptation and duly went off to the final. When he returned to his work on Monday he was promptly given the sack. A reflection of the times in which he lived. A chap could be let off for a criminal act arising out of the Cup mania, but a long-serving employee takes half-a-day off work and the penalty is dismissal. In those days of high unemployment and cheap labour some employers easily became despotic!

A further consequence of victory for the Everton team was a summer tour of Denmark. With the exception of White and Geldard, both of whom had been selected to play for England in Italy and Switzerland, the Everton team embarked for Copenhagen early in May. Everton played half-a-dozen matches with Danish sides of varying quality. Dean enjoyed himself immensely, and both he and the team were fêted wherever they went. Everton won all their games, including one by 10 goals to nil. Dean, however, only managed to score two goals in that game. He says that at that time a number of ex-footballers from Britain were resident coaches to Danish teams, as indeed they were in many other continental countries during the thirties. The high standard and perhaps even the superiority of continental soccer today owes much to the solid foundations built by British coaching in the pre-war period.

Dean was very impressed with some of the Danish teams and although Everton were much superior, the football of their continental rivals was exceptionally skilful and only their finishing power, a failure to take advantage and score goals, was deficient. It was not only football that occupied Dean's interest on that tour. It was whilst he was in Copenhagen that he learned of his success in backing the winner of the English Derby the horse tipped by Lord Derby which could be said to be another consequence of the Cup final. The cycle of success which Dean experienced seemed to know no bounds. But as with most wheels of fortune the ups are well matched by the downs. The following season was to be a less fortunate one for Dean and indeed for his club.

17 300th League Goal

WHEN THE LEAGUE FIXTURES opened in the autumn of 1933 the economic climate of the country was showing distinct signs of improvement. The number of unemployed had dropped by 700,000. Despite the progress on the home front, foreign affairs were the subject of some concern. The rise of Nazism and fascism in Germany, Italy and Japan, although worrying some people in Britain, seemed to have little impact on the general public. The Empire was troubled by events in India but no-one in Britain thought its stability was ever in question. The British Empire was something on which the sun never set, physically or metaphorically. In 1933 Germany and Japan had left that great institution, the League of Nations, which was to become a declining force in the search for world peace. The bubbling cauldron of international events went unnoticed by the majority of Britons, who were preoccupied with their own serious economic problems.

Nevertheless sport, particularly football, continued to attract a devoted following. Indeed during the 1933-34 season an expansion of interest took place in international soccer, to a greater extent than in some of the serious political developments. Hunger marches by the unemployed of Scotland and the North of England continued to be organised despite the drop in workless. However, their pleas for work were generally ignored. There were also plenty of hungry footballers about, a situation which created increased competitiveness in the professional game.

During the first half of the 1933-34 season an Austrian national football team visited Britain and astonished soccer fans by drawing a game with Scotland at Hampden Park. The Austrian style and high standard of play amazed the football critics. Another event which also took place at the time was the visit, for the first time in history, of a football team from South America. The team represented a combination of players from Chile and Peru, and matches were arranged with several English clubs. No South American team had ever performed in Britain prior to 1933. Fascinating when one thinks of the progress made by those countries in the game since then. If the sport had taken over from politics at that time it is possible that world peace might have endured!

During that season a good example of the political domination which was developing in sport occurred. A German soccer team playing a fixture in France was banned from performing abroad for a whole year. The reason? For failing to give the Nazi salute when on the field. The French team had threatened to cancel the match if the German players had insisted on making such a demonstration. The German team agreed not to give the salute and consequently was summarily punished by the Nazi-controlled football authority.

The season looked particularly bright for Everton. There were no political ties involved for them, thank goodness, and Dean continued as captain. The team had proved an enterprising, skilful combination, and as Cup-holders this made them an additional attraction. The club also had the knack of successfully nursing players in the reserves with a goodly number proving themselves in the first team to become internationals. Indeed during that period players like Geldard, Gee, Britton, Stein, White, Coulter, and Mercer were very good examples.

Of course it takes time to develop players, and the team for the new season was more or less the same as that with which Everton had won the Cup. Seemingly the team could be relied on to do well and provided injuries did not undermine their prospects, high class football would grace Goodison Park for some time to come. However, it was a quiet opening, and with four games played Everton had gained only as many points. But Dean was in form and had scored in each of those matches. In one he celebrated his 300th League goal, against Birmingham on September 2. It was a unique record. In only nine full seasons and playing in 310 games he had registered 300 goals. And he was still only 26 years of age!

Then tragedy struck. The season was not a month old. Everton were playing Arsenal in a game at Goodison and the home side were combining well with Dean at his sparkling best. Spectators had just marvelled at Dean's famous back-heading trick, which had deceived the Arsenal goalkeeper Moss, the ball going to Dunn to score a simple goal. Then Dean was seen to be limping badly, but nevertheless carried on to finish the game. Afterwards it was reported that he was suffering from a sprained ankle. Two days later he was admitted to a nursing home and had to be operated on for the removal of two pieces of bone from his left ankle. He had had a similar operation on his other ankle in November 1929 which had put him out of

168

the game for a considerable period, an absence which had a dramatic effect on the fortunes of the club at the time. That was the season Everton finished bottom of Division One and was relegated. Of course everyone knew Dean was a tough customer and expected him to make one of his remarkable recoveries. Alas, it was not to be, for he was out of the side for six weeks and once again the club's fortunes took a nose-dive.

Dean returned to the team on November 4 to play in a match against Huddersfield in which Everton were beaten 0-1. The reports of the match noted that Huddersfield was the youngest club in the League, the club not having been admitted until 1910, a fact which made their brilliant successes in the twenties all the more remarkable. In the match Smith, the youngest club's oldest player, had scored the decisive goal and was described as the best man on the field. He had joined Huddersfield in 1913 and was still performing brilliantly at 39 years of age. Smith played for England many times at outside-left but he had switched to the right wing for his club following the transfer of Alec Jackson, the Scottish international, to Chelsea.

The match was, however, another tragedy for Dean and his club. The master, making a welcome return from six weeks' absence, was injured once again. This time it was a knock on his knee and he limped rather badly for the greater part of the game. Nonetheless his performance was highly praised. He used his head to very good effect despite being hampered by his injury. Whatever happened to him the man never gave up. But the injury necessitated a cartilage operation and the result was that he did not return to the team for a considerable time.

At that stage Everton were lying fifth from the bottom of Division One and things looked decidedly glum. Dean was out of the nursing home within five weeks and acknowledging his amazing constitution hopes were raised that he would be back in the side before Christmas. In fact he soon joined the team for light training and went off with a party of players to Everton's favourite resort at Buxton to recuperate. Hopes were dashed however when Dean was declared to be unfit. Everton, although realising that their star centre-forward was almost irreplaceable, were compelled to enter the transfer market and commenced negotiations with Chelsea in the hope of signing Hughie Gallagher, the Scottish international centre-forward. The approach proved abortive and Everton continued by utilising Tommy White as Dean's deputy. The club was indeed fortunate in having a player of White's calibre. What a marvellous, versatile asset White proved to be. He scored regularly and whenever Dean returned White would readily revert to his centre-half position. The club went on assiduously searching for another centre-forward, trying to find one of Dean's class, but like any other club in such circumstances the search was in vain. Such class just wasn't available.

Subsequently Dean was given a trial with the reserves, scored a brilliant hat-trick and naturally it was anticipated he would be ready to play in the Cup-ties which commenced in January 1934. Alas, this proved to be over-optimistic. He did not join the side until February 24, when he turned out against Blackburn Rovers at Ewood Park. His performance then showed that his confidence in his legs having the capacity to stand up to the rigours of first team play was somewhat shaky and therefore it was to be some time before he was anything like match fit. His reappearance in the Everton side was given wide publicity and it was evident that the magic of his name had not diminished by his absence.

At Blackburn the crowd turn-out was substantially increased, rather astonishing for a match between two teams not doing anything very spectacular. The large attendance could only be due to the fact that Dean was playing. Many travelled from Merseyside to see the great man once again. Dean gave a magnificent performance by his heading skills and reports of the game made much of this, particularly in view of the wet conditions which prevailed throughout the match. Dean's display was said to be an object lesson for Everton's two young inside-forwards, Cunliffe and Higham. A wet ball in those days required great expertise to control, particularly with the head, and the game at Blackburn, played in heavy rain, produced the obvious hazards. Many players performing under those conditions were afraid to use their heads at all and some even found difficulty in kicking the ball. It is on record that players suffered injuries from actually kicking a rain soaked ball and heading, of course, was even more dangerous.

The season had only six weeks to go and it was evident that Dean would not recover quickly enough to make the contribution normally expected of him. The team had been without its captain for most of the unfortunate season and struggled with the utmost difficulty to ensure a safe position in the League table and so be free from the dangers of relegation. This they managed, however, gaining a final placing of 14th in Division One. The effect of losing their idol was most apparent. Everton recorded their lowest goal total since Dean joined the club, and such a famine was not to occur again until 1947. The 1933-34 goal total was 62 – just two more than had been registered by Dean alone in 1928!

Despite the poor season and Dean's absence, his consistency never flagged, his tally for the period being 9 goals in 12 games. It was the first time in ten seasons he had failed to score more than 20 goals. Some players have scored more than 20 goals in consecutive seasons but their consistency tends to break down after four years. The Everton centre-forward still had a record that could not be challenged. The season had been a disastrous one for Everton and even more calamitous for Dean. The club had been eliminated from the FA Cup at the first hurdle, and the trophy was eventually won by Manchester City, the team Everton had defeated in the final at Wembley in 1933.

Because of his long absences through injury, Dean found he had plenty of time to spare and as a man partial to gambling he had bought himself a greyhound, which he raced successfully on a number of occasions. It was, however, a time when the Government was attempting to clamp down on all forms of betting and introduced a Bill to impose many restrictions, which included greyhound racing. The economic depression, which caused so much poverty, had the effect of inducing more and more people to indulge in betting, a vice they no doubt thought of as their only hope of ever gaining any security. Perhaps the Establishment thought that if gambling could be reduced, people would more easily tolerate the low incomes which the depression imposed. But more restrictions tended to have the opposite effect on people, and instead of limiting the vice only served to increase it. An example of this was prohibition in the USA. Gambling in Britain continued to flourish in the back streets, despite the Bill.

Another curtailment of a popular scheme – cigarette coupons – was introduced by the Government. This was a system whereby working people smoked themselves silly to obtain gifts, the most popular of which were often essentials, like boots and shoes, the luxury items being beyond the reach of most. Nevertheless, there were 'haves' and 'have nots' in 1934 just like today, and some were arranging cruises to exotic places with luxury liners sailing from Liverpool at the rate of about ten a month. Indeed, it became a boom trade catering for the people who could afford to pay. It was on one of these ships that the Everton team embarked for a tour of the Canary Islands in May 1934 to play three fixtures with the local

Spanish clubs. Dean had fully recovered from his injuries and captained the Everton side for the tour. Of course it was a well-established tradition to arrange an end-of-season holiday abroad and the Everton players were regarded as the lucky ones, belonging to one of the few wealthy League clubs that could afford to do it.

After such a depressing season, no doubt the Everton players felt in need of the holiday, but their stay in Tenerife, according to Dean, was marred by the heat, the flies, and he adds, the sight of people who were even poorer than many of those back home in Britain, who were suffering the deprivations of the economic depression. Of the three games on the tour Everton won two and drew one. In the first match Dean had a goal disallowed, although the referee apparently took account of it at the end of the game. After picking the ball out of the net the Spanish goalkeeper placed the ball to take a goal kick and Everton, like well behaved guests, didn't bother to argue, but the referee had in fact noted it as a goal for Everton. Dean says that the Spanish players showed remarkable skills and ball control but were not too well acquainted with the rules of the game, the latter deficiency also extending to referees!

The matches were helpful to Dean, who recovered all his old confidence and achieved match fitness, ready to resume a full programme in the next few months when the English season commenced. But knowledge of Dean's fitness did not inhibit the Everton directors from continuing their search for another centre-forward. They were increasingly aware of the risks of not having someone to deputise for Dean, particularly in the light of their experience of the past season. During the rest of the summer they publicly made their intentions clear about their quest for a high class centre-forward, and Dean had sufficient nous to understand that such a policy was justified even if he was the player who may eventually have to stand down. Although the chances of obtaining someone as an adequate replacement were extremely remote, a fact the directors, supporters, and everyone else in football had to accept, Dean's self-effacement caused him not to recognise that particular aspect of the situation.

The result was that Dean became even more attentive to keeping fit. During the summer he joined the Caledonians, a Merseyside baseball club, and found a place in the team almost immediately. Baseball was very popular in south west Lancashire at that time, particularly in Liverpool. Dean became an outstanding baseball player, was eventually selected to play the game for England, and to this day proudly retains many souvenirs of his participation in the sport. Dean will tell you how he once met Babe Ruth, the great American legend of baseball. But the meeting did not take place because of Dean's connections with the game in Britain. It arose out of Dean's fame as a star footballer.

Everton were playing Tottenham Hotspur at White Hart Lane and Dean, along with his team-mates, was enjoying a rest at half-time when Babe Ruth entered the dressing room. 'Where's this guy Dixie Dean?' Ruth quizzed. 'I just gotta meet him!' Dean, whose name was not unknown in the USA, was predictably modest about his fame and the American's approach embarrassed him. However one of the other players introduced the Everton centre-forward. Ruth shook Dean warmly by the hand and said admiringly, 'Your name is well known in the States even though we don't play your sport much over there.'

'And your name is even better known over here,' said Dean, 'although we don't play baseball much.'

'I see,' Ruth responded, 'but what do you make out of this game, Dixie? It looks as though it pays pretty well.'

'You're joking, mate,' retorted Dean, 'I make eight pounds a week, plus a few quid if I'm on the winning side.'

'But all that crowd out there,' Ruth gestured, 'there's as many there as we get for a World Series. You must get a share of the gate – surely most of them have come to see you, haven't they?'

Dean, when recalling the conversation, asks 'how do you answer that?' Babe Ruth made a fortune out of baseball over a career which lasted 20 years ending in 1934. But even he could scarcely have provided greater entertainment value to the sporting public than that given by Dean. It seems that these two stars had a lot in common, except for the money they made from their efforts. It is a strange coincidence that Ruth scored a record 60 home runs in 1927, at the same time Dean was scoring his record 60 goals.

Although he was the outstanding sporting hero in Britain, Dean and his achievements were perhaps not recognised in the way they might have been in other countries where sporting genius receives a national response of a more tangible nature. Is it a quirk of the British that they too often fail in this respect? It has been demonstrated that many in the sporting field who are simply brave losers are frequently accorded more recognition in Britain than those who are outstanding winners.

18   Memorable Cup Run

ALTHOUGH FOOTBALL is generally regarded as a working class sport it would be surprising if it did not draw a large proportion of its support from other walks of life. Of course there are many working class people in these days who rise to become members of the Establishment and although often losing touch with their origins rarely forget the sport on which they were nurtured, which more often than not is the game of soccer. Even the upper crust, brought up on more exclusive sports, are beckoned by the soccer bug and go on to develop a keen interest. Supporters of the game include many eminent men and women who are just as susceptible to the emotive aspects of watching football as those from the so-called lower orders. When recalling the 1934-35 season Dean was surprised to learn in 1976 of a connection on this very point.

Dean was invited in April 1976 to present the 'Footballer of the Year', trophy to Kevin Keegan. He duly attended the function which is organised each year by The Football Writers' Association and takes the form of a dinner held in a London hotel for the purpose of celebrating and presenting the award. In addition to Dean and Keegan the other distinguished guest was the Rt Hon Michael Foot, MP, who had only a few days previously been pipped at the post in the election for the Prime Minister's job in succession to Sir Harold Wilson. Dean was most pleasantly surprised to hear Mr Foot declare himself a devoted soccer enthusiast, and having worked in Liverpool in the thirties he was a keen supporter of Everton, holding a special affection for the former Everton centre-forward.

To prove that his claim was no idle boast, invented to pander to the occasion, Mr Foot revealed that his enthusiasm for Dean and his men of Everton reached the point whereby he composed an Ode to Everton FC, which was in fact published in the *Liverpool Daily Post* in 1935. Mr Foot, whose allegiance to the Labour Party is perhaps better known, went on to describe some aspects of soccer, a game which he asserted as being the greatest ever conceived by mankind. He praised Dean as an idol he was meeting for the first time. Then he decided to recite his ode, which had been inspired by the great men of the Merseyside club. Dean was demonstrably delighted, and no wonder. Here it is:

ODE TO EVERTON FC

When at thy call my weary feet I turn
The gates of paradise are opened wide
At Goodison I know a man may learn
Rapture more rich than Anfield can provide.
In Coulter's skill and Geldard's subtle speed
I see displayed in all its matchless bounty
The power of which the heavens decreed
The fall of Sunderland and Derby County.
The hands of Sagar, Dixie's priceless head
Made smooth the path to Wembley till that day
When Bolton came. Now hopes are fled
And all is sunk in bottomless dismay.
And so I watch with heart and temper cool
God's lesser breed of men at Liverpool.

Although Mr Foot was obviously keen to prove his connection with Dean, it had to be borne in mind that the principal guest for whom the function had been organised was the recipient of the Footballer of the Year trophy – none other than Kevin Keegan, a player from the Liverpool club and a man of Anfield!

Michael Foot's poetic inspiration had reflected his sadness at Everton's failure in the 1934-35 season to get to Wembley following the Cup run which took the team to the sixth round, only to be beaten 2-1 by Bolton Wanderers. He remembered the season when Dean came bouncing back to fitness and with remarkable consistency played in 38 League games and scored 26 goals. Following the previous year's lack of success, Everton's worries were lessened to a great extent by Dean's continued availability. Absence of their centre-forward not only meant the loss of a star player, but also an excellent captain. Dean had been skipper since 1931 and his experience, good humour, fair play and inspiration were rare qualities, difficult to replace.

By 1934 most League clubs employed managers, posts which nevertheless had a limited authority compared with the wider role of their successors, who in today's football claim a far greater measure of independence, particularly from directors. In 1934 the Everton club continued its policy of operating without a manager, control of team affairs being left to the co-ordinate of secretary, directors, and to some extent the captain. Dean, therefore, was consulted on some aspects of team selection and general matters of policy connected with the playing side of the business. His knowledge and shrewd approach proved valuable assets to the administration, in addition to his obvious talents on the field of play.

During that period, however, managers were gradually assuming more power and influence. The example set by Arsenal's Herbert Chapman, whose successes as a manager became legend, obviously had some connection with this development. When Chapman died and George Allison was appointed as his successor it was reported that Allison's contract included a salary of £3000 per year – no mean sum in those days. But it has to be said, as most followers of soccer know, that being a manager of a League club was, and still is, an extremely insecure occupation.

Dean has no firm opinions on the subject of managers in football. During the major part of his career he never played with a club run by a manager. Everton, for example, won five championships and two FA Cup finals without the services of a manager. It was some 18 months after Dean left Everton that the club finally bowed to making a managerial appointment. Dean of course, knew many of the managers who were ex-players, some of whom he had admired on the field. One suspects that Dean, having been brought up in an environment where managers were taboo, did not see much necessity for them.

There were some managers whom it was suspected issued unsportsmanlike instructions to their players on how to stop men like Dean scoring goals. In the modern age there are managers who admit to giving such directions. In contrast to this there was a manager, Dean is pleased to recall, by the name of Johnny Cochrane of Sunderland, who following a game in which the Everton centre-forward scored three goals against the Roker Park side, presented Dean with a £5 note, commenting, 'That's for scoring the finest hat-trick I have ever seen.'

Everton appointed a manager in 1939. He was a former secretary of the club, and a man for whom Dean had little respect. That the first manager of the club should be this person brought expressions of regret from Dean. He alleges that his own reputation suffered under the autocratic administration which the man operated as secretary to the club. According to Dean the secretary preferred serious charges against him which were proved to be false. One accusation made by the secretary was that Dean neglected his duties as captain by indulging in persistent drunkenness; that he had been seen pub-crawling as far away as Blackpool as well as in the environs of Merseyside. The evidence was brought before the Chairman, Mr Cuff; and a hearing arranged. Dean was able to prove that on the dates on which it was alleged he was drunk he was actually attending meetings and other functions in the company of the Chairman! So Dean was cleared of all such charges, but he never forgave the secretary, whom he regarded as being deliberately malicious.

Following the incident of Dean being charged with drunken behaviour, it was discovered that a man who bore a striking resemblance to the Everton centre-forward had in fact been adopting the role of an imposter touring the pubs and generally taking advantage of the position. Of course, it was not the first time that a famous person had been abused in that way. However, Dean felt that the secretary was too anxious to exploit any gossip to slander him. According to most people associated with the Everton club this was the only sour relationship that Dean experienced in all the years he was at Goodison Park. Naturally, not having any particular regard for managers, Dean was not impressed with the appointment that was finally made at Everton!

In August 1934 Dean embarked on his twelfth full season as a professional footballer – his tenth with the Everton club. He was then 27 years of age and although he had suffered a crop of injuries, many of major proportions, the previous season had been the first in his career during which he had appeared in less than 25 League games. It had also been the first season in which he had scored less than 21 goals. Such consistency was indeed remarkable. He was to go on in the 1934-35 period to play 38 League matches and 5 Cup games, in all of which he captained the Everton side. The team did not win any trophies but the results were relatively successful, the club finishing 8th in Division One with 44 points and reaching the 6th round of the FA Cup.

Dean's preoccupation with the captaincy may well have affected his goal-scoring habits. The role of captain was, however, one in which he mellowed and became a vintage wine in a sense, his performances so mature that they were savoured by soccer connoisseurs and never failed to excite or whet the appetite of all followers of the game. Dean gave a great deal of his attention to team work, but individually provided more opportunities for his colleagues to score goals and generally demonstrated an astute football brain in all that he did. Nevertheless, by any standards, his ability to score goals continued to be exceptional, maintaining as he did an average of almost one goal per match. His return to fitness was reflected in the team's vast improvement during that particular season.

The FA Cup run provided almost as exciting a venture as the club had ever experienced – even including their Wembley triumph in 1933. The 4th round replay against Sunderland in 1935 will be talked about as long as English football is played. It has been described as the match of the century – some say the most thrilling and skilful soccer match of all time. Archie Ledbrooke and Edgar Turner in their book *Soccer from the Pressbox* devote a whole chapter to the Everton v Sunderland Cup replay of 1935. They say among other things . . .

> . . . it is difficult to believe that any other first-class game has combined good football, dramatic incident, and full scoring in such abundance. Although Dean did not score any of the goals, Dean's job that day was more to marshal the attack than score goals himself.

There seems little doubt that this game was appreciated far beyond the boundaries of Merseyside and the Wear, and will go down as one of the classic games in the annals of football.

Sunderland's team in 1935 was regarded as one of the best in the land. In particular the forward line played skilful attacking football which matched the reputation of the great Everton forward line. In January 1935 when meeting Everton in the 4th round of the Cup at Roker Park they were second in the Division One table with their opponents only three points behind lying sixth. Soccer fans regarded the draw as the best tie of the 4th round and all anticipated a classic duel. Alas, it turned out to be a disgrace of a football match, tempers more in evidence than skill. During the game Dean had his shorts ripped off and had to go off the field for a new pair. On form or not, Dean was always treated as a danger man, and opponents seemed prepared to adopt desperate measures against him. In attempting to head a ball Dean could outleap most, and tugging at his shorts was a commonplace tactic to impede him, often resulting in him having to renew that essential part of his attire.

In the Sunderland match his pants were ripped to shreds. It was January, and frosty. Cold enough, according to Dean's account of the incident, for brass monkeys to complain. He walked to the touchline making, he says, unsuccessful efforts to pull his short shirt (he always had a few inches taken off his shirts) over the parts he was reluctant to have exposed to the women whom he could see scattered in the crowd at that side of the ground. 'Not,' Dean drily remarks, 'that I had much to cover up – it was so bloody cold, you understand!' A Geordie woman sitting in the front of the stand, however, stared with great fascination and suddenly called out, 'Ye buggar to heel man, isn't it funny!' Whilst Dean was in the act of changing his shorts the attention of the peeping Toms was diverted to witness Everton score the vital goal which produced the 1-1 draw and so earn the Merseysiders the replay at Goodison Park. Cunliffe, Everton's clever inside-forward, had volleyed the ball home from a free kick taken by Britton.

The Cup replay against Sunderland took place on the afternoon of January 30 1935 before 59,213 spectators. The ground at Goodison could have held many more but due to control problems many thousands were left outside. When the teams came out on to the pitch the referee called up both teams and lectured the captains on the necessity of maintaining discipline among their players. He warned them that he would not stand for the nonsensical behaviour which had occurred in the game at Sunderland. This appeared to have a salutary effect, for the game was played in a fine sportsmanlike manner and produced highly skilful football performed at a great pace throughout. One outstanding feature of the play was that the ball scarcely left the ground and out of the ten goals the game finally produced, not one was scored with the head.

Fifteen minutes from the end Everton were leading 3-1. Then Connor scored for Sunderland to make it 3-2, thus halting some fans who were making their way towards the exits. With only seconds to go came the goal of the match. Gurney, the Sunderland inside-forward, was ten yards out, with his back to the Everton goal, when the ball came across to him at shoulder height. Gurney somersaulted to make an overhead kick. He heard the crowd respond to the goal he had scored but did not see himself. The ball went into the net like a rocket, leaving the Everton goalkeeper Sagar helpless. The score was 3-3, and immediately the final whistle was blown.

Extra time was ordered and during this period the thrills multiplied, growing more intense with four more goals, three for Everton and one for Sunderland. The final score was 6-4 for Everton, with Dean not credited with one goal! He had, nevertheless, led his men brilliantly, and participated in a match which on Merseyside at least will never be forgotten. The six Everton goals came from three players. Coulter on the left wing scored a hat-trick, Geldard on the right netted two goals, and Stevenson one. It was revealed that Coulter, who scored in extra time, had played in a semi-conscious condition for the last half-hour after heading the ball. The crowd had its money's worth not only in the witnessing of the game but also in the pleasure of its memory in later years.

If an Everton supporter is questioned about what he thinks was the most memorable match in the club's history, it's odds-on that he will decide on the 1935 Cup replay with Sunderland. Even if he was born a generation later, his forbears having described the event to him, he will say that that was the historic occasion Everton will always remember. No doubt the story will continue to be passed on in legendary fashion. Dean, of course, would wish that he had been on the score sheet, but can take credit for his share – he was captain of the victorious Everton side. Strangely enough Everton had beaten Grimsby Town in the previous round of the Cup by scoring six goals, and Dean was not on the score sheet in that game either.

In those days Goodison Park was a venue for quite a number of international matches, much more often than it is today. One week after the Sunderland game, England met Ireland at the Everton ground. The England team contained no less than five Arsenal players with only one Everton player, although the Merseyside club, with three men in the Irish team, were well represented on the field. Dean was not even considered for the England team. He had played his last game for his country at the age of 25. He was never to play for England again, despite the fact that he was still the most dangerous centre-forward in the First Division, continuing to score goals at a rate of almost one per game. It was anticipated that Dean might have been selected for the Ireland match because when internationals were played in a provincial town it was usual to pick an outstanding local player to give a boost to the attendance. The matches were always arranged to be played mid-week, which meant an afternoon kick-off as there were no floodlights to facilitate later starting times.

The economic problems in 1935 continued to provide a drab backcloth to life. Soccer remained as an essential safety valve in diverting attention from the grimmer aspects of existence which masses of people had to endure. The 'means test', a method whereby unemployed members of the community were subjected to the grossest indignities to obtain what was a lower than subsistence rate for their families' survival, continued to be justified by politicians, although some from all parties did condemn the procedure as brutal and barbarous. Men were driven to spend a shilling of the pittance they received in benefit (money perhaps that should have been spent on their families) to attend a football match in an attempt to uplift their spirits, a habit which no doubt restrained them from a severe reaction against a society which imposed such inhuman conditions. Some politicians who supported the 'means test' condemned the unemployed who dared to spend money watching football matches, accusing them of indulging in an extravagant and irresponsible pursuit! The fools did not realise that soccer was a morale booster which possibly helped to save the country from civil unrest, particularly under the savage conditions of the time. But it appeared that some moralising members of the establishment were blinkered when it came to comprehending such aspects.

Another diversion of the time was the extensive news coverage given to murders and other crimes which seemed to provide morbid interest for the masses of people who read the popular press. The thirties produced many sophisticated crimes involving lengthy court hearings for the accused, and these roused public interest on a scale which has probably not been seen since. There was much else going on both in Britain and the rest of the world to attract the public interest. Speed records were regularly being broken by machines on land and in the air. A man named Hore-Belisha was, however, reforming transport conditions on the roads of Britain, introducing for the first time a speed limit of 30mph for cars; Lawrence of Arabia was killed riding a powerful motorcycle when he was involved in an accident on a country road in the south of England; Mussolini was occupying Abyssinia through aggression – an event which alerted the world to the dangers of fascism; purges were being conducted on a murderous scale by Stalin in Russia. In Britain the year was rounded off with a General Election which returned a National Government.

Although some improvements in the economy were being announced, a great measure of insecurity existed which haunted the majority of the population collectively and individually. The professional footballer was no exception and although relatively well paid he had no future when his playing days were over, a stage usually reached in his late twenties. He had no training for other employment and even a highly successful player could not save enough to assure for his future security. Serious injury was the most frightening prospect for most professional footballers. A benevolent fund existed, but this could only afford to pay token payments to players in extreme distress. Dean appeared in matches arranged to raise money for the benevolent fund. He gave his services free, but he says he has never benefited from the fund, even in his retirement. The intense competition in soccer was a root cause of insecurity, no different perhaps from that which existed in industry. In football even a good performance in one match did not always ensure a place in the team for the following fixture. Without doubt it was a precarious profession.

Dean, with a wife and family to support, was sufficiently realistic to know that within a few seasons or even sooner he would be replaced. Everton were already searching for a deputy for him and although his skills had not diminished, the number of injuries he had sustained were taking their toll. Only his exceptional physical constitution, his tenacity and perseverance, had kept him going, plus of course a consistent combination of outstanding ability and experience in the position he occupied.

But in the competitive labour market, like his fellow professionals, Dean knew he would find it most difficult to find alternative employment when his career in football ended. And he had to face the fact that such clouds were on the horizon. He had no ambitions of entering the main opening for ex-players, that of management, an occupation even more hazardous than the playing side of the business. Dean, however, reflecting the common outlook of the times, accepted the hazardous prospects and thought of them as bridges to be crossed only when he actually came to them.

Warney Cresswell, the Everton full-back and long-time colleague of Dean, was a player who had given outstanding service to his club. In 1935 he was aware that the twilight of his career had arrived and he turned his thoughts to going in for management. Tranmere Rovers had announced that Bert Cooke, their secretary for almost 20 years was to be sacked and Cresswell was tipped to take over as manager. Dean, recalling his experience of Cooke, had some uncomplimentary comments to make about the Tranmere secretary, and expressed approval of the club's decision. But, despite the faults that Dean adduced to Cooke's administration, it could not be denied that under Cooke's direction Tranmere had produced two of the most distinguished centre-forwards in football history. He had also turned out many other players of outstanding ability. In addition to Dean and Waring there was Ellis Rimmer, the Sheffield Wednesday international outside-left (a Birkenhead lad who played with Dean at Tranmere) remembered as the hero of the Wednesday team that won the FA Cup in 1935. Rimmer had the distinction of scoring in every round, including two goals in the final.

Other players to emerge during Cooke's reign at Tranmere were 'Bunny' Bell and 'Nibbler' Ridding, both of whom made their reputations as centre-forwards in First Division football. With the sale of all those players Bert Cooke assisted substantially in the continued solvency of Tranmere. At the time of the sacking of Cooke, other troubles occurred in the Third Division club. Allegations involving club finances were made by one director against another, resulting in a court case.

Warney Cresswell's ambitions to become manager at Tranmere were apparently thwarted by the fact that Everton would not release him without payment of a transfer fee which no doubt Tranmere could not afford. It seemed that Everton suspected that Cresswell could take up a player-manager role and had this in mind when demanding a transfer fee. Cresswell did not get the job, but a few months later left Everton to manage Port Vale, the team from the Potteries.

Before Cresswell took up his new position, however, he joined the Everton party of players on a summer tour of Switzerland, making a return visit to the country which had so cordially welcomed the club in 1928. Dean and Cresswell were the only survivors in the Everton team who had gone on the previous tour. On that occasion the club had been received as champions of the English League and Dean acclaimed as the greatest goal-getter in the world of football. The Swiss had then accorded the team, and in particular Dean, a rousing welcome. The 1935 party of players included King, Williams, Jones, Britton, Gee, Thomson, Mercer, Geldard, Cunliffe, Stevenson, Stein, and Leyfield.

As usual with Everton's continental tours, the excursion was highly successful despite the team losing one match 2-3 against Basle. Everton's reputation was still high and the Swiss produced souvenirs of the club's history and reports were that these were in great demand throughout the country during the tour. Dean was given a rousing reception wherever he went. Off-duty in any public place he attracted crowds of autograph hunters and sightseers who followed him in the manner given to 'pop' stars and even indulged in chants of 'Dixie'. Dean accepted it all with his usual modesty and aplomb.

The Swiss fixtures involved playing against sides of varying quality, a feature of almost every continental tour Everton had conducted. In one game under floodlights the English club won 10-1 which wasn't bad, considering it was the team's first experience of performing under such conditions. Dean recorded a hat-trick, the first he had ever scored with a white ball. The white ball was essential he says, because the lighting left a great deal to be desired. The Swiss were, however, very keen to develop the use of this new aid to soccer, a progressive attitude which was a long time coming to the minds of the administrators of English football. The use of the white ball was not legalised in Britain until 1951.

The tour was marred by an accident to Stein, who sustained a broken leg in the first match. He was admitted to hospital and spent the rest of the tour there. He was well cared for, but it was a tragic blow not only to Stein but also to the club, which could ill afford injuries to any of its players. No other injuries occurred to the players, but the incident served as a strong reminder to the Everton directors that they still had to find a deputy for Dean. Although Dean was now restored to fitness, the risk of injury to him continued to plague their minds. The search for an understudy would be intensified, but where would one be found? It was to be another 18 months before the club succeeded in its quest, and as it turned out, the wait was well worth it – a thought generously expressed by Dean himself!

19 Injury Strikes Again

EVERTON'S OPENING FIXTURE of the season was at home to Derby County, a team of much talent, which included a number of well-known international players, and was well fancied to take honours of one sort or another during the coming season. The Derby line-up included Sammy Crooks, Dally Duncan, and Hughie Gallagher – the latter a centre-forward of high class and one of the few that could be compared with Dean. Everton won the game 4-0 before 44,000 spectators and such a convincing victory naturally raised high hopes for a successful season. Dean scored the opening goal with a fine shot and George Green, the *Liverpool Echo* cartoonist, described it as 'an old Everton custom'. When Dean was on top, so were Everton. Another feature of the game was the performance of a new player 'Dusty' Miller, an inside-forward who had laid on three of Everton's four goals. So supporters, club officials, and players brimmed over with confidence at the prospect of success. Like many similar situations in the past, alas, it was not to be as expected. Quite the contrary in fact.

The season was only one week old when Everton played their old rivals Liverpool in a derby game at Anfield and were thrashed 6-0. Not only was it the most humiliating defeat the Goodison men had ever suffered at the hands of their neighbours, but in the process Dean was injured and had to leave the field during the first half. McDougal, the Liverpool defender, had stamped on Dean's foot with such force that the centre-forward's toe was broken. Dean alleges that it was no accident, the foul being deliberate. Nevertheless, Dean returned in the second half (there were no substitutes allowed) and bravely attempted to play some part in redeeming the position for his side, which had been losing 4-0 at the interval. It was obvious he was in great pain and limping so badly he was unlikely to finish the game. Eventually he went off 15 minutes before the end. Few players would have survived as long as that but such dourness was typical of the man. He always kept going, a characteristic which drew the admiration of spectators almost as much as the skills which endeared him to them. Dean had his toe in splints for some weeks and did not play again until the middle of October. In the meantime Everton suffered further defeats and for a considerable period lay perilously situated at the bottom of the League table.

It seemed that as a result of Dean's injury posterity has been denied a visual record of the great man's wizardry in kicking, dribbling and, in particular, heading a football. Just after his injury it was announced that the Football Association, in liaison with the Gaumont Film Company, was in the process of producing a film (on the subject of soccer) with the cooperation of League clubs in various regions of the country. Production had commenced twelve months earlier and the film unit was about to visit Goodison Park to take action shots of four Everton stars. The idea was to cover all aspects of play – kicking, heading, passing, and some tactics. Dean was the undisputed master of heading a football and as the film was to be used for instructional purposes, mainly to aid schools and clubs, Dean's skills in that direction could scarcely be omitted. But he was unable to participate (due to his injury) and this would prove a great loss for posterity. One would have thought that in producing a film of that kind the sponsors would have ensured that only the best would be filmed. To record Dean in action was essential, even if they had to wait. But Dean never even saw the camera crew, or the producers, or indeed the film when it was completed! One wonders what happened to that piece of celluloid? Is it hidden away somewhere in our sporting archives?

Dean's absence caused Everton to try out a number of players at centre-forward, including the old standby Tommy White, and a new player, Harthill, recently imported from the Midlands, was brought into the position. But Everton continued to struggle around the bottom of the table. After ten matches the club had conceded 26 goals and scored only 13. Dean was declared fit to return to the Everton team against Chelsea on October 19. Chelsea were doing rather well and were certainly no pushover, but Everton beat them 5-1. Dean's presence was a tremendous boost to the team's confidence. The maestro scored a great goal with his head, providing the sort of inspiration that team and spectators alike found most welcome. However, it was clear that Dean took care not to use his feet too much but supplied adequate compensation by using his head to great effect. Even a man of Dean's courageous character was justifiably tentative about the healing of a broken bone.

During that period the Everton team had the misfortune to

have three players injured and the forward line was frequently changed, thus becoming rather ragged. Just before Christmas, Dean was considered to be out of form and was sensationally dropped from the team. In his defence the local Press argued that working with a forward line that lacked co-ordination, any centre-forward would appear to be out of form. Early in the New Year Dean was brought back to the side and again began scoring goals. Everton consequently made a fair recovery, escaping the relegation zone and finishing the season in 16th position, something which at one time appeared to be beyond their highest expectations. No doubt the club also drew some consolation from the fact that their neighbours at Anfield finished three places below them in 19th position!

Despite the recovery and the satisfaction of escaping relegation, the season was full of disappointments, proving a sad period for Everton. Tom McIntosh, the club's beloved secretary, died – a tragic loss not only for Everton but for Dean in particular. Tom had been like a father to Dean, establishing a warm and friendly relationship which had commenced on the day, over 10 years earlier when, in the Woodside Hotel, Birkenhead, McIntosh first met the young centre-forward and signed him for Everton. Dean says that McIntosh was highly respected by all the players. He adds that sometimes solace is gained, and the mourning relieved in such cirumstances, if the successor continues to hold and apply some of the qualities of the lost predecessor. But in Dean's view the appointment of Theo Kelly to the secretary's post was an event which only served to make the death of Tom McIntosh an even greater tragedy. Dean was still club captain and as such had to work closely with the secretary. The secretary's post at Everton loosely combined the role of manager, because the club still refused to follow the fashion of most League clubs and designate a 'manager' as such. Kelly was appointed in February 1936 at a time when Dean had just returned to the side after being dropped from the first team. But Dean says there was no significance in this.

Dean's position at Everton during that period was subject to much speculation in the Press. His name was being linked with a transfer to Heart of Midlothian. There was, however, no truth in the story. No doubt this kind of gossip led to the manager of Blackpool approaching Dean and making him a very attractive offer to move to the seaside club. Dean went off immediately to see Mr Cuff the Everton Chairman and inform him of the meeting. The Chairman told Dean that he was wanted at Everton and as far as he was concerned William Ralph Dean was part of the Everton club and it was intended that he should remain there for life, even when his playing days were over. Of course, Dean's playing days were not yet over. His contribution to the Everton revival in the latter part of the 1935-36 season had been invaluable. In the penultimate match against Birmingham, Dean scored a hat-trick, a performance which was described as brilliant and as good as anything he had ever done. But once again injury struck. During the game a Birmingham defender, when challenging Dean in the air, had come down heavily, striking Dean's back and fracturing the great man's shoulder blade. But Dean carried on in that game giving further demonstration of his exceptionally strong constitution. It was thought in fact that he would be available for the final match of the season against Preston which was to be played one week later!

What an important game that could have been for Dean. Following his hat-trick against Birmingham it was discovered that he required only one goal to equal the great Steve Bloomer's long-standing record of 352 League goals, the highest total achieved by any footballer during a professional career. It had taken Steve Bloomer 22 seasons to reach that figure and here was Dean, after only 13 full seasons, ready to break that record. Leslie Edwards, the *Liverpool Echo* sportswriter, arranged for Bloomer (who was retired from football) to come up to Liverpool and watch Everton's next game against Preston in order that he might witness Dean either equal the record, or even break it. The Everton team announced in Edward's column the evening before the match included Dean's name. But due to injury Dean was not allowed to play and it was a disappointed party (which included Dean and Edwards) that met Steve Bloomer at Central Station Liverpool on the day of the match. So was lost another climax to an exciting chapter in the phenomenal football life of this man Dean. Although many thousands of spectators were disappointed at being denied witnessing an historic soccer event they were nevertheless consoled by an Everton victory of 5-0 over Preston.

In an interview after the game Bloomer, a great sportsman, expressed regret that Dean had been unable to play – a factor which had denied him the purpose of his visit. Bloomer emphasised, no doubt bearing in mind the gossip about Dean's decline, that Dixie was still the finest centre-forward and had many years of good football left. Praise of Dean's amazing skills poured from Bloomer (a man who knew what football was all about) thus providing, for the record, reliable testimony to Dean's greatness. Steve knew, however, that inevitably Dean would break that record.

Everton's search for an understudy to Dean continued and to that end the club had signed on 'Bunny' Bell, the Tranmere Rovers centre-forward, who had distinguished himself earlier in that season by scoring nine goals for Rovers in a Third Division game against Oldham Athletic. Although Bell had some good games for Everton (he deputised for Dean in the Preston game and scored) he was not really the understudy Everton were looking for. Tommy White, perhaps the most versatile player Everton or any other club ever had, often proved the best deputy for Dean. But even White was not always available because he seemed so busy taking up the stand-in for other positions and his availability for the centre-forward berth was therefore limited. Dean praises White as one of the greatest all-round players he ever knew.

When talking about the animosity between himself and the secretary, Dean says that White also had good reason to dislike Theo Kelly. Indeed, Dean alleges, Kelly once threatened to stop White's benefit. This resulted in an altercation between White and Kelly which ended in fisticuffs. Dean, who never once lost his temper on the football field, admits that he had occasion to strike Kelly when arguing over an administrative threat which had been made to him. Dean alleges that the secretary's policy was to try and get rid of the long-serving players only for the purpose of establishing greater autocracy, which the older players tended to resist. Dean appears to intensify his criticism when talking of Kelly and makes such caustic remarks as 'He didn't even know what shape the ball should be!' Such difficulties and clashes of personalities no doubt arise in every football club, but it did seem in those days that many administrators were employed who ought to have had a greater knowledge of the game they were serving. Nevertheless, Kelly holds the distinction of being appointed as the first official manager of Everton, an innovation made following the club's championship win in 1939, the last full season before the war. Kelly was subsequently to revert to the Secretary's job when Cliff Britton, a former player, became Everton's manager in the late 1940s.

The end-of-season tour of the continent which the Everton club traditionally arranged, was, in 1936, destined for Germany. Because of Dean's injury the party did not include him.

Perhaps it was as well. Last time Everton toured Germany in 1932 the Nazis were in the process of assuming power. In 1936 the Hitler regime was well established and subjecting all sport, including football, to political controls. Most people will remember the Olympic Games held in Germany that summer, and the nasty political and unsporting discourtesies which Nazi leaders indulged in throughout the events. When Dean had toured Germany with the Everton team four years previously he had been involved in an incident concerning the observation of Nazi salutes. He would not be there this time and therefore would escape from such embarrassments. However, it has to be said that the Everton tour, according to all the reports received from those who did go, was a great success.

As soon as he was fit, Dean spent the summer playing baseball and indeed was to represent England at this game before the football season resumed at the end of August. His baseball activities attracted much attention. Dean had joined the Caledonians, a Liverpool baseball club, one of many that made the game popular throughout the North West of England in the thirties. The game was perhaps less popular in the South but London's Harringay fielded a very good side and in a challenge match played in London in 1936 defeated Caledonians 16-7. Dean was a member of the defeated team but reports of the game in the Press praised Dean's skills. 'Dixie Dean made three hits and took two splendid catches, pleasing all the critics with his display.' Dean was later selected for the England team which met 'The Yankees', an all-American baseball side, at the White City Stadium in the Summer of 1936. Dean is very proud of the medal he holds to commemorate the event.

20   Record Goal Crop

PRE-SEASON TRAINING started in July and although Dean was usually the first player to report, one or two others beat him to it in 1936. Such a break with tradition was due to Dean's preoccupation with baseball that summer. The Everton officials were more than pleased, however, with how well and fit Dean was when he did report. Dean was entering his twelfth full season in the service of the club and as captain and centre-forward he held a fair measure of responsibilities, which of course required him to be in the peak of physical condition. The pre-season practice matches were played, each of which attracted the usual 10,000 spectators. In the second of these matches Dean suffered a split eyebrow sustained in a heading duel with Walkden, a new centre-half who had been signed in the close season. Compared with the more serious injuries with which he had been afflicted, this seemed but a minor calamity, but it would be a great tragedy if the injury prevented him from playing. Dean was on the threshold of establishing new goal-scoring records, apart from the fact that his club depended on his services in so many other directions. Fortunately his eye injury proved no real handicap, and he was declared fit to play in the opening fixture.

The first match was an away fixture against Arsenal, the famous London side, and this presented a situation which provided for a number of strange coincidences. Dean had made his debut for Everton in a match against Arsenal in March 1925. He was then a raw lad of eighteen. In May 1928 Arsenal were the side against whom he scored that memorable hat-trick to complete 60 goals in a season – a feat which created an all-time record for the First Division. Now, just over eleven years after his debut, Dean had the opportunity to equal or break the 22-year-old record established by Steve Bloomer, who had scored 352 goals during a career which stretched over a period from 1892 to 1914. And once again Arsenal were the team against whom Dean was poised to make further soccer history. The London side was at that time a team of internationals enjoying a success never matched in the annals of British football. But as captain, and a remarkably unselfish and loyal club man, Dean was only concerned about the result of the match, always ready to subordinate his individual aims for the good of his beloved Everton. His team were going to win if possible and Dean was determined that his own ambitions would not divert him from that purpose. His team colleagues would readily testify to that.

The prospect of Dean creating another goal-scoring record no doubt helped to increase the size of the attendance the Arsenal game attracted, and the sporting Press had kept the pot boiling by their eager anticipation. The special interest in Dean did not deter both teams serving up a brilliant and exciting game, which Arsenal won 3-2. The irrepressible Dean scored to equal the Bloomer record, with the goal appropriately coming from his priceless head. Coulter took a free kick which found Dean's curly mop for the great man to glide the ball superbly into the net. Dean was given a rousing ovation by the Arsenal crowd, warm congratulations from the players and, of course, the referee, who was none other than Lol Harper, the man who was in charge of the game against Arsenal in 1928 when Dean scored his 60th goal. Another coincidence!

According to Dean, Harper was the most respected referee of the period. He was a man for whom players and spectators alike held a deep affection. At that point in time, in 1936, the Football Association were expressing serious concern about the development of rough play on the field, which prompted the issue of an edict to referees and clubs urging greater discipline and control. Harper's name was one that was generally accepted need not be included to receive the FA instructions on the subject of control. Harper was regarded as a prince of referees, scarcely ever being criticised for his handling of a soccer match. Dean describes his first experience of observing Harper's approach. Dean explains that following an incident between two players, tempers flared and Harper called the two men to him, gave them a fatherly talk, and admonished them. But as the players walked away Harper recalled them, only to present each with a peppermint, a supply of which Harper always carried. 'Suck on that and forget your animosity', Harper sweetly advised. Dean adds, 'the curious thing was that somehow this approach successfully calmed the situation, no doubt because Harper had such a wonderful personality and communicated easily with the player.' One is left to wonder what measure of success a referee would have in cooling a situation by offering sweets to the antagonists in modern football?

Having equalled the Bloomer record, within a few days Dean had a further opportunity to pass the 352 goal mark. Everton's second match of the season was a mid-week fixture against Sheffield Wednesday at Goodison Park, and Everton supporters were keen to witness another historic event in the life of their idol. Over 50,000 were at the game and it seemed that almost as many photographers were in attendance. The cameramen surrounded the pitch anxiously waiting to discover which goal would be defended by Everton's opponents, so that they might occupy a suitable position to snap the immortal goal expected from Dean. The goal came, again from that magnificent head, and coincidently was almost a facsmile of the famous 60th coal. A corner kick, taken from the same spot as in 1928 floated over for Dean's magical head to connect and glide it home. The crowd erupted and the roar was reported to have been heard in the centre of Liverpool over three miles away. Even Dean, normally so undemonstrative, clutched his hands high in the air and leapt with joy. The sports writers used up their stock of superlatives to describe the goal including, 'He rose like a salmon to a fly!' September 2 1936 was a day to remember. Dean had scored 353 League goals in just over 12 full seasons in football, playing in only 379 games. What made it more remarkable was that 313 of those games were in the First Division of the Football League. A record and an average never to be surpassed. Moreover, his football career had not by any means ended. Dean's record is made even more exceptional when it is considered that it was achieved in the face of the enormity of injuries he received, which he so bravely overcame during the making of it. When he was absent for weeks through injury he was usually back to form immediately he returned to the team, and for five of those seasons he also did a captain's job – a duty he never once neglected.

Many reporters descended upon Dean for interview immediately after the game with Sheffield Wednesday. Those who did not already know Dean expressed their astonishment at the modesty of the man. Of course, the breaking of the record brought out the usual comment and analysis from sports critics and commentators. Comparisons were made between the differing situations which faced Bloomer in achieving his record and whether or not Dean's task had been made easier by the changes in the offside laws in 1925, a factor it was felt that had subsequently simplified the task of goal-scoring. On the other hand Bloomer had taken 22 seasons to collect 352 goals, compared to Dean's 12 seasons, 9 of which were played the First Division. The arguments about the merits of goal-scoring by different generations of players will no doubt go on, and opinions will vary *ad infinitum*. But the fact is that of all the men who have played since 1925, not one has come near to emulating Dean's records.

Analysis can show that goal-scoring, either on a club or individual, basis, has followed such a varied pattern that almost any theory which can be conceived can be proved. As with most statistics, many conflicting assessments emerge, often suiting whatever answer is desired. For example, in modern soccer the alleged scarcity of goals causes some concern and reference is often made to Dean's 60 goals in a season as being the figure which even First Division champion *teams* are not now expected to exceed. But do these alarmists know, for instance, that Derby County, runners-up in Division One in 1936, scored only 63 goals? Moreover, between 1928 and 1937 only eleven first Division teams exceeded a total of more than 100 goals in a season, whereas between 1956 and 1959 seven teams passed the century mark in Division One. Arsenal exceeded the 100 goal mark three times during the thirties, at a time when defensive tactics were being developed so intensely. Since 1892, out of all the clubs scoring more than 100 goals in a season, none, with the exception of Everton, have produced a player to record as many League goals as Dean as a share of those totals. So whatever comparisons may be made in relation to conditions which existed at any particular time, one thing is certain – Dean's prolific goal scoring was something more than exceptional.

December 1936 was an eventful month for the nation. One major and traumatic event was the abdication of King Edward VIII, which caused a constitutional crisis unprecedented in modern England. Football was, of course, much less important an issue, but at the same time as the country solved the crisis by passing the Constitutional Amendment Bill which provided for the Duke and Duchess of York's accession to the throne, Everton appointed an heir to a monarch who had reigned for many years. On December 31, only a few days after the nation appointed a new Sovereign, Everton signed a boy named Tommy Lawton from Burnley to inherit Dixie Dean's throne. Their long search was over at last.

It was intended that the Lawton boy would be Dean's understudy. After a few weeks in the reserves the signs were clear that Lawton would be everything the Everton directors had been searching for. To understudy a star like Dean must have been an unnerving experience for any youngster. Fortunately for Lawton, perhaps, he was helped by Dean's generous nature, which was devoid of the usual petty jealousies that often govern the relationships of stars and their understudies. Dean went out of his way to encourage the lad, even arranging such extramural activities as heading practice and other special types of training, the master offering all his knowledge and experience without let or hindrance.

Dean says Lawton was blessed with much talent. Indeed, many observers of the youngster made the comment, 'It was just like seeing Dean arrive once again as he did in 1925.' Lawton however, was not ready to take over, and even if he had been he could hardly have replaced Dean, who was turning on performances to match anything he had ever done in his early days, and on many occasions during the 1936-37 season even surpassed some of the brilliant displays of the past.

Even after 13 seasons and at 30 years of age, Dean was still the marked man of English football, attracting the attention of opposing defences no less than in his former years. As a result he continued to suffer injuries, but during this particular season he was never out of the side for more than one game at a time. He played in 36 out of the 42 matches despite having to cope with half-a-dozen injuries during the season. He had suffered the loss of two cartilages, had damaged both ankle bones, and his legs were scarred and bruised, the marks of years of rough treatment, yet he went on to score 24 goals in 36 games.

On November 7 1936 Dean played his 400th League game and celebrated it with a hat-trick against West Bromwich Albion. In those 400 games he had netted 362 goals. Another League record and also one for the club. He had registered 335 goals for one club. Sports writers raved about Dean's exhibition of centre-forward play. In the West Brom game one of Dean's goals came from a penalty (which has been referred to elsewhere) and the goalkeeper punched the ball out, but Dean's reflexes, undiminished by time, were so quick that he coolly ran forward nodding the ball back, out of the goalkeeper's reach, into the net.

Everton met Sunderland at Goodison Park on February 6 1937, a fixture which continued to attract intense interest following the memorable Cup replay between the two sides in 1935. In this 1937 game Dean served up a model of centre-forward play, unsurpassed by him in his long career in soccer. And some people were writing him off as finished

– definitely past his best! Detailed reports of the game published in the *Liverpool Echo* and *Daily Post* provide for the record some evidence of Dean's scintillating display.

Modern football enthusiasts too easily swallow the myth that soccer in the thirties was stereotyped and barren of ideas; that only present-day football has developed sophisticated methods and flexibility. For example, they point to Di Stefano, the Real Madrid and Spanish international player, as the paragon of modern centre-forward play, a view with which Dean himself agrees. the report of Dean's magnificent exhibition of football in the Sunderland match could quite easily be mistaken for one about Di Stefano who, 30 years afterwards, produced similar displays of skill, except perhaps that Dean had a greater capacity for scoring goals. On numerous occasions during that game Dean was defending in his own goalmouth, heading away corner kicks, yet moments later up in the front line attacking his opponents' goal, dribbling, spraying passes equally with head or foot, and generally demonstrating all the attributes of a superstar forward of the modern post-war era.

In this match Dean scored two goals, one of which was particularly outstanding, even measured by his own high standards. He had just been helping out in his own penalty area when he gathered the ball on the right in his own half of the field. With great dash and superb control Dean feinted to move one way but went in another direction, selling a beautiful dummy, causing two opposing players a dilemma of direction, and he then took an oblique path towards goal. Suddenly, from over 30 yards, he released a rocket of a shot with his right foot. The ball fairly sizzled as if projected from the muzzle of a bazooka, crashing into the far corner of the rigging, leaving Mapson, the Sunderland goalkeeper, astonished and utterly helpless. The ball had entered the net without any curve in its flight trajectory, as in usual with long shots of this kind, and Dean's seemingly jet-propulsed drive must have been one of the most powerful and explosive shots ever seen on a football field, even making a Bobby Charlton blinder look like a pass back to the goalkeeper. A visual action replay would have to be made to confirm the truth of how that goal was scored. Spectators who attended the game continue to refer to it as incredible.

The sportswriters who witnessed the Dean goal inevitably rapturised about its great merit. One wrote 'It would find the highest place in Dean's records long after he had given up football.' What a pity it couldn't have been recorded visually. It was, of course, a suitably crowning effort for one of the most remarkable displays of football skill produced by an individual player. The critics were unanimous in their praise – never had they seen Dean in a more effervescent mood, combining dash, dribbling, kicking, and heading power of rare character. It was incredible to think that the man was then 30 years of age, and what's more he had suffered so many injuries after playing continuously in top class soccer for a period of 14 seasons.

When one analyses football, past and present, it is an exercise which inevitably involves a whole variety of comparisons in respect of conditions and relative standards, often producing subjective conclusions. It is not surprising that varied opinions emerge on what is regarded as change or otherwise in the game, even when making assessments within one decade or a period of several. Some may look back 50 years and gain the impression that football in the twenties was an entirely different game. Those who are old enough to have actually witnessed the football scene continuously over the last half-century would no doubt support the view that any changes perceived stem only from differences in style and approach; that there is still room even in the modern game for a player of exceptional skill to defy managerial control and stamp his personality on the sport, the bounds of which remain fundamentally the same today as ever they were.

In attempting to get the history of soccer into perspective, one is reminded so often of the old adage that there's nothing new under the sun. In the football context an event reported in 1937 serves to highlight this. A report in the sports pages of the Press told of a book sale at Sothebys, the London Art dealers, at which a rare book, described as the 'first book on football' was sold for £2-10s. The book, entitled *Gioco del Calcio*, was stated to have been printed in Florence in 1580 and dealt with a game closely resembling modern football. What was meant by 'modern football'? The period from 1888 to 1937?

When reflecting on something like a 350-year-old comparison a different kind of image and perspective is projected. It is reasonable to predict that the distinctions modern writers may draw between the football of 1930 and the football of 1976 will not be interpreted as such by football historians 200 years hence. Posterity will probably see the game as fundamentally the same from 1926 to a date (whenever it does actually change) which most certainly will be post-1977!

Having said that, which is prompted by comparisons with Dean's outstanding display against Sunderland in 1937, it is of interest to remember that Everton was at the time nursing, as understudy to Dean, a player who blossomed into a centre-forward unquestionably accepted as belonging to the post-war era of 'modern football'. That player's name was Tommy Lawton, who was playing in the Everton first team during the latter part of the 1936-37 season. Dean was in such good form that he could scarcely be discarded, and so Lawton was brought in to play at inside-forward and demonstrated his potential to no small degree.

It is interesting to look back on that time and read the names of both Dean and Lawton on the same score sheet of a number of matches during that season. Dean did suffer one or two minor injuries and his absence gave Lawton the opportunity to substitute at centre-forward, making it evident that it was his true position. It was one of those strange quirks of fate that at a time when Dean was playing so superbly, Everton should find the deputy they had been searching for. The Directors were obviously anxious to establish Lawton as the regular first-team man. But Dean, the idol of the Everton fans, was still shining brightly, and this presented the club with a dilemma of selection that they could well do without. Next season, however, was to produce a situation in which this dilemma, rather sadly for Dean, would be resolved.

Everton finished 17th in the First Division – one place lower than the previous season. Yet at the beginning the side had given strong indications of much greater achievement. Such are the fortunes of football. Perhaps the season's outstanding success in Division One was Charlton Athletic, a team that had climbed from the depths of the Third Division in successive seasons and in their first period in the top sphere gained the distinction of being runners-up to Manchester City for the championship. The point in making reference to this is the strange pattern revealed by the goal-scoring figures of both teams.

As champions Manchester City scored a total of 107 goals, but Charlton Athletic, runners-up only three points behind, registered a mere 58! In view of the fact that the story about Dean is predominantly concerned with the subject of goal-scoring during a period in which it is sometimes alleged scoring goals was all too easy, the inconsistencies thrown up by the two top teams in both 1936 and in 1937 are relevant. Sunderland and Derby had produced a similar situation in 1936.

The theories bandied about of the effects on goal-scoring brought about by the change in the offside law in 1925 tend to denigrate subsequent individual performances, particularly those of Dean. In defence of Dean and his contemporaries, such theories ought to be given closer examination. The example of two teams, Derby and Charlton, obviously success-ful, finishing as runners-up but scoring such a low total of goals, serves to illustrate that all-round goal abundance at that time is simply a myth. In fact throughout the history of First Division football from 1888 to the present day the average number of goals scored by teams in any season has consistently fluctuated, ranging between 1.3 and 1.9 goals per match. Proof perhaps that at no time have goals ever been easy or indeed ever in profusion.

When assessing Dean's contribution, it is revealed that he averaged over 0.9 of a goal per game throughout his career which means that he supplied on average 50% or more of the goals scored by his team in all the matches he played. Such analysis once more emphasises what an amazing record he achieved even when judged by the criteria of any period in the history of football. In 1936-37 Dean scored 24 goals in 36 League games. His grand total for his League career at the end of that season was 375 goals in 423 games. The aggregate included 37 hat-tricks.

It is worth explaining that a hat-trick in those days meant scoring three goals consecutively in one match. There is a tendency in the modern game to credit a player with a hat-trick if he scores three goals in a match regardless of whether the goals come consecutively. Dean's hat-tricks were the genuine type and the number he scored will probably stand as a record as long as League football is played.

Dean was credited with another hat-trick during 1936 which did not go down on the football score sheet. It was a family hat-trick – a trio of consecutive success much more important than the kind of success he had gained on the football field. This was scored when his wife presented him with a third son in September. And as the 1936-37 season was to be his last in top-class football, he would be very much more concerned with providing for his wife and sons in future than contemplating his scoring feats in soccer.

Although Dean was very much aware that his 14 years in soccer must in itself bear ominous signs that the curtain would soon fall on his career, he had no idea that it was in fact so imminent. Fairly secure in mind he went off on the 1937 close-season tour of Denmark which Everton had arranged, joining a party of fourteen players which included Morton,

Jackson, Cook, Jones, Britton, Gee, Mercer, Bentham, Gillick, Cunliffe, Stevenson, Coulter, and, not least, the young Lawton.

Dean did not play in all the games on that tour of Denmark, Lawton taking over at centre-forward for most of the fixtures. Lawton showed much prowess but Dean did not seem to worry too greatly about the prospect of the lad replacing him. Indeed, Dean took every opportunity to encourage the boy and unstintingly made available to him all the benefits of his vast experience. The tour was a great success, the club enhancing the already good reputation it held in that country.

During the team's absence on tour during May and June a number of important events occurred at home. There was the Coronation of the new King, George VI, and the nation celebrated with all the pomp and circumstance warranted by such an occasion. There were flags galore, street parties, coronation mugs, coronation fashions, and every conceivable function was arranged which could provide a basis for a general binge. The Everton players, of course, had their own private celebrations, and the Coronation was an additional excuse to indulge. Who could blame them?

There were still a couple of million people unemployed, even though the economy was at that time stimulated to some extent by an arms build-up, caused by the threatening war clouds which appeared on the horizon. The pageantry of the Coronation came as a colourful diversion in what was still a time of acute economic depression which, for those who thought about it, was worsened by the prospects of war. Dean had opened a sports shop in his home town of Birkenhead and the business prospered temporarily, but small shops did not guarantee much profit in those times. He says a schoolmaster bought £80 of equipment from him but failed to cough up the money when the bill was later presented. Dean never traced the man, and the debt had to be written off. The business finally closed, leaving him with no security for his post-playing days.

However, on the football front some major changes for the better were being arranged, the old diehards of the Football Association for once donning a more progressive coat than had been worn in the past. The FA had decided to legalise payment of talent money for players of clubs that registered success in League and Cup. For example, a Cup final team would be allowed to share talent money which would provide a princely bonus of £12 to each player. Reporters sarcastically drew attention to the generosity of such terms by referring to the 1937 Cup Final, when the clubs involved, Sunderland and

Preston, each received £5000 as their share of the gate. On that occasion each of the players had been paid the miserable sum of £8. Now players were to receive a further £12. For those who performed and entertained in a Cup final the combined rewards would be £440 out of takings of £10,000! Still, it was an improvement which showed the way to better things.

Another change of rule imposed by the FA was the introduction of the arc, or 'D' – an additional marking on the pitch to be made at the centre edge of the penalty area to show players where they could stand to ensure that they were at least ten yards from the penalty spot when a kick was taken. Rules were also changed to provide for a free kick to be taken inside the penalty area. In some ways this ought to have enhanced the prospect of scoring more goals. The weight of the ball used in international matches was also reviewed at that time and it was proposed this be increased from 14 to 16 ounces. With the all-leather ball then in use, increasing the weight presented more problems on wet pitches. Absorption of water could further add to the weight. In those days some players actually injured themselves when heading or even kicking a heavy ball in bad weather. But Dean's international days were over, and interest in the ball change from his point of view was purely academic.

21 End of an Era

WHEN DEAN TURNED UP for pre-season training in the autumn of 1937 he had little idea it would be the last time he would engage in such activities at Goodison Park. He was fit and well and armed with great experience and skill, so there was no apparent reason why he shouldn't continue with the Everton first team for at least another couple of seasons. He was still captain, and looked forward with keen interest to the opening fixtures. Everton had a first-class playing staff which included many internationals and prospects looked good. Alas, Everton were out of luck. Dean played in the first three games, all of which were lost. Indeed, Everton scored only one goal and had seven goals against them in that dismal trio of matches. In the third game against Blackpool, Dean had several teeth loosened in a collision with Finan, the seasiders' centre-forward. Although dazed, Dean carried on in the match and gave a brilliant performance. However, he was left out of the side in the following fixture, Lawton being promoted to the first team, where he occupied the centre-forward berth for the remainder of the season.

Dean recovered from the injury sustained in the third game, but was recalled to the first team on only two other occasions during rest of the season. The second and last occasion was an away game against Grimsby Town, a match which turned out to be Dean's very last appearance for Everton's senior side. One assumes that had it been known in advance that this game was to be Dean's final bow, a ceremony would have been arranged to administer the last rites both to commemorate and lament the event. It would be hard to find another player in the long history of the Everton club who rose to such eminence, who served more loyally, or consistently contributed so much to both the club and the game in general, as this man Dean. Such were the fortunes of a professional soccer player.

It is difficult to imagine that the administrators of the Everton club could possibly overlook the fact that when Dean played his last League game for the first team on October 23 1937 it was his 399th for the club and he only needed to appear once more to celebrate an anniversary which would most certainly have been a commercial attraction and a deserving tribute to the greatest player ever to serve at Goodison Park. It is odd that a man with such an outstanding record should be denied playing one more match in order to complete 400 League appearances and appropriately round off a wonderful career with the club.

In order to fully appreciate how thoughtless and ungrateful the administrators were in their attitude towards Dean it is pertinent to draw attention to the profits the man must have made for the club. This star centre-forward never ceased to be an attraction in every one of those 399 appearances with the Everton club. He must have added at least 5000 to the attendances of each matches he played in, which means Everton benefited to the tune of about two million extra paying spectators – a tidy sum of money! The situation remains a mystery. Dean did not quibble at the time, probably because he did not attach much importance to statistics. His attitude on this score was incredibly naive, but this was due perhaps to the fundamental modesty of the man.

In retrospect, his relegation to the reserve side was really ignominious, but he accepted the position without complaint, continuing to render his club great service even in that minor capacity. That the reserve side led the Central League by a considerable margin of points during the rest of the season was significant. The reserve team completed the season with a total of over 100 goals and won the championship of that League by a distance. Although Dean was to leave just prior to the end of the season, he was entitled to, and was duly awarded a championship medal.

The Central League included a majority of reserve teams from Division One clubs in the North and Midlands. Reserve sides of top Southern clubs played in the London Combination and each year a representative match was arranged between both Leagues. Dean was selected to play for the Central League against the London Combination in a match played at Newcastle on November 13 1937, and although his side lost 2-3 Dean scored one of the goals. The reports said that Dean gained little encouragement from his reserve colleagues and might have scored more goals had support been forthcoming. Nevertheless whilst in the reserves he made his mark and received all the honours that situation could offer.

Dean continued to lead the reserve team until the beginning of March 1938. 'Bunny' Bell, another of Everton's deposed centre-forwards, also played in the second string at inside to

Dean for most of that season. But whenever a substitute forward was required for the first team, Bell was selected and Dean ignored. Bell played well and it is no reflection on him to suggest that Dean ought to have had an opportunity to return to the senior eleven. Dean was resigned to the fact that Lawton was successfully occupying the throne from which he had been deposed and indeed Lawton ruled so effectively that he had become the leading scorer in the League. The first team, however, did not reflect the success of the young centre-forward, hovering for the greater part of the season rather perilously around the bottom six places in Division One.

The continuing absence of Dean's name on the first class soccer scene, in spite of the fact that he was available and showing much of his old skill, albeit in the reserve side, inevitably led to speculation about his future. Rumour and counter-rumour about his position circulated wildly on Merseyside. Dean was still the idol of thousands, and they demanded some official reassurance on what the future held for their hero. The club made repeated public statements that their intention was to retain Dean and he could be expected to remain with Everton, to end his football career at Goodison Park, an assurance which provided some satisfaction for all his admirers.

With such enunciations about Dean's future so firm in their minds, the proclamation made on March 11 1938 that Dean had been transferred to Notts County, a Third Division (South) club at a fee of £3000 hit the Merseyside soccer public like a bombshell. The local Press reacted by indulging in extensive comment on the decision. Some said that no football event, at least on Merseyside, had ever caused so much controversy. Many were intrigued by the transfer fee of £3000, coincidentally the precise sum Everton had paid for Dean in March 1925, exactly 13 years before. As inflation followed a modest path during those years, Everton were credited with pulling off the best deal in football history. The club had received 13 years priceless service from Dean and in the end this had involved no real outlay. Something like buying a Rolls Royce, running it for 13 years, obtaining more than the anticipated maximum mileage, then to re-sell it, and recover the whole of the purchase price! Dean, however, was not a piece of machinery, but an exceptional human being who proved to be more exceptional than any custom-built motor car!

Dean had been the greatest name in football for more than a decade, and news of his departure was more astonishing and sensational because of the contrary statements put out by the Everton club so shortly before the transfer. Following the announcement the Everton administration refused to make any further comment or to explain in any way their *volte-face*. Sports writers in the local press then voiced their criticism and put the best interpretation on the event they could possibly conceive, apparently not taking any risk of offending the Everton club. The sports pages argued that it must be assumed that Dean's transfer had been agreed and conducted only with the best interests of the player in mind. Such a line, it was hoped, would pacify many supporters and so stifle any continuing controversy about the issue.

Dean's account of the situation did not altogether match the sportswriters' assumptions. Dean says his decision to leave Everton was brought about by the continuing sour relationship he had with Theo Kelly, the club's secretary. Dean alleges that Kelly adopted an autocratic and disagreeable attitude to all the older players, particularly to himself, and this he found intolerable, hence the decision to transfer. Dean also suspected that Kelly had something to do with his exclusion from the first team throughout that season. So when Dean became aware that under FA Rules March 16 was the date beyond which transfers became restricted, he opted to take the first offer that came along prior to that date. A number of clubs had for some time expressed interest in him but these he had ignored, his firm intention being to stay with the Goodison Park Club. But when Harry Parkes, the Notts County manager, arrived to discuss the position Dean felt he had to take the opportunity to get away from the Everton secretary, a man he says he had come to dislike so much. Dean quite naturally was very attached to Everton, holding a deep affection for everything it stood for, and therefore he had no real desire to leave. After all, the club had been the vehicle for all his great success. But he had to get away from the man who was likely to be secretary for a long time to come. Dean was convinced that if he remained at Goodison the situation could only lead to a serious confrontation.

The transfer was completed on the afternoon of Friday March 11 1938 and according to Dean, Theo Kelly was the only Everton official present. Furthermore, Dean says, when the papers had been signed Kelly withdrew without a word, not even a goodbye. Dean also adds that no player or other member of the Everton staff came to say farewell and so he packed his bag and left for Nottingham the same afternoon with Harry Parkes.

That a player of Dean's eminence, one who contributed so much to the Everton Club, should be allowed to leave unnoticed seems incredible. Dean, however asserts that this is exactly what happened. In normal circumstances if any employee leaves a job after 13 years' service, even if it is undistinguished service, colleagues gather to say farewell and sometimes present a memento of their good wishes. What happened to Dean was an appalling reflection on the way football was administered in those days. Dean says he did not return to Goodison Park for many years. Everton did not redeem its position in relation to Dean's departure until the 1939-45 war was over, when due compensation was made to Dean through a remarkable event referred to later in the story.

Dean's transfer to Notts County proved a less successful venture than either he or the County manager anticipated. Harry Parkes was very pleased with Dean's performance in his first three games for the Third Division side. Parkes expressed optimism and estimated that Dean would be good for another four seasons, by which time he hoped Notts County would be back where the club belonged – in the First Division! Alas, it was not to be. Dean was injured in the third match, his ankle bone (what was left of it) being chipped, and by the time he had recovered, the 1937-38 season was over. Once again injuries had taken their toll.

Dean spent the summer in the Isle of Man and returned fit and well to face the new season. He was appointed captain of the County side and hopes were raised once again that Dean would lead his new team to great success. After only six games Dean was again injured, a bone in his instep being broken. Although the increased risk of playing in the harsher type of game involved in Third Division football was something Dean appreciated before he transferred, he was a fearless character and paid little heed of such hazards. On his reputation alone, he put fear into the defence of every team he played against, but in the Third Division it led to tactics of less finesse than those employed against him when he played in the higher sphere. It became inevitable that he would suffer injury more frequently than hitherto.

It was the last time he was to play in English League football. Dean went into hospital to be operated on for the injury to his instep. He says it was the fifteenth operation of his career and his legs were already covered with the scars left by previous surgery. The doctors expressed wonder at how a man could continue to play professional football having suffered so much damage to the legs, such vital pieces of equipment to a soccer player. Of course, the game can also be played by using the head and there was no one better at that than Dean. But even that was a spot where he had suffered a smashed skull from which he had fully recovered! This time his leg operation led Notts County to accept that as far as they were concerned Dean had to be regarded as a write-off, and they would allow him to leave if he wished.

The County's administration was extremely generous to Dean and continued to pay him wages, keeping to the contract until such time as he found some other opening. Then, out of the blue, the manager of Sligo Rovers, a soccer club in the Republic of Ireland League, wrote to Dean asking if he would scout for him and in particular would he urgently recommend a centre-forward of ability who would be prepared to sign for the Irish club. Dean felt he had recovered from his injury sufficiently to offer himself as the player they might be looking for. Highly delighted, the Sligo manager immediately responded, accepting Dean's proposal. Notts County duly released him and in January 1939 he went off to Ireland.

22 Ireland-The War-
Retirement

IN 1939 WHEN DEAN SIGNED for the Irish club, Sligo, the IRA
was active, and feelings in some parts of the Republic were not
exactly conducive to the ready acceptance of an Englishman
playing in one of their soccer teams. Dean was not much
interested in politics, but he recognised that there might be
difficulties. His arrival in Sligo, however, gave no sign of any
public animosity. Indeed he was given a warm welcome by the
club officials who were still rather amazed at having captured
such a famous footballer. Supporters soon came round to
welcome the new man. Sport, particularly soccer, appears to
transcend all political barriers, and before long the former
Everton and England star became extremely popular and as
much an idol of the local fans as he had been with Merseysiders, many of whom were of Irish extraction.

Dean is full of praise for the Sligo club and says he had a
great affection for the local people. The whole community
seemed to go out of its way to grant him his every wish. Hotel
accommodation was provided free and the famous Irish
hospitality knew no bounds. Dean sums it up with the story that
one day not long after he had arrived in Sligo he was sitting in
the hotel dining room waiting for tea to be served. The waitress
approached him rather nervously and addressed him with
some hesitance. 'Im terribly sorry Mr Dean, but do you know
what, we only have fresh salmon for tea today!' 'My goodness,'
Dean thought, 'if serving such an item warranted an apology
then I'm prepared to remain here forever!' But his sojourn was
interrupted by the war. Dean looks back on his time with the
Irish club as one of the most enjoyable of his football career.
His golf improved, and as a scratch player he competed with
many of the top Irish professionals whilst he was there.

Dean's record with Sligo from January to May 1939 was that
he appeared in 11 matches and netted eleven goals, thus
maintaining the consistency he applied to goal-scoring
throughout his career in whatever standard of football he
played. Sligo Rovers are very proud of this particular period in
their history. Not many clubs in the football world can boast
that the great Dixie Dean once played for them. Indeed, only

three League clubs in England are privileged to be able to say this, and Sligo is the only Irish club to be honoured in this way.

Over 30 years later, in 1970, Sligo Rovers once again appeared in the Irish Cup Final and the club invited Dean to attend the match with a request that he lead the team out on to the field. The club paid all Dean's expenses from Liverpool to Dublin, and although he was delighted to be asked and looked forward to the weekend, he accepted the air ticket with reluctance, openly confessing that he hated flying. However, the captain of the flight regarded Dean as a very important passenger and allowed him to take over the controls of the aircraft in an effort to soothe the great man's fears!

Much of the pleasure Dean derived from his stay in the land of the shamrock in 1939 came not only from the idyllic surroundings of the Bay at Sligo, the Ox and Dartry mountains, the lakes, the wonderful salmon fishing, and the Rosses Point golf course, but also because the Sligo team achieved unprecedented success during the short time he spent with them. For the first time in the club's history Sligo Rovers reached the Irish Cup Final and at the same time were runners-up in the League, a position never previously attained. Rovers were therefore highly satisfied and gave much credit for their success to the presence of Dean in their side. The Cup Final was a close affair, resulting in a draw. The replay was played in Dublin, Sligo losing 0-1.

Celebrations followed, and Dean became the hero of the hour. A crowded hotel function which he attended demanded the showing of the prized runners-up medals won by the Sligo team. The medals were duly passed round a cheerful, exuberant, and intoxicated group of supporters. By the end of the evening, Dean's Cup medal had not been returned and the conclusion was that it had been purloined. Dean, who had always been diffident about such symbols of honours won at sport, reacted to the situation without fuss. But the club officials and many supporters became very much concerned, and as their pride in Irish hospitality was injured, they made every effort to recover the medal, without success. Dean was given a rousing farewell and presented with various gifts including an envelope containing £60, and his passage back to England was paid for. What Dean felt as more important was the goodwill he had established, and there was no hiding the fact that it was a grateful Irish community that bade him farewell, hoping he would return the following season to play and help bring further honours to their local football.

Nearly seven years later, the war over, and Dean ensconced as licensee of a pub called The Dublin Packet, a small parcel was delivered one morning. There was an Irish postmark, but no message of any sort. Inside was the runners-up medal that had gone missing at the reception in 1939. An uneasy conscience after all those years? We shall probably never know.

Dean went back to his wife and family, who had remained in Nottingham during the time he was in Ireland. In the summer of 1939 the war clouds thickened and it became obvious that he would not be able to continue with Sligo. When war was declared he and his family decided to return to Merseyside to be near relatives and friends. Dean had no job, and awaited his call-up to the forces. In the meantime he obtained employment doing a menial and dirty job at the lairage in Birkenhead. It might have been thought that this local sporting hero would have no difficulty in obtaining an easier and more lucrative kind of employment, but stars of his profession meet the inevitable fate of becoming forgotten in economic terms when they lose what they once had to offer. Dean remained at his job in the abattoir until he was enlisted in the Army in 1940.

Most of the famous names in sport, particularly professional footballers, were being recruited into the services as physical training instructors and given rank and status. Dean did not seek such advantages and went into the infantry as a private, joining the Kings (Liverpool) Regiment, and doing his primary training at Formby near Liverpool. At no time was he offered a role which his background ought to have prompted the Army to give. Whilst at Formby, however, he was asked to organise a football team from the recruits to play a representative team of ex-footballers who were all in the PTI section of the services. His team of unknowns, he says, whacked the professionals 8-3! He was not invited to play in any of the many representative games which were organised during the war to entertain the troops. He did, however, appear for Cambridge Town as a guest player against an RAF team – a match in which his side won 15-1! Dean scored eight goals, and the report in the local paper said that six of his goals came in 39 minutes!

Dean volunteered to transfer to the Royal Tank Regiment, where he became a mechanic instructor with the rank of corporal. He recalls that he occasionally played some soccer with his own unit but rarely at any higher level, except for the club mentioned.

When he was demobilised at the end of the war Dean took

over a public house in Chester called The Dublin Packet. Here he literally hung up his football boots together with his many trophies and stayed there for a lively and interesting 15 years. Many of the pubs in Chester are no doubt widely known by virtue of their situation in a historic Roman city which draws visitors from all over the world. But The Dublin Packet became an even greater attraction with Dean as the landlord. When he took over in 1946 the pub's name became almost as well known as that of its proprietor. Stars of sport, stage, and screen frequently called in to pay their respects.

As time went by, Dean's achievements in the football world seemed to attract more attention and began to look even more phenomenal than ever in retrospect. During the immediate post-war period sportswriters were constantly making reference to the great man and each article published concluded by mentioning his retirement to The Dublin Packet. So its fame spread. Visitors, distinguished and otherwise, called at all times of the day and night. Lester Piggott, whom Dean knew quite well, was once engaged at a race meeting in Chester and after an early morning training gallop called round to the Dean pub at 6.0 a.m. He knocked on the side door, eventually opened by Mrs Dean.

'I'm Lester Piggott. Mr Dean said I could call round any time', the famous jockey explained.

Mrs Dean shouted towards the bedroom, 'Bill, there's a Mr Piggott here to see you, he says he's from Leicester!' Another regular visitor to the pub was Dean's old friend and rival Elisha Scott, who had retired to his native Ireland.

In the fifties the BBC featured a television programme *The Hall of Fame* which honoured sporting stars of the past, and Dean's name could scarcely be excluded, so a TV production team and camera crew visited The Dublin Packet to film Dean in his retirement. Raymond Glendenning, the famous sports commentator who presented the programme on television, accompanied the BBC team and was first to enter the pub. Dean was in the act of pulling a pint for a customer as Glendenning entered the bar.

'Good afternoon, Dixie,' he said, raising his homburg hat. 'I'll swap you this for one of those up there,' pointing to the row of international caps hanging from a beam.

'Not bloody likely', retorted Dean, 'I couldn't wear your kind of hat.' Strange to relate, Dean does not now possess a single cap – they were never returned after being loaned to a private club in Liverpool for display at some charitable function. The

Hall of Fame programme which featured him was broadcast, but Dean says he never saw it – again typical of his diffidence. A group of sporting enthusiasts in 1971 revived the idea of a 'Football Hall of Fame' and chose Dean as one of the first candidates for such an honour. As a result he was presented with a beautiful trophy to commemorate the event.

In the early fifties, during the time he was at the Chester pub, Dean accepted an invitation to play in a charity match between teams made up of ex-Everton and Liverpool players. The game was played at South Liverpool's ground under floodlights and attracted a large crowd. Dean appeared, but he was then in his mid-forties, rather porky and out of training. He naturally occupied the centre-forward berth on the ex-Everton side. Many of the spectators had never seen the great star play, and were prepared to make allowances for his age and weight. But what they did see was a revelation in heading skill. Many talk about it to this day. They say they have never seen a professional footballer head a ball with such power and accuracy. A flick of his head and spell-binding passes were made from the centre of the field to the wings as effectively as could ever be done with the feet. Dean went off at half-time but the younger element in the crowd had seen enough to convince them of his greatness. 'It is true what they say about Dixie' was the general feeling.

In 1961 Dean decided to give up the publican's life in Chester and return to Merseyside. The Everton club had reclaimed his interest (Dean says he never ever lost his attachment to Goodison Park) and John Moores, the football pools tycoon who was Everton's Chairman at the time stepped in and offered Dean a job as a security officer with his organisation in Birkenhead. Dean accepted, but subsequently transferred to the Liverpool offices of the firm. There the job entailed him rising at 4.30 a.m. each morning to travel from Bebington in order to report for duty in Liverpool at 6.00 a.m. This he did for several years until he reached the age of 65 when he retired on a pension. Dean finished his working life in the same fashion as when he started his first job at ten years of age, regularly getting up at an unearthly hour in the morning! His amazing constitution had served him well right up to the end.

Due entirely to the efforts of John Moores, the Everton club redeemed its position in relation to Dean. After 13 years' loyal service, Dean had left Goodison Park in 1938 without so much as an empty handshake. Everton had produced many famous

212

players, but none had remained so loyal or achieved so much fame under the club's banner for as long a period as this man. Obviously John Moores realised this and set about doing something positive to offer, albeit belatedly, some token of appreciation for Everton's famous son. So, in the spring of 1964, arrangements were made to play a testimonial match in honour of Dean. As far as is known no club in history has done this for a player 26 years after he left the club. There might have been some who thought such a venture too much of a risk – after all, a war had intervened and a new generation had been born and the main question to be answered was – how well would the ex-star be remembered? Would his name still be popular enough to attract people to attend such an event? Those who may have had such doubts need not have worried. Dean is a legend – a folk hero, particularly on Merseyside, the image more clearly in focus as time goes on. Sporting history it seems, will forever embrace the name of Dixie Dean.

The testimonial match was arranged on a Scotland v England basis, the teams to be drawn from the Everton and Liverpool clubs, both of which had sufficient players of each nationality to provide two good sides. The game was played on the evening of Tuesday April 7 1964 at Goodison Park and even the optimists were astonished by the attendance. The *Liverpool Echo* gave full coverage to the report of the game and commented 'Where else in this country would a crowd of 40,000 turn up, towards the end of the season, to watch an exhibition match for a player who last appeared for the club more than 26 years ago? Of course the player they were honouring was exceptional – so was the gate.' The gate receipts came to nearly £10,000, a tidy sum at that time, and John Moores arranged for the money to be held in trust for the man who had been so generously honoured.

The event opened with Dean walking out to the centre circle to take the kick-off. Although his usual attitude was one of diffidence, this time he could not hide his emotions, for there he was standing in the centre of Goodison Park – a spot he had not occupied for more than a quarter of a century. The crowd rose to him, cheering him to the echo, revelling in the sheer nostalgia of the occasion. The former star walked off alone waving shyly in response to the rapturous applause that followed him all the way to the touchline. He wondered how many of those cheering thousands had ever seen him play? Many of course were old enough, and no doubt shed a few tears over this reminder of the glorious football occasions this man had had, now only a memory never to be seen again. For Everton supporters, both young and old, the Dean legend is emotionally inscribed on their hearts and will continue to be on generations of fans to come. That memorable evening in April 1964 provided predictable evidence of that. Many Liverpool supporters attended the game and when asked why they went to honour a man from the camp of the opposition (a mortal sin to many on Merseyside) the general response was 'Dean, in spite of the blue jersey he wore, gave me hours of pleasure and entertainment, the like of which may never be seen again – and after all, he was a scouser!'

When Dean retired in 1972 he settled down in Bebington with his wife, his three sons and daughter being already married and living away from home. Not long afterwards he was taken ill and admitted to hospital, where for a time he was on the danger list. Once again his remarkable constitution helped to pull him through. In 1974 he suffered a major tragedy when his wife died suddenly from a heart attack. Barbara, Dean's daughter, was there to look after him. He now resides with Barbara, her husband, and a young granddaughter to whom he is devoted. None of his sons followed him into the football profession, but Dean says that Barbara has the spirit, courage, and other qualities which would have equipped a boy to succeed in professional football.

In his retirement Dean continues to retain an active interest in soccer. Proof that his fame is not forgotten comes from the fact that he is constantly receiving invitations to attend various charitable and social functions where his presence is regarded as a star attraction. Wherever he goes he is soon identified and devotees of football gather round him to pay homage. Recently he went on holiday to a remote part of Cornwall where a visit to the local inn brought out most of the village to see him and ask for a souvenir autograph. No effort on his part to hide his identity was successful. He frequently receives letters and postcards from a variety of sources at home and abroad, all to wish him well and thank him for the pleasure he gave to people in the old days. Again recently (in 1976) a group of schoolboys wrote to him from Sweden seeking answers to questions on the subject of soccer. It is remarkable that almost 40 years after he finished playing he is so clearly remembered by the public.

As an after-dinner speaker Dean is now much sought after, particularly to attend functions arranged by sporting organisations. He has a droll and ready wit and adopts histrionics remarkably like Jack Benny, the famous Hollywood comedian. It has already been mentioned that in April 1976 Dean attended the Football Writers' Association annual dinner in London to present the Footballer of the Year trophy, a task which also required him to make an after-dinner speech. About 600 denizens of the sporting Press formed his audience, all shrewd men of the world, including Mr Michael Foot who is not unknown for his power of oratory. With all due respect to the other speakers, Dean's effort was the most amusing and appropriate and came out as the star performance. After the dinner Malcolm McDonald, famous centre-forward of the present day was asked did he know of Dixie Dean? 'Dixie Dean? Of course! I remember once my name was included with his in the same sentence in a Press report – I was never so proud or flattered.'

Following the presentation of the trophy to Kevin Keegan as Footballer of the Year, the Press gave Dean a silver salver on which was incribed:

To Dixie Dean. 60 goals in a season,
more than most teams score today.

Dean in his retirement would no doubt pursue an even more active interest in the game but has been impeded to some extent by his inability to walk very far. This handicap cannot be unrelated to the leg injuries he suffered, living proof of the sacrifice he made to the game. But worse was to come. In November 1976 his doctor diagnosed a thrombosis and immediately ordered Dean to hospital, where he underwent a major operation in an attempt to save his life. The specialists were not very confident that the surgery would be successful. Indeed, Dean's family was warned that he might not even recover from the pre-operative stages of treatment. Within a few months of his 70th birthday, Dean was operated upon and survived, but one week later it became clear that despite the great skill and effort of his doctors his right leg could not be saved. His life was in danger and there was no alternative but to amputate. So Dean underwent a second operation within a fortnight and again survived. Testimony not only to the surgeon's skill, but also to the great man's remarkable constitution. It was the *seventeenth* major operation he had been through during his life.

Within five days of the amputation, Dean was able to get out of bed for short periods and, with some assistance, hobble about on crutches. Consistent with his nature, he showed no sense of shock or self-pity. He was cheerful and confident of his recovery, despite having to give up his regular indulgence in a pint of bitter and being forced to become a non-smoker for the first time in 40 years. He told his old joke (about having appeared in more theatres than Morecambe and Wise) with more emphasis than before.

Professional footballers of the past, even some who made an outstanding contribution to their sport, retired from the game and were then forgotten. Of course, from time to time their names are the subject of reminiscence but age or natural causes and even tragedies that subsequently affect them do not always make news value half-a-century on. There are some players who, at the time of their successes, were regarded as being unforgettable – even immortal – but subsequently live and die in obscurity. So do their achievements. A great pity, but that is the way of the world. Success in the football business is more then usually ephemeral. Perhaps the test of any sportsman's claim to immortality is when increasing reference to his achievements is made as time goes on. Time is the best judge and jury of most things in life. In Dean's case interest in him and his particular contribution to football had not diminished in 1976 despite the fact that 40 years had passed since he last played in first-class football. So when the news of his serious disablement was revealed, the football world was profoundly shocked, a reaction which found wide expression through the media.

Dean continues to be respected as a sporting phenomenon, but perhaps even more as a person, by sports writers everywhere. The views of his misfortune prompted a spate of articles in the local and national Press about the man and his remarkable contribution to soccer. Whilst in hospital Dean received hundreds of letters from well-wishers far and near, all the envelopes vaguely addressed 'Dixie Dean, Merseyside', but all were delivered. You can still address a letter to 'Dixie Dean, England' and the Post Office would find him – because who hasn't heard of Dixie Dean? Even *The Times,* that paper for top people, featured a lengthy article about Dean to report the news of his unfortunate disablement. The writer of the article, Geoffrey Green, described Dean as 'the greatest centre-forward of all time,' – praise indeed! Geoffrey Green concluded the article, 'There was poetry in him. If only England had his like today.' Few will disagree with that statement.

Dean's consistency in never giving up on the field of play was a commendable contribution, but is now a debt he has to pay.

Moreover, despite the hacking his legs received he always resisted the temptation to retaliate, responding only in a truly sporting fashion, with skill, patience and good humour, rare qualities for a player who occupied such a vulnerable position, one which might have offered him reasonable excuse for violent reaction. In this day and age Dean can be set as a shining example of the heights soccer can reach, levels which make the game one of the greatest ever conceived by man.

Religious orders canonise those individuals who by their virtuous application enhance their cause and by their example to followers are likely to perpetually draw inspiration. Sport, which has millions of disciples (probably more numerous than some established religions), indulges in similar canonisation of its heroes. Some of the sporting saints do not last as long as their holier counterparts, because no doubt in most cases their achievements are subsequently emulated. The old saints march out and the new saints come marching in. As Dixie Dean's achievements give no sign of being surpassed, it may be safely predicted that in the context of the religion of football his name will be recognised in perpetuity as that of a saint. Amen.

> And when it is over we'll drink a blithe measure
> To each Laird and each Lady that witnessed our fun
> And to every blithe heart that took part in our pleasure
> To the lads that have lost and to the lads that have won
>
> *Sir Walter Scott*

Dixie Dean wishes to thank all those people who sent him their good wishes, and so helped sustain his spirits during the difficult period of the operation on his leg. In particular, he wishes to place on record his grateful thanks to the doctors, nurses, and all staff of the Birkenhead General Hospital, without whose skill and care he would not have survived. To his family physician, Dr.John Blaney, he says he owes a special debt of thanks.

W. R. (Dixie) Dean's Goal Scoring Record in English Football

Season	Club	Division	League Games	League Goals	FA Cup Games	FA Cup Goals	Internationals/Representative Games	Internationals/Representative Goals	Goals Total
1923-24	Tranmere R.	3	2	0	0	0	0	0	0
1924-25	Tranmere R.	3	27	27	1	1	0	0	28
1924-25	Everton	1	7	2	0	0	0	0	2
1925-26	Everton	1	38	32	2	1	0	0	33
1926-27	Everton	1	27	21	4	3	5	12	36
1927-28	Everton	1	39	60	2	3	15	37	100
1928-29	Everton	1	29	26	1	0	7	8	34
1929-30	Everton	1	25	23	2	2	0	0	25
1930-31	Everton	2	37	39	4	9	2	3	51
1931-32	Everton	1	38	45	1	1	2	1	47
1932-33	Everton	1	39	24	6	5	2	4	33
1933-34	Everton	1	12	9	0	0	0	0	9
1934-35	Everton	1	38	26	6	1	0	0	27
1935-36	Everton	1	29	17	1	0	0	0	17
1936-37	Everton	1	36	24	4	3	1	0	27
1937-38	Everton	1	5	1	0	0	0	0	1
1937-38	Notts Co	3	3	0	0	0	0	0	0
1938-39	Notts Co	3	6	3	0	0	0	0	3
TOTALS			437	379	34	29	31	65	473

Total Games 502
Goals 473

Average for League 0.867 goals per game
Average overall 0.936 goals per game

Some highlights of W. R. (Dixie) Dean's Goal-scoring achievements in First Class Football

60 Football League goals in one season (1927-28) in the First Division. An all-time record for any Division in the Football League.

100 goals overall in 1927-28 including Cup, League, International, representative, and charity games. An all-time record.

100 Football League goals before he was 21 years of age. An all-time record. *(Equalled by Jimmy Greaves in 1960.)*

200 Football League goals in 199 games achieved at 23 years of age. An all-time record.

300 Football League goals in 310 games. An all-time record.

362 Football League goals in 400 games. An all-time record.

379 Football League goals in 437 games. An all-time record.

349 League goals for one club (Everton) in 399 games. A record for any club.

37 Hat-tricks in his career. An all-time record.

200 goals in 198 games for one club (Everton). An all-time record.

More than 20 League goals in 9 consecutive seasons.

More than 30 League goals in 4 seasons.

Broke Steve Bloomer's career record of 352 goals (made in 22 seasons) by achieving 353 goals in just over 12 seasons.

Averaged 0.94 goals per game throughout his career. Highest average of any player appearing in over 400 games in English football.

473 goals in 502 matches including Cup, League, International, representative and first class charity games.

W. R. (Dixie) Dean's International Appearances for England

Date	Opponents	Venue	Result	England Scorers
12. 2.1927	Wales	Wrexham	3-3	Dean 2, Walker
11. 5.1927	Belgium	Brussels	9-1	Dean 3, Rigby 2, Brown 2, Hulme, Page
2. 4.1927	Scotland	Hampden Pk Glasgow	2-1	Dean 2
26. 5.1927	France	Paris	6-0	Dean 2, Brown 2, Rigby, Rollet O.G.
21. 5.1927	Luxembourg	Luxem-bourg	5-2	Dean 3, Bishop, Kelly
22.10.1927	Ireland	Belfast	0-2	
20.11.1927	Wales	Burnley	1-2	(O.G. by Wales)
31. 3.1928	Scotland	Wembley	1-5	Kelly
17. 5.1928	France	Paris	5-1	Dean 2, Stephenson 2, Jack
19. 5.1928	Belgium	Antwerp	3-1	Dean 2, V. Mathews
22.10.1928	Ireland	Goodison Pk Liverpool	2-1	Dean, Hulme
17.11.1928	Wales	Swansea	3-2	Hulme 2, Hine
13. 4.1929	Scotland	Hampden Pk Glasgow	0-1	
28. 3.1931	Scotland	Hampden Pk Glasgow	0-2	
9.12.1931	Spain	Highbury	7-1	Crooks 2, Smith 2, Johnson 2, Dean
17.10.1932	Ireland	Blackpool	1-0	Barclay
	16 Matches		18 Goals	

W. R. (Dixie) Dean's Football Honours Representative Appearances Football League

Date	Against	Venue	Result	
21. 9.1927	Irish League	Newcastle	9-1	Dean 4
10. 8.1928	Scottish League	Ibrox Pk Glasgow	6-2	Dean 2
22. 9.1928	Irish League	Belfast	5-0	Dean 2
7.11.1928	Scottish League	Villa Pk Birmingham	2-1	Dean 1
7.11.1931	Scottish League	Celtic Pk Glasgow	3-4	
21.10.1936	Scottish League	Goodison Pk Liverpool	2-0	
	6 Matches	9 Goals		

W. R. Dean's Medals and Honours

Football League Division I Championship Medal (Scored 60 goals in 39 games)	1927-28
F.A. Charity Shield Match Winners Medal (Scored 2 goals)	1928
Football League Division II Championship Medal (Scored 39 goals in 37 games)	1930-31
Football League Division I Championship Medal (Scored 45 goals in 38 games)	1931-32
F.A. Charity Shield Match Winners Medal (Scored 4 goals)	1932
F.A. Cup Winners Medal (Scored 5 goals in Cup Matches)	1933
16 International Caps for England (Scored 18 goals in 16 matches)	1927-1932
6 Football League Medals (Scored 9 goals in 6 matches)	1927-1936
Central League Championship Medal	1937-38
Republic of Ireland League Runnersup Medal (Scored 11 goals in 11 games)	1938-39
Republic of Ireland F.A. Cup Runnersup Medal	1938-39

221